COM  / LIFE

101 873 398 1

'Community' continues to be a persistent theme in political, philosophical, and policy debates. The idea of community poses fundamental questions about social inclusion and exclusion, identity and belonging.

Drawing on a wealth of international empirical examples and illustrations, this book reviews debates surrounding the idea of community. It examines changing patterns of community life and evaluates their importance for society and for individuals. As well as urban, rural and class-based communities, it explores other contemporary forms of community, such as social movements, communes and 'virtual' gatherings in cyberspace.

Truly multidisciplinary, this book will be of interest to students of sociology, geography, political science, and social policy and welfare. It provides a fascinating overview of contemporary debates surrounding the idea of community.

Graham Day is Senior Lecturer in Sociology at the University of Wales, Bangor. His research interests include community and locality studies, economic and social restructuring, rural/urban sociology, national identity and the sociology of Wales.

Sheffield Hallam University
Learning and Information Services
Withdrawn From Stock

THE NEW SOCIOLOGY

Series Editor: ANTHONY ELLIOTT, University of Kent, UK

The New Sociology is a book series designed to introduce students to new issues and themes in social sciences today. What makes the series distinctive, as compared to other competing introductory textbooks, is a strong emphasis not just on key concepts and ideas but on how these play out in everyday life – on how theories and concepts are lived at the level of selfhood and cultural identities, how they are embedded in interpersonal relationships, and how they are shaped by, and shape, broader social processes.

Forthcoming in the series:

Religion and Everyday Life
STEPHEN HUNT (2005)

Culture and Everyday Life
DAVID INGLIS (2005)

Community and Everyday Life
GRAHAM DAY (2005)

Self-Identity and Everyday Life
HARVIE FERGUSON (2005)

Consumption and Everyday Life
MARK W. D. PATERSON (2005)

Globalization and Everyday Life
LARRY RAY (2006)

The Body and Everyday Life
HELEN THOMAS (2006)

Nationalism and Everyday Life
JANE HINDLEY (2006)

Ethnicity and Everyday Life
CHRISTIAN KARNER (2006)

Risk, Vulnerability and Everyday Life
IAIN WILKINSON (2006)

Cities and Everyday Life
DAVID PARKER (2007)

COMMUNITY AND EVERYDAY LIFE

Graham Day

Routledge
Taylor & Francis Group

LONDON AND NEW YORK

First published 2006
by Routledge
2 Park Square, Milton Park, Abingdon, Oxon OX14 4RN

Simultaneously published in the USA and Canada
by Routledge
270 Madison Ave, New York, NY 10016

Transferred to Digital Printing 2006

Routledge is an imprint of the Taylor & Francis Group, an informa business

© 2006 Graham Day

Typeset in Garamond and Scala Sans by Taylor & Francis Books
Printed and bound in Great Britain by Antony Rowe Ltd,
Chippenham, Wiltshire

All rights reserved. No part of this book may be reprinted or
reproduced or utilized in any form or by any electronic, mechanical,
or other means, now known or hereafter invented, including
photocopying and recording, or in any information storage or
retrieval system, without permission in writing from the publishers.

British Library Cataloguing in Publication Data
A catalogue record for this book is available from the British Library

Library of Congress Cataloging in Publication Data
Day, Graham.
  Community and everyday life / Graham Day. ·
     p. cm.
  Includes bibliographical references and index.
  ISBN 0-415-34074-8 (pbk.) -- ISBN 0-415-34073-X (hard back) 1.
Community. I. Title.
  HM756.D38 2006
  307--dc22

                                        2006003799

ISBN10: 0-415-34073-X (hbk)   ISBN13: 978-0-415-34073-1 (hbk)
ISBN10: 0-415-34074-8 (pbk)   ISBN13: 978-0-415-34074-8 (pbk)
ISBN10: 0-203-46317-X (ebk)   ISBN13: 978-0-203-46317-8 (ebk)

CONTENTS

SERIES EDITOR'S FOREWORD

'The New Sociology' is a series that takes its cue from massive social transformations currently sweeping the globe. Globalization, new information technologies, the techno-industrialization of warfare and terrorism, the privatization of public resources, the dominance of consumerist values: these developments involve major change to the ways people live their personal and social lives today. Moreover, such developments impact considerably on the tasks of sociology, and the social sciences more generally. For the most part, however, the ways in which global institutional transformations are influencing the subject-matter and focus of sociology have been discussed only in the more advanced, specialized literature of the discipline. I was prompted to develop this series, therefore, in order to introduce students – as well as general readers seeking to come to terms with the practical circumstances of their daily lives – to the various ways in which sociology reflects the transformed conditions and axes of our globalizing world.

Perhaps the central claim of the series is that sociology is fundamentally linked to the practical and moral concerns of everyday life. The authors in this series – examining topics all the way from the body to globalization, from self-identity to consumption – seek to demonstrate the complex, contradictory ways in which sociology is a necessary and very practical aspect of our personal and public lives. From one angle, this may seem uncontroversial. After all, many classical sociological analysts, as well as those associated with the classics of social theory, emphasized the practical basis of human knowledge, notably Emile Durkheim, Karl Marx, Max Weber, Sigmund Freud and George Simmel, amongst many others. And yet there are major respects in which the professionalization of academic sociology during the latter period of the twentieth century led to a retreat from the everyday issues and moral basis of sociology itself. (For an excellent discussion of the changing relations between practical and professional sociologies see Charles Lemert, *Sociology After the Crisis*, 2nd edn, Boulder: Paradigm, 2004.) As worrying as such a retreat from the practical and moral grounds of the discipline is, one of the main consequences of recent global transformations in the field of sociology has been a renewed emphasis on the mediation of everyday events and experiences by distant social forces, the intermeshing of the local and global in the production of social practices, and on ethics and moral responsibility at both the individual and collective levels. 'The New Sociology' series traces out these concerns across the terrain of various themes and thematics, situating everyday social practices in the broader context of life in a globalizing world.

In *Community and Everyday Life*, Graham Day offers a comprehensive tour-de-force of sociological debates concerning the concept of 'community'. His review is at once social-theoretical, tackling the notion of community in the writings of leading sociologists from Emile Durkheim to Zygmunt Bauman, and empirical-analytical, ranging widely from the analysis of local associations such as Neighbourhood Watch to global forums such as Live Aid. This breadth of concerns makes the book immensely rewarding, but as Day argues, there are substantive intellectual reasons why any assessment of the concept 'community' must engage such varied theories and disparate phenomena. One is that 'community' may well be one of the most elastic terms in social science, stretching from the promised pleasures of local bonds to the warming moral values of social solidarity. Another is that community is one of those words which, as the distinguished cultural theorist Raymond Williams noted, is always invoked positively, much like notions such as 'imagination' and 'democracy', of which everyone seemingly approves. This goodwill towards the idea of community is charted by Day with great skill and erudition. Throughout this lively study, Day is out to demonstrate that the concept of community has served as a bridge or link in sociological studies for rethinking the relations between self and society, identity and culture, security and freedom, opportunity and risk.

Day in particular draws our attention to the *politics of social theory* and of how 'community' emerges in various guises, both flattering and unflattering, as a result. He addresses the complex, contradictory social arrangements underpinning expressions of community by reassessing the contributions of classical and contemporary social theory. From Durkheim's analyses of social solidarity to Etzioni's call for stronger communities, Day critically examines both pessimistic and optimistic sociological critiques of meanings attributed to community. Perhaps what is most instructive in this connection is his deft mapping of how both theoretical and popular conceptions of community encode broader cultural understandings of the role of shared human values in the production and reproduction of social life. And it is precisely the politics around the idea of community, I would suggest, that marks this book out as important. At a time in which global transformations bite further and further into the fabric of communal relations, restructuring and reconstituting the performance and play of community dialogue in cities across spaces of the globe, it is imperative for sociology to attempt to clarify the conditions in which men and women living in their communities can seek to address the imbalances and disturbances of today's politics. From the distressed (and largely forgotten) citizens of New Orleans who attempt to reconstitute their communities in the wake of hurricane Katrina to those immigrants from North and Central Africa rioting on the streets in Clichy-sous-Bois as civil war erupts on the streets of Paris in 2005, redefining the possibilities and perils of community in these early days of the twenty-first century is a key task not only for practical sociological life but also for the public political domain more generally. Graham Day's book offers its readers a glimpse into the full sociological and political stakes of such interventions and of the reasons for the continuing significance of the idea of community.

Anthony Elliott

Canterbury 2006

PREFACE

THE SIGNIFICANCE OF 'COMMUNITY'

Public consternation was expressed a few years ago, when a single mother and her young son were found to be living a life of almost total social isolation in a well-to-do British suburban village. They came out only at night, never spoke to their neighbours, and were housed in conditions of great squalor. Expressing his shock, the local Director of Social Services commented that it was a 'strange sort of community' which could so neglect its members. Yet odd circumstances of this sort are reported quite regularly in the media. People can die and lie undiscovered by those around them for days, even weeks; neighbours engage in fierce, sometimes bloody, disputes over seemingly trivial matters like the size of their hedges, or the tidiness of their yards; groups of juveniles make life miserable for those who live nearby by behaving noisily or committing 'anti-social' acts of vandalism. More structured conflicts and divisions also occur. Barriers are put up to keep certain kinds of people out of neighbourhoods: the wealthy try to exclude poor people from their living spaces by erecting gates and fences; vigilante groups are formed to take action against those who are deemed undesirable; differences of religion, ethnicity, or sexual orientation are used to define boundaries between groups, and often to locate them in particular places. Some of the most disturbing social confrontations occur across these boundaries, as the various groups struggle to expand or defend their territories. Almost always in the course of such events, questions will be raised about why people cannot get along better with one another, why they cannot show greater responsibility towards their neighbours, and what has become of the idea of community.

In all these examples, it could be said that behaviour falls short of the highest standards of social cooperation, in which people ought to show concern and consideration for one another. Instead, we see processes of distancing and separation, failures to empathize, and lack of common courtesy. While it would be absurd to blame every social failing on defects of community, it is certainly the case that very often problems with community are held to be responsible for aspects of social life which worry people greatly, including loneliness, crime, fear and disorder. Sometimes the solutions are felt to rest with governments, or outside agencies like the police and welfare organizations, but frequently the root causes or explanations are believed to belong closer to home, with the immediate social relationships and motivations of those involved. This is the sphere normally thought of as community, those contacts and dealings which we have with one another in the course of our daily lives, and which form the context of our immediate social circle. Of course, the picture is by no means entirely negative, since individuals and groups also dedicate great efforts, time and resources to doing things on behalf of their communities, not least through their membership of voluntary bodies and organizations in the so-called 'community' sector.

The idea of community touches people's lives today in many ways, forming a significant influence on how they live and relate to one another. People are addressed in the media, in politics and through social policy as members of communities of various kinds (the gay and lesbian community, ethnic minority communities, faith communities), and frequently identify themselves as belonging to particular communities of taste or interest.

Communities are objects of regeneration, participation and intervention. There is a growing field of employment and training for different types of community workers. Businesses deploy ideas of community to gather local support, or to win market share by appealing to particular groups. All such uses of 'community' raise fundamental social questions about inclusion and exclusion, the privileging of some social relationships over others, and the formulation of particular as opposed to general interests. Activity conducted in the name of community poses issues of power, leadership, and representation. It seeks to bring people together by emphasizing what they have in common, while overlooking or subordinating their differences, and this generates basic arguments as to which social characteristics really count in deciding how people can and should unite or divide in social action. As rival communities compete for the allegiance of individuals, individuals engage in struggles to define, and delimit, the extent and demands of community. These topics are of obvious interest to sociologists, although they have tended to find the notion of community to be a troublesome and perplexing way of handling them. Various attempts have been made to dispense with it, and to find replacement terms. Nevertheless, after a period of relative dormancy, recent sociological debates have brought the idea of community back into prominence. It is also closely related to a number of other concepts which have gained recent sociological and political currency, such as 'trust', social capital, and civil society. The popularity of the theme of community in political, philosophical, and policy debates makes it likely to continue to hold the attention of sociologists for some time to come. The aim of this book is to explore the meaning of this tricky concept, and see how effectively sociologists have applied it as a means of empirical research.

1

THE IDEA OF COMMUNITY

According to the authors of a basic dictionary of sociology, the term 'community' is 'one of the most elusive and vague in sociology and is by now largely without specific meaning' (Abercrombie *et al.* 1984: 44). In view of the complexity and slipperiness of so many sociological concepts, this is a notable claim. However, there are many who would agree that 'community' is a concept that has been worked to death: its range of meanings is so wide and diverse, its connotations so inconsistent, and at times downright dangerous, that it deserves no place in any serious social analysis. Indeed, for about as long as sociology has existed, critics have poured scorn on the value of the concept and its ability to tell us anything really useful about the nature of society. Yet it remains nevertheless one of the most common points of reference, not only among social scientists, but also for policy makers, politicians and the general public. Precisely because it is so elastic and various in its meanings, the idea of community continues to grip people's imaginations, and even grow in significance as it takes on new applications.

The essential meaning of community might seem obvious enough. It refers to those things which people have in common, which bind them together, and give them a sense of belonging with one another. Clearly this is a fundamental aspect of society, perhaps its very core. But as soon as one tries to specify more firmly what these common bonds are, how they arise, and how they can be sustained, the problems begin. We would not be social beings if we did not feel some sense of identification and solidarity with the others around us and share in their experiences and expectations; yet there are limits to how far we can empathize with every one of them, or feel obligated towards them, or look to them for succour and support. As humans, we are boundary-drawing animals, and we erect barriers between ourselves and others, quite as much as we identify with them. The idea of community captures these elements of inclusion and exclusion, pointing towards those who belong together, and those who are held apart. This is why some would place it at the heart of social analysis, despite the difficulties it engenders. Nisbet's description of community as the most fundamental and far-reaching of sociology's unit ideas (Nisbet 1967: 47) points both to its importance, and to the need to treat it with considerable caution, lest it become too diffuse and all-embracing. The same applies to many popular uses of the term in everyday contexts; all too often 'community' signifies something vague and ill-defined, an excuse for not thinking hard enough about what exactly it is that people do have in common. References to the international or world community, the scientific and business communities, or even the human community, are obvious instances, but so are many routine appeals to more particular communities to act, or take a stand, or express an interest of some kind. When one asks to whom precisely this refers, and what exactly they are required to do, answers are frequently lacking. So 'community' is a highly problematic term, alluring in its promise but to be approached with extreme care.

CLASSICAL SOCIAL THEORY AND THE IDEA OF COMMUNITY

Ideas of community have been embedded in social theory since its origins, and were absorbed fully into the framework of classical sociology. The formative works of the discipline are pervaded by concerns with the question of how societies were held together, what gave collectivities and groups their unity and distinctiveness, and the extent to which such social ties were being strengthened or undermined by social change and development. 'Community' represented one significant way of speaking about group-ness, and distinguishing it from conditions of isolation or individualism. At a minimum, community involved people doing things, and being, together, rather than separate and alone. In the writings of Emile Durkheim, for example, there was a preoccupation with differing forms of social solidarity. Sets of people were united either because they were so alike, a form of solidarity Durkheim called 'mechanical', or because although different, in crucial respects they were complementary, and this gave them an 'organic' unity (Durkheim 1964). Both types of solidarity could be seen as giving rise to forms of community, centred respectively on similarity or interdependence. In Durkheim's theory of social change, the worry was that the emergence of organic solidarity might be threatened by excessive individualism, and a loss of readiness to cooperate on behalf of common purposes. Instead of combining their efforts into a collective project, people might allow selfish interests and competitiveness to divide them, so that society would lapse into a condition of disorder and 'anomie'. Durkheim's approach encapsulates a number of the major themes associated with discussions of community and its fate, including a contrast between different types of social order, a normative preoccupation with the regulation of society to maintain successful cooperation, and a sense of fear that prevailing social conditions might render this impossible. Not surprisingly, Durkheim provides a fertile source for later reflection on the nature of community.

The context for Durkheim's arguments, as for the general shaping of the foundations of academic sociology, was the nineteenth-century European experience of industrialization and modernization. His concern with developing the conceptual and analytical underpinnings for sociology is therefore heavily influenced by some of the empirical developments taking place at the time, such as the rise of modern industry and the accompanying growth of towns and cities. For example, he makes connections between evolving forms of social solidarity and the changing 'moral density' of society, as measured by patterns of population concentration, migration and geographical mobility. These are seen as exerting a pressure on the social division of labour, which in turn conditions the kinds of communal relations that are likely to develop. Thus the changing nature of community is influenced, or even determined, by a wide range of material and institutional forces. Again, this theoretical framework has exercised a major influence on subsequent explorations of how different sorts of community relate to factors such as the size of a population, the continuity and stability of its social relationships, and its capacity to assimilate new members.

While Durkheim has been one of the most influential of sociology's forebears, very similar observations and concerns can be found among most of his contemporaries. Setting out his own sociological scaffolding, Max Weber paid a great deal of attention to the nature of the 'communal', asserting that it was a characteristic to be found within most social relationships (Weber 1978). It consisted of the mutual orientation of social actors towards one another. That is, they were not solely concerned with their own interests, but almost always paid some heed to the wishes, needs, and behaviours of others. Relationships which were long-lasting, and went beyond the achievement of immediate ends, were especially likely to generate communal sentiments of belonging together. Weber instances associations within military units, school classes, workshops and offices, as well as religious brotherhoods and national communities. The physical proximity of neighbourhoods made them an especially likely source of mutual dependence, so that the neighbour is 'the typical helper in need'; thus neighbourhoods show a particular tendency to form 'communities of interest' (Weber 1978: 41, 361). However, the potential for community can be found wherever people engage in social interactions.

In the preceding generation, Karl Marx had examined ways in which social classes could come to form distinctive kinds of 'community', those which were aware of themselves and united around the pursuit of clearly formulated economic interests. The collective organization of classes was seen as owing much to the local and occupational groupings which formed around different industries. Marx also dealt with the shift from localized communal relations towards more universalized relationships which occurred across different historical epochs. In early history, he believed, people were embedded deeply into their communities, and the primitive forms of property were communally owned. History saw the emergence of the individual and private property, the dissolution of communal ties, and the exposure of the worker as a 'free' person to the vicissitudes of the market (Marx 1973). Despite their very different theoretical and methodological stances, and political outlooks, there are some interesting convergences between Marx and Durkheim in the way in which they treat the long-term transformation in the significance of community. Both sought to discover and promote ways in which future society could regain the strength and value of communal bonds, Marx through his vision of a communist society, and Durkheim by the revival of guild-like occupational communities.

A special mention must be reserved here for Tonnies (1955, originally published in 1887), if only because customarily he is seen as the theorist with the most direct influence over later sociological work on communities, and as offering the most explicit version of the kinds of theoretical distinctions we have begun to outline. Weber refers to the 'pioneering' work done by Tonnies in setting out a specific contrast between 'community' (*Gemeinschaft*) and 'association' (*Gesellschaft*). Unlike Weber, who saw these as intermingled and continuous aspects of social relations, Tonnies is often regarded as setting the precedent for treating them as opposing, mutually exclusive, sides of a dichotomy. Certainly they represent different principles of social organization. For Tonnies, *Gemeinschaft* involves 'a lasting and genuine form of living together' which is oriented towards the achievement of ends, through 'coordinated action for a common good'. *Gesellschaft* implies instead an orientation to means, calculated action on the part of individuals who engage in 'artificial' relations for what they can get from one another.

This is a fundamental classification which runs through all types of social interaction, corresponding to what Tonnies perceives as the distinction between 'natural' (spontaneous, organic) will and 'rational' will. As propensities, these are not necessarily exclusive of one another, but should be seen as 'model qualities' whose relationship is dynamic and fluctuating. Hence 'the force of *Gemeinschaft* persists, although with diminishing strength, even in the period of *Gesellschaft*, and remains the reality of social life' (1955: 272).

As handled by Tonnies, therefore, *Gemeinschaft* and *Gesellschaft* do not designate real social entities or groups, but abstract properties. Nevertheless, Tonnies makes a number of observations which encourage the confusion of such ideal type characteristics with 'real' instances. He informs us that the rural village community is 'an outstanding example' of *Gemeinschaft*, and that in general *Gemeinschaft* signifies the 'old' and *Gesellschaft* the new. Yet he also notes that *Gemeinschaft* could attain new levels in towns, and in work-based or religious groupings. It was the city which appeared to be the ultimate enemy of *Gemeinschaft*, although even here it could persist in certain forms within the urban context. The distinction made by Tonnies lends itself to being incorporated into analyses of change which see a general movement taking place from *Gemeinschaft* to *Gesellschaft*, from community to association. He set an influential precedent himself by researching the disintegrating effects of industrialization and modernization upon community life in his native Schleswig-Holstein.

In the course of constructing his theoretical polarities, Tonnies assimilated into his definitions a number of characteristics which subsequently have been assumed to go together. 'Community' stands for real ties of interdependence and emotion between people who form part of an organic, bounded, entity, often linked to place or territory. 'Association' refers to exchanges among individuals who engage in essentially boundaryless, contractual relationships; the ties between them are merely convenient. Tonnies suggested that community arose 'naturally' on the part of those who encountered shared experiences, for example through common origins and backgrounds. This applied most obviously to relationships within the family. Such an understanding of community encouraged an emphasis on mutual agreement or consensus, and the maintenance of established relations. The exercise of 'rational' will on the other hand was directed more towards future-oriented and instrumental objectives, so that association was more temporary, and subject to constant deliberate revision and improvement. Commercial or business transactions might typify *Gesellschaft*.

The notion of community as natural and 'organic' goes along with expectations that it will be valued for its own sake, and represent a situation of at least relative stability and homogeneity (Noble 2000). Understood in this way, community seems inevitably to belong more with the social order of the past, while the features of association fit more closely the world of the present, and its domination by commercial organizations and public bureaucracies. Rightly or wrongly, as Noble comments, the distinction appears to crystallize a lot of things that people feel they encounter in the real world, and a good deal of later research and commentary on community could be summed up as taking the form of a debate with the ghost of Tonnies, and his conceptual apparatus. Among the points at issue is whether the term 'community' ought to be equated with a distinct pattern of social relationships that is the outcome only of certain limiting conditions. This is where a concern with the conceptual specification of its meaning blurs into a series of assertions about empirical examples. Locating 'community' in the settled social relations of the past, and equating it with situations of stability and persistence, biases the discussion in a predominantly conservative direction, and both Durkheim and Tonnies have been accused of fostering a backward-looking sociology. More practically, Tonnies encouraged the belief that the quintessential expressions of community were to be found in close conjunction with relationships of kinship, or even blood, and proximity, such as were more characteristic of early, and rural settings than they are of modern life. He also asserted that they were closer to the circumstances and inclinations of women, and poor people, than those of men and social elites; hence, he proposed, *Gemeinschaft* belonged in the realm of 'nature', rather than that of reason.

It was in the surroundings of the city, and the modern industrial organization, that the 'associational' patterns referred to by Tonnies were most likely to thrive, where the emphasis was on short-term, purposeful exchanges among self-conscious individuals. These could be regarded as being at the opposite end of the spectrum from the types of behaviour and attitude typical of relationships within families and households, or in small, intimate, social groupings. However, simply describing it in this way sets up a whole series of mental oppositions between the settled and the changeable, short-lived and long-term, conscious and unconsidered, things which have an intrinsic worth or meaning and those which are useful only because of what they can bring about. Whereas certain of these features might seem to flourish best within community, the others appear antithetical to it, and show more affinity with the values and ethics of the marketplace, or with the reasoned actions of policy makers and officialdom. In their different ways, the institutions of the market and of the state appear especially distant from the true nature of community as depicted by Tonnies, giving us a sense that community exists somehow outside, or between, the market and the state.

We must remember that Tonnies and Durkheim were writing at a time when the disappearance of a rural peasantry and its semi-feudal conditions of existence was still visibly taking place around them in Europe. They were witnesses to the emergence of modern society, and the associated experiences of industrialization and urbanization were relatively new, and raw. Insofar as either sought to ground their arguments in empirical research, they relied heavily on contemporaneous studies of the decline of traditional social orders by authors such as Maine, Spencer and Gierke, and faithfully reproduced their accounts of the importance of ancient custom, collective regulation, and common ownership. Tonnies relates the existence of *Gemeinschaft* to the 'folk cultures' and customary laws that were to be found among those who enjoyed a long-established settled relationship with the land and ties of blood. The development of modern social relationships implied the destruction of these kinds of bonds, and with it the threat of a loss of community. Teasing out these conceptual and empirical relationships offers an almost unlimited potential for questions and problems. To what extent, for instance, should we confine the term 'community' to situations in which there is no rational deliberation, no calculation of benefit, and no conflict? How common are such situations? If rationality is hostile to community, how can we contemplate the explicit creation, or development, of communities designed to serve particular purposes? Can community ever be planned? A glance at contemporary advertisements for public sector jobs will indicate that there is no shortage of those who believe it is possible to do so. Applicants are invited to join projects which are concerned with such objectives as 'building communities as well as homes' (Swan Housing Association) or 'creating and co-ordinating a thriving community' (Blackburn with Darwen Borough Council: *Guardian* newspaper, 21 July 2004). How realistic are these aims, if they involve artificially engineering something as 'natural' as community? And what are we to make of enterprises such as 'community planning' (Marris 1982), 'community development' (Barr 1996), or 'community architecture' (Wates and Knevitt 1987)?

THEORY'S TWENTIETH-CENTURY LEGACY

Dichotomous representations of the contrasts between rural and urban, traditional and modern, spontaneous and rational permeated sociology throughout its early development, formed a prominent feature of the works of the Chicago School in particular (Wirth 1927; 1938; Redfield 1947), and persisted well into the 1960s (Frankenberg 1966; Pahl 1966). Whenever theories of historical change were formulated by sociologists, it was apparent that the conditions deemed most favourable to community fell on one side of the divide, and everything that was conducive to development and progress on the other. Hence community became identified with traditional social orders, like those of the feudal and agrarian past, or with 'less developed' modern contexts, and change was construed as its enemy. The association is sufficiently strong to make it seem that every concept of community had implicit within it a criticism of urban/industrial society (Ennew 1980: 1). These tendencies arose from the bundling together of several characteristics into a single package, often presented in the guise of an 'ideal type', which was acknowledged to exaggerate and simplify what would be found in any actual community, and yet prone to be handled as if it was real. The work of Tonnies was presented in black and white terms by many of his followers, as if it was self-evident that *Gemeinschaft* referred only to the rural village and/or the extended family, whereas urban living and freely chosen social relations were incompatible with community. Durkheim's analysis of changing social solidarities underwent a similar process of interpretation and simplification. The result is an inclination to presume that, providing some of the features of community can be detected, then the others must also exist; or, conversely, that if certain dimensions are missing, then what we have is not in any sense a proper community. The temptation to preempt what ought to be matters for empirical investigation is shown in definitions of community such as the following:

> a territorial group of people with a common mode of living striving for common objectives.
>
> (Durant 1959)

> a specific population living within a specific geographic area with shared institutions and values and significant social interaction.
>
> (Warren 1963: 2).

Nisbet's (1967: 47) definition of community as encompassing 'all forms of relationship which are characterized by a high degree of personal intimacy, emotional depth, moral commitment, social cohesion and continuity in time' is loaded with positivity. Except for the numbers typically involved, this could be an idealized description of marriage, or close friendship. Likewise Lee and Newby (1983: 52) remark on how the term has been used to denote 'a sense of common identity, enduring ties of affiliation and harmony based upon personal knowledge and face-to-face contact'. These statements seem to settle very tricky questions by fiat, leaving us to determine only how far actual examples measure up to the conceptual purity they provide. Nearly always, this makes real cases appear to fall short of an ideal, because there are bound to be some respects in which the simple correspondences built into the definitions cannot hold. Consequently, community remains an elusive prospect, a goal that is tantalizingly plausible and yet never quite achieved. This leads some to conclude that it is best regarded as an ideal, a philosophical dream, rather than a real phenomenon.

COMMUNITY UNDER THREAT

Classical theories of community were abstract and general; in modern parlance, they were not evidence-based, and their authors carried out no detailed studies to confirm their intuitions. Tonnies has been especially influential in crystallizing a dominant conception of community as a spontaneous outgrowth of close social and geographical relations. His account of *Gemeinschaft*-type relationships implies that the people involved will share a body of experiences, habits and memories, and display what Durkheim refers to as 'common ways of thinking and feeling' (1964: 79). This will happen almost innately, simply by virtue of being members of a community. It is not necessarily the case that the classic sociologists wholeheartedly endorsed community as a value, or an end in itself. On the contrary, it can be argued that in general they welcomed social progress and development, and saw the fading away of strict communal bonds as a price to be paid for the freedoms and opportunities of modern society (Kumar 1978; Little 2002: 18). However, many who followed in their footsteps came to lament the change, and to formulate a zero-sum equation in which 'association' could grow only at the expense of, or as a substitute for, community. The 'loss' or 'decline' of community became a leading theme in sociological writing (Stein 1964; Lee and Newby 1983), and was attributed to many different influences, chief of which included industrialization, rationalization, and urbanization. An entirely typical, early example is Zorbaugh's claim that

> The community is gradually disappearing. And its disappearance is the result of the fundamental processes of the city's growth – mobility, centralization, succession, and the consequent breakdown of culture and public opinion within local areas, the rise of social distances, and the organization of sentiment and interest on the basis of vocational activity rather than contiguity of residence.
>
> (Zorbaugh 1929: 271)

Zorbaugh's statement is packed with assertions about the causal relationships which lie behind the loss of community, of a sort that were widely rehearsed by sociologists, planners and others throughout the twentieth century.

Later contributions have done their best to move away from some of the more simplistic polar oppositions. Frankenberg (1966) and others insist, for instance, on the importance of constructing some form of continuum, rather than dichotomy, so that different examples can be arranged between extremes in appropriate ascending or descending order. In his theoretical review of British sociological and anthropological case studies of community, Frankenberg fixed them somewhere between the 'truly rural' and the 'thoroughly urban', according to differences in characteristic patterns of social structure and social relations. Although this was said to be no more than a 'morphological continuum', a classificatory arrangement of social types, Frankenberg notes that the tendency of direction of change is clear:

As we move towards the urban end of the continuum redundancy in social relations decreases, social relationships become less complex, processes are formalized and bureaucratic forms introduced. Elements of behaviour are stripped of latent and not so latent side-functions.
(Frankenberg 1966: 282)

In other words, the more 'urban' the situation, the more the aspects of community are shed. Social relationships are simplified, to become focussed around explicit aims and purposes. They become more specialized, and single-minded. There are marked echoes of Tonnies' analysis, though strangely Frankenberg makes no overt reference to the German theorist, drawing instead on the work of a number of more recent British and American social anthropologists. Frankenberg's version of the 'truly rural' seems to fit the model of *Gemeinschaft* in every respect, while he uses a range of variables such as density, complexity, breadth of social roles, differentiation, connectedness and individuation to measure deviations from it. Again this makes a certain kind of established rural social order seem the very epitome of community, whereas other later, and supposedly more sophisticated, forms of social organization are departures from it. The general movement is *from* community *to* something different.

A similar attempt to elaborate the distinction drawn by Tonnies and break it down, at least in theory, into a number of distinct and separable elements was made by the American sociologist Talcott Parsons. In his system of pattern variables, said to characterize all forms of human action, Parsons included contrasts between orientation to the self or to collectivity, and between value-attitudes that were particularistic or universalistic; ascribed or achieved; and affective or affectively neutral (Parsons 1951). Whilst multiple combinations of these variables were theoretically possible, in practice they appeared to cluster together in ways that reproduced the more simplistic models. As conventionally described, 'community' seemed to unite orientations towards others (the group or collectivity) with particularistic, ascribed, and affectual ties, so as to engage people's sentiments of belonging with a specific set of others, who were given rather than chosen. At the other extreme, there were the universalistic, achieved, and emotionally neutral orientations typical of modern formal organizations, or encounters between strangers on city streets.

There is a close connection between the sense of community as an integrated whole, in which a number of distinctive features fuse together, and the broader thrust towards harmony, cooperation and integration in functionalist social theory of the kind advocated by Parsons. It has often been claimed that the concept of community displays an intrinsic affinity with functionalist theory, so that examinations of communal relations fall easily into making claims about the functional necessities which shape them. Parsons himself took the restricted view, that community referred essentially to a particular kind of social grouping or collectivity, 'the members of which share a common territorial area as their base of operations for daily activities' (1951: 91). Within this delimited area, it should be possible to trace the ways in which different aspects of life were drawn into functional connections, each serving the needs of the others. Not just the members, but the social structures within which they were caught, would 'belong together', to form some kind of unity. However, Parsons did not limit his use of the word community to this special type of geographical, and rather strictly demarcated collectivity, since when conceptualizing society as a whole he also spoke of the 'societal community'. In other words, the communal impulse is quite central to his model of society as something bound together by a consensus of sentiments and values. At the largest scale, a society itself constitutes some sort of community, and is integrated by more than rationally calculated means and ends. So far as the development of particular communities was concerned, Parsons saw that the individual 'base of operation' was becoming more extended in range through the development of mobility and communications, such as commuting 'by mechanical means'. This meant that 'daily activities' could take place over larger and larger social spaces, stretching the bounds of community, possibly to breaking point.

According to Parsons, all societies are patterned into communities, and all individuals will belong to some such community or communities. Communities could be organized at various levels of inclusiveness, and some communities might contain others. Although an individual's entry into a community could be by choice, once inside it, a great deal becomes ascribed – Parsons mentions the obligation to pay local taxes. Local residence is also said to predispose actors towards relationships which are 'diffuse' rather than specific; that is, living alongside one another puts pressure on neighbours to form connections which go beyond any specific context. Like kinship, ethnicity and class groupings, communities tend towards an emphasis on the particular, ascriptive, and diffuse; they are indeed social groupings, rather than formal organizations. Where societies are constructed on the basis of a predominance of universalistic or achievement-oriented values, with imperatives for mobility and choice, then close ties of community solidarity will represent something of a threat to the system as a whole (Parsons 1951: 187); commitments will be driven to move towards more 'associational' arrangements, or to identification with larger groupings, such as the nation. There are very strong traces here of the evolutionary dynamic found in the classical theories of Spencer, Durkheim and Tonnies, which sees 'genuine' community as ultimately incompatible with advanced societies, and even raises the prospect that actual communities may be antagonistic to some of the values and imperatives of social progress. From the point of view of writers like Parsons, there is a definite tension between the pull towards loyalty to a community, and the openness and flexibility demanded by a modern developed economy and society.

POPULAR AND THEORETICAL CONCEPTIONS

The world of social theory is specialized, and at times opaque, and its influence on 'ordinary people' possibly remote, and hard to assess. Yet we can discern many ways in which these theoretical preoccupations about the meaning of community converge with everyday usages. Indeed, one of the issues touched upon by critics is the extent to which theorists, as happens in other fields, may rely too much upon popular and vernacular understandings of the term, letting them contaminate what should be more precise and reasoned analyses. Those inclined to do so can find ample excuses in social theory to dismiss community as a falsely romanticized, over-unified, sentimental construct. One does not have to go far to find references to community which underline the extent to which its use is bedevilled by 'nostalgic and romantic notions of a mythical past' (Pahl 1996: 89) or prone to draw upon 'fictionalized memories of a golden past' (Mayo 2000: 39). The cultural critic Raymond Williams (1976: 65–6) opined that 'community' was unique among the terms of social organization, in never being used unfavourably. This chimes with Tonnies' assertion that 'the expression bad *Gemeinschaft* violates the meaning of the word' (1955: 38). Consequently community can be used as a tag-word to confer a positive aura upon notions which might otherwise seem unattractive – like 'community policing', 'community discipline' or practices like 'neighbourhood watch'. The recent revival of enthusiasm for community among advocates of communitarianism such as Etzioni (1995) and Tam (1998) relies heavily on the assumption that communities are a good thing, and that individuals ought to be prepared to subordinate their selfish interests and desires to the common good. Merely referring to some set of people as a 'community', as in the 'gay and lesbian community', 'ethnic community', or 'rural community', can confer a spurious sense of caring and togetherness on what may prove to be no more than a disparate collection of individuals and groups (Hoggart 1988: 3). Consequently, community has become one of the most abused terms in the rhetoric of politics and policy making, employed promiscuously to harness the positive feelings and support that accompany motives of altruism and solidarity. Agencies that purport to be 'working for the community' can expect to be given the benefit of the doubt, since they have the interests of others at heart. Few would think it as sensible to proclaim that they were 'working just for ourselves'!

Among those who do appeal in this way to notions of community, there is a strong sense of regaining lost ground; it is commonplace to hear talk of the 'recovery' of community, or its 'regeneration'. This would fit the argument that, over time, community has been lost, or subjected to degeneration, and in that sense belongs somewhere in the past. Warning against romantic conceptions, Giddens (1990: 101) nonetheless explains that community was a marked feature of pre-modern social conditions, but underwent a decline with the advent of modernity. He has in mind especially those 'clusters of interweaving social relations' that tended to be concentrated on particular places, or 'local milieux', consisting in the main of relatively immobile and self-contained local populations. In pre-modern circumstances, such local communities were the foundation of wider social organization (1990: 80). Now, they have far less significance in the lives of most people; they have dissolved in the face of modern means of transport and communication. In fact, in the developed societies, the destruction of the local community is said to have 'reached its apogee' (Giddens 1994a: 101). This does not prevent Giddens, in his more activist political writings, from putting 'community' somewhere near the centre of his recommendations for a stronger focus on personal responsibility and active citizenship. For him, communities are among the cornerstones of a 'new progressivism' which seeks to combat the 'decay' of community and assist in the process of community renewal and rebuilding (Giddens 1998; 2000). Giddens is less forthcoming about where exactly in contemporary circumstances we are to find, or rediscover, such communities.

Amitai Etzioni has similar preoccupations. As the most celebrated recent advocate of communitarian values, he seems to accept the loss of traditional community as a fact, but wants to reverse the value that he believes other sociologists have put on this process. Whereas he contends that they have hailed it as a liberation from constraint, and release of individual rationality, he wishes to see the restoration of its 'old fashioned values and . . . sense of obligation' (1995: 117). He identifies a 'network of reciprocal obligations and care' as the central feature of community; it is a 'place in which people know and care for one another'. Etzioni's sociology has its roots in the subsoil of American structural-functionalism, and in his work he reproduces the Parsonian concern with the centrality of shared values and normative consensus to stable social order. Going further back, there is an obvious debt to Durkheim. Etzioni argues that community has a powerful moral dimension, and exerts a 'moral voice' which is able to enforce certain kinds of behaviour and rule out others. Thus the community into which people are born is the mainspring of social morality, and later developments in moral attitudes and individual values are adjustments around commitments originally formed in communities. However, recent decades have seen a weakening in the powers of communities, so that they now require some 'major fixing' to redress the excesses of individualism and greed. There is an entirely familiar refrain to Etzioni's comment that it is 'mainly in instances in which there is no viable community, in which people live in high-rise buildings and do not know one another . . . that the social underpinnings of morality are lost' (1995: 33).

The merging of theoretical and sociological analysis with everyday practical concerns is very evident in Etzioni's writings. He offers a diagnosis of various contemporary social ills with which many ordinary people, and newspaper journalists, would concur, and finds the solution for them in stronger communities. However, he is quite mistaken in supposing that sociologists have adopted only one attitude toward community and its characteristics. They have always been divided in opinion, and as many, if not more, have regretted the disappearance of close-knit community life as have applauded it. Etzioni makes his recommendations look new and radical only by ignoring the large numbers of sociologists and social commentators who have celebrated the virtues of small town and village life, the solidarity of various ethnic communities, and the warmth of relationships to be found among those who share common interests and goals, a tradition into which he fits quite comfortably. Indeed, his intellectual opponents criticize him for adopting the conservative, or even reactionary, stance that goes with a rejection of everything that is modern. Traditional conceptions of community tend to emphasize primordial attachments to the family, and to ties of kinship and place, as the bedrock of social solidarity. All of these appear to be challenged by the growth of modernity. Hence, it is not surprising that for Etzioni and those who share his perspective, they also need to be reinstated. Although hedged in by various qualifications and reservations, there is undoubtedly a desire among communitarians to see conventional forms of family life strengthened, along with the bonds between neighbours and friends. Going against the grain of most recent social analysis, Etzioni even claims that there are signs of a slowing down in the readiness with which people will flit between places, and a new eagerness on their part to put down local roots. Within such a framework, community itself acquires a distinctly conservative thrust. It is both a force for conservation, of values and social controls, and a step back into the social conventions of earlier years. Whereas classical sociology looked to times before the rise of modern industrial society to discover communities that were effective and strong, Etzioni finds his examples as recently as the 1950s; but the sense that things since have taken a turn for the worse is just as powerful. As he depicts it, the second half of the twentieth century represented an unrelenting decline from social harmony, solidarity and responsibility into self-centred individualism, 'rampant moral confusion and social anarchy' (1995: 24). The restoration of community will bring back a sense of discipline and moral persuasion, and help provide the antidote to crime, vandalism and social irresponsibility.

Whether or not they would accept Etzioni's proposed solutions, there is a powerful conviction amongst many sociologists that to find true examples of community one needs to look to the past. It is widely contended that modern advanced societies have witnessed the eclipse of people's ability to identify themselves with spatially located communities of place, and possibly also their ability to fashion alternative, substitute, versions of community more appropriate to contemporary circumstances. Whereas in early conditions it is accepted that most people inhabited social relations that were fixed, and organized largely around close family and neighbourhood connections, community of this sort is now considered to be a rare phenomenon, increasingly overwhelmed by the twin forces of corporate planning and government intervention (Crook *et al.* 1992), or market and state. More generally, the pressures of modern life are held to be hostile to the kinds of secure and predictable existence which were characteristic of earlier times. According to Savage and Warde, for instance,

> Modernity is intrinsically disorderly because it obliges individuals to experiment, to hope, to gamble, and to be ambitious. Its social life lacks the predictability and the certainties that characterise societies governed by tradition. Individual creativity is exchanged for the security of calculable social obligations and the sense of belonging that emanate from fixed social bonds.
>
> (Savage and Warde 1993: 150)

This raises questions about the basis for any strongly collective identity in the modern world, but makes it extraordinarily unlikely that it will be found in anything like the old patterns of community organization. Similar fears were expressed thirty years earlier by Stein (1964: 329) when he argued that community could not withstand the weakening of personal bonds that went with the decline of national, regional and family ties. Ultimately he feared this would jeopardize even the individual's capacity to sustain a coherent self-image. Giddens (1990) makes the same connection between modernity, and the undermining of stable social relations and a secure sense of the self.

Commentaries from a range of different perspectives can agree on this diagnosis, if not on how it should be counteracted. There is common ground, for example, between Etzioni's definition of communities as 'social webs of people who know one another as persons and have a moral voice' (1995: x) and Raymond Williams' conception of community as the sphere of 'direct and directly responsible relationships' (1989: 112). In each case, the idea of community is employed as part of a critique of the present, and its social failings. Both writers assume that obligations are stronger where people actually know and understand one another, and both see these kinds of relationships as under threat from contemporary change. Where they differ is in the direction taken by their politics. While Etzioni lays stress on the recovery of community, and the reinstatement of old ways of doing things, Williams looks more to an extension of community, and the translation of its values of immediacy and directness into a larger realm, through political action, culminating eventually in a whole society in which people could be motivated by 'habits of mutual obligation'. Where Etzioni emphasizes the disciplines imposed by community, Williams enjoins us to see it as a means through which people can seize control of their own destinies. The latter's debt to Marx's utopian vision of a future (communist) society is revealed when he asks how it could possibly be that people should *not* want to live in real (*sic*) community, which offers them so clearly a much better way to live than the conditions of the present (1989: 119). Here, full community lies somewhere in the future, though it draws on the strengths of the past. Yet even so, we find similarities between Williams' goal of an ever expanding awareness of community, and Etzioni's description of how different layers of community can nest inside one another, from its local and 'less encompassing' varieties up through the national and ultimately international and even global forms of community (Etzioni 2004).

WHAT FUTURE FOR COMMUNITY?

The readiness with which the idea of community can be embraced within the politics of the right, left and centre reminds us of those who would caution against its evasive nature: surely, to be acceptable to theorists of such different political persuasions, it must lack any definite meaning. As Mayo puts it, it seems to describe everything, and therefore nothing (1994: 51). Yet we have also seen that there is a fair degree of underpinning consensus, that community represents a particular kind of social bond, involving direct personal relations and intimate knowledge of others; also that the existence of this kind of relationship is associated with the presence of certain definite social conditions, which may or may not have been more likely to occur in the past than they are now. The question posed by much of the theoretical discussion among sociologists is whether or not the possibilities for ties of this sort to exist between people today have been exhausted by the tendencies of social change. Under contemporary conditions, is it possible to designate sets of social relationships that will foster the kinds of solidarity, and commitment to shared purposes and interests, that have been associated with communities in the past? This has been a central preoccupation among those who have turned their attention to the problem of community, for example those working in the field of urban sociology, who have worried away endlessly at the problem of finding ways of creating social bonds between those who inhabit the fragmented worlds of modern cities (Savage and Warde 1993; Harvey 2000).

For his part, Williams was sceptical about any general claim that community is a vanishing prospect; instead, he traced a series of major social changes through which it evolved from its 'primitive' early forms into a more explicit, and politically ambitious, pursuit of shared ideals. He also showed how the thesis of the loss of community formed part of a much larger narrative, that of society's decline from some bygone golden era (Williams 1975). Although in social theory this became closely associated with industrialism, and the rise to dominance of capitalist social relations, it extended much further back in time, to the very beginnings of social analysis, and carried with it always a certain social nostalgia. The ancient Greeks and Romans were already regretting the disappearance of orderly relationships, and the intrusion of urban and commercial values into their civilizations. This is a perspective that is especially attractive to those who feel that their own interests and powers are under attack, and can be shored up best by bringing about a 'return' to erstwhile community relations. This gives a variety of social groups, including those based on gender, ethnicity and class, a vested interest in upholding particular versions of community, with their associated patterns of social hierarchy and privilege.

Williams offers an alternative vision: not that community will disappear completely, but that it will be transformed into new kinds of awareness, increasingly detached from the limitations of particular places, neighbourhoods, and experiences. In his terms, community becomes a political project, a function of the mobilization of collective powers, and therefore is compatible with the conscious pursuit and realization of shared values and goals. Engagement in community does not necessarily mean having to eschew reason and foresight in favour of emotion. He considers this interpretation to be closer to the nature of those historical communities which he identifies as having been built through processes of social defence and opposition, usually in response to experiences of inequality and power, rather than laid down merely through habit and inertia. Although he accepts that many accounts of community would locate it within the framework of social and economic relations that are 'settled, reciprocal, and of an avowedly total kind' (1975: 48) – in other words, as part of a static social order – his own position is that community can be conceived of as an active process through which individuals and groups strive to realize their potential. Indeed, he distinguishes between a 'community of struggle', one that involves people in fighting for and gaining their economic and political rights, and the 'mutuality of the oppressed', found among those who have been pushed to the margins of society (1975: 131), for whom community is simply a defensive social arrangement.

Williams was not a sociologist, although in some aspects of his work he aspired to be one. As a cultural theorist, a prime interest lay in articulating what he referred to as the prevailing 'structures of feeling' characteristic of certain social groups, or during certain historical periods (Williams 1961). The sense of the loss of community was one such theme, running through popular cultures as well as conveyed in works of literature and social criticism. It is so pervasive and powerful as to suggest that communities face a continual threat of social entropy, which drags them towards disorganization, fragmentation, and individualization. Time and again this seems to be their expected fate. Williams sought to refute this. Throughout his own extensive writing on the topic, his touchstone remained the notion of a 'knowable community', supporting the kind of direct, face-to-face contacts through which we can 'find and value the real substance of personal relationships' (1975: 203). Once again there is a strong evaluative, even moral, component to this definition. It reflects the social environment Williams had experienced when growing up in the 1920s in the 'border country' of rural south Wales. He admits that such relationships are more difficult to sustain in larger and more complex social settings, where community and identity become more problematic, and need to be worked at harder, and other kinds of knowledge become important in addition to immediate experience. But the vision of his youth provided him with a critical tool for assessing other patterns of social life, and in this he was typical of many of his generation. The experience of actually having lived through what appeared to be the retreat or even collapse of community was shared by numerous others who adopted broadly similar criteria of the decent society.

In Britain, the idea of community provided a binding concept in the work of many who were influential in establishing sociology as a recognized intellectual discipline, following the Second World War. Their analyses of social problems and social changes were bound up closely with perceptions of how community in general, and real communities in given places, were being torn apart by fundamental shifts of political and economic power. There is a lengthy tradition of empirical exploration of such matters, which acquires a specifically British inflection in the preoccupation with examining how it relates to questions of class and class awareness (Young and Willmott 1957; Goldthorpe *et al.* 1969; Devine *et al.* 2005). In America, a comparable line of inquiry has centred more on issues of ethnic diversity, and the assimilation of migrant groups in urban settings (Park 1957; Whyte 1957; Suttles 1968), although there is some cross-over of concerns in later work. British sociology has produced nothing exactly equivalent to the 'Chicago School', with its depth of research and consistency of theoretical direction (Dickens 1990; Saunders 1986); but it would be possible to construct something not altogether different from the record of 'community studies' and those later investigations which have explored the importance of locality for people's identity and ability to act together (Bell and Newby

1971; Crow and Allen 1994). In much of this work, community has continued to serve as a benchmark against which the strengths and weaknesses of newly emerging social patterns can be measured. Usually the comparison works to the detriment of the new, because it does not fulfil the expectations and hopes associated with older ways of living.

This is one reason why some have lost patience with the concept. Though it is not alone in this respect, since similar problems afflict the use of other prominent social science concepts, it has proved especially difficult to disentangle the descriptive from the normative aspects of community. The temptation to mix supposedly objective assessments of the state of modern social relations with evaluative judgements upon them helps explain why the idea has drawn so much criticism. Already we have seen how easily discussions can blur the distinctions between prevailing patterns of social relationships, the quality of the resulting personal involvements, and aspirations for a better kind of social order. Several attempts have been made to argue that for the sake of clarity and rigour, these aspects must be kept apart (Bell and Newby 1976; Lee and Newby 1983; Willmott 1986), but it has proved almost impossible to sustain the separation, and as yet no one has come up with a convincing set of alternative concepts. It is hard to do so while 'community' remains so firmly embedded within the everyday thought and speech of social actors. Hence the frustration expressed by influential figures in sociology like Pahl (1996: 92) when he asked the question 'if sociologists have exposed the myths and fallacies of the idea of community . . . [why] does a dead idea refuse to lie down?' The answer must be, because actually it is not deceased; for some people at least, it continues to fulfil a useful living purpose.

THE RETURN OF COMMUNITY

Given that sociologists have been proclaiming the death of community for more than a century, it may seem surprising that recent years have seen its revitalization as a concept. Yet theorists at the cutting edge of contemporary sociology continue to reflect upon its importance. For a term so often dismissed as antiquated and confused, it displays an extraordinary resilience. An example would be the prominence of the term in the writings of Zygmunt Bauman, one of the foremost exponents of the sociology of postmodernity (Bauman 1992; 2000; 2001a). Time and again, Bauman informs us that the social conditions of the twenty-first century are incompatible with community, and yet he points out how widely and diversely the idea is deployed. Bauman cites the words of the eminent Marxist historian Eric Hobsbawm (1994: 428), to the effect that the term was never used 'more indiscriminantly and emptily than in the decades when communities in the sociological sense became hard to find in real life'. Again this must make us question what it is that people are actually seeking, and perhaps finding, within the notion of community, and how this relates to the proposed 'sociological sense' of the word. Bauman joins Hobsbawm in putting a negative gloss on this 'quest' for community: it is interpreted as a reactive response to the uncertainties and insecurities which are endemic in social life today. Bauman argues that contemporary society has released individuals from most of the restraining influences which once surrounded them, and especially from the 'ascribed, inherited and inborn determination of social character' (Bauman 2001a: 149). This leaves people free to make their own choices, but also highly anxious about their place in society. Increasingly therefore they turn to contexts where they can feel 'at home', and comfortable, amongst those who resemble them in their tastes and interests. This puts the emphasis upon certain voluntary types of community, or 'modes of togetherness', for which Bauman has produced a range of different labels. From the tone of his discussion, it is obvious that he considers most or all of these to be spurious and deceptive, because they cannot provide the 'real' security and protection that once were taken for granted. As ever, it seems that the notion of the 'true' community hovers over current conditions, and casts some dark shadows upon them. According to Bauman, it is in the search for community, real or fabricated, that some of the worst aspects of social exclusiveness, racism and fascism, are brought into being.

Castells (1997) occupies similar territory with his assertion that the construction of communities intended to resist the pressures of contemporary life forms perhaps the most important type of identity building project in our society. Thus 'the construction of social action and politics around primary identities, either ascribed, rooted in history and geography or newly built in an anxious search for meaning and spirituality', is said to constitute the most distinctive social and political trend of the 1990s (1997: 22). Recourse to communities organized around identities that are given supposedly by history, biology, or geography would seem to lead naturally towards groupings which are defensive and exclusive. Yet there is also a more positive message in Castells' conclusion that, in resisting powerful processes of individualization and social atomization, people may cluster together in organizations that, over time, will 'generate a feeling of belonging, and ultimately, in many cases, a communal, cultural identity' (1997: 60). He instances the growth of urban and environmental social movements, and also the possibility that people will utilize electronic communications to build virtual communities around their shared interests. Lash and Urry (1994: 50) concur that the difference between these 'new communities' and traditional *Gemeinschaften* is that people are not born into them, but must make them through their own choices and actions. This may lead in the direction of narrow and aggressive definitions of belonging, or it may result in more open-ended and inclusive types of social movement. Whichever way it goes, it seems that far from disappearing as an issue, new kinds of community are 'ever more frequently invented, so that such invention of community, such innovation becomes almost chronic. It is no longer the exception, but the rule' (Lash and Urry 1994: 316). Contrary to claims that community is defunct, this implies that it has taken on a new lease of life, albeit in quite unexpected and non-traditional forms.

CONCLUSION

In confronting community, we are dealing then with an idea which contains many possibilities and paradoxes. While some speak of its terminal decline, others see it flourishing in new and exciting forms, more adapted to modern circumstances. These rival claims rest on radically different understandings of what community actually involves. The various approaches we have been considering locate community among a number of contradictory pulls; hence the recurring references to tensions between individualism and collectivism, conservatism and progress, factual description and moralization. We have seen how the term community simultaneously invokes a particular way of organizing social relationships, a general (and desirable) quality of sociability and mutual regard, and a summons to undertake joint social action. Some regard community as an established fact, a 'taken for granted' reality, whereas others view it as a mission to be accomplished. The first position is represented by Abrams and McCulloch (1976: 165), when they describe community as an 'encompassing social fact' of lived interdependence, which gives rise to feelings of fondness and solidarity, through social relationships that are largely unconscious, and which therefore tend to deny individual choice and volition. Here community imposes itself upon people. However, this rather fatalistic interpretation is challenged by others who construe community as something which people actively pursue, as 'a metaphor for people's longing for a better life' and 'an imaginary framework for political mobilization' (Farrar 2001: 80, 111), or as a measure of the gap between life as it is actually experienced, and life as it could be imagined (Lee and Newby 1983). In the context of a rapidly changing social world, conceivably there has been a transformation in the central meaning of community, from one interpretation to the other: from providing the secure and stable setting for everyday social relationships to a state of affairs in which 'to speak of community is to speak metaphorically or ideologically' (Urry 2000: 134) about what it is that different sets of people are trying to achieve, in the face of a reality that seems to be increasingly fragmented, fluid, and chaotic.

2

COMMUNITY STUDIES

THE IDEA OF COMMUNITY STUDIES

In the opening decades of the twentieth century a variety of influences contributed to the emergence of a form of social research known as the 'community study', which occupied a position of some significance during the early development of academic sociology. Brook and Finn (1978: 141–3) list well over a hundred British and American sources produced between the late 1930s and early 1970s in which the concept of community plays a central part (for a full account of such researches, see Bell and Newby 1971; also Frankenberg 1966; Stein 1964). Relevant influences included the work of social surveyors and statisticians, who collected data on different local populations and sought to understand how they varied from one another, for instance in their demographic profiles; social anthropologists, whose emphasis on understanding the distinctive 'ways of life' of small social collectivities through techniques of participant observation and 'total immersion' showed how even very unfamiliar and sometimes bizarre patterns of behaviour could make sense once they were set properly in context; social geographers, who were interested in drawing contrasts between urban and rural types of community, and seeing how they developed over time; and political scientists, for some of whom the ideals of 'small town democracy' and community activism held particular value. The different tools and methodologies used by these various groups of social scientists were combined in a somewhat eclectic style of work, which converged on the investigation of relatively small and supposedly self-contained social units, regarded as constituting distinct and varied social worlds, or 'communities'. The community study was intended to show what was distinctive about a particular community, and to provide an account of how it worked that was as complete as possible. It was a 'holistic' enterprise, aimed at a total understanding of a community's nature.

The community study approach can be identified practically with three main kinds of locale: the rural or village community; small towns; and working class communities. There is a substantial body of primary and secondary literature for each of these, of which only a fraction can be mentioned here. While there are some key differences between them, so that often they were intended to provide quite contrasting sociological reference points, from the point of view of analysing the nature of 'community' it is also possible to extract some common themes, and derive some general conclusions across all three domains. Indeed, the extent to which valid generalizations could be taken from case-study materials in this way became one of the major debating points of the literature. However problematic it may be to do so, studies carried out in the three distinct contexts have contributed to some influential general models, which have informed ideas of what 'real' communities ought to be like, and served as starting points for subsequent empirical research. Together they generated a perception of 'community' as a particular kind of social structure or environment, with some very specific characteristics, within which certain typical patterns of action and belief would be likely to appear. It is against this benchmark that much of the subsequent, more critical, writing has been done.

Broadly speaking, we might refer to such studies as giving us a conception of the nature of *traditional* community that underpins many of the assumptions with which subsequent students of community have approached the field. Although few may believe that anything like this type of community exists now, in the twenty-first century, accounts of their earlier existence still provide standards of desirable social relations and the associated 'good life' which exert an influence upon contemporary expectations. Many of the more philosophical and theoretical reflections on the nature of community involve some kind of reference back to what is known, or assumed to be known, about these particular settings. They are, of course, a limited sample of possible social situations, as Byrne indicates when he writes (1995a: 15) that 'most community studies were either of small rural contexts, of one class special cases, or of rural towns. There isn't a proper UK community study of a large industrial city'. However, this begs the question as to what a community study of an entire city might look like. Many took from the classic studies the conclusion that such a study would not be possible beyond a certain level and scale of size and complexity, and indeed that in such circumstances the very idea of 'community' might not apply. Although it might contain one or more communities within it, a city as such was unlikely to be a community.

THE OUTLINES OF TRADITIONAL COMMUNITY

For each of the three contexts, the prevailing interpretation depended substantially on ideas of proximity, continuity and stability as forming the crucible within which the ties of community are forged. While these conditions are not altogether incompatible with change, the kinds of change which were seen as occurring 'naturally' in such communities were believed to be gradual and controlled, whereas abrupt transformations and unexpected changes brought disorder, and possible collapse. In these terms, community itself came to be conceived of as a source of stabilization, ensuring the conservation of social relations. In the majority of studies, considerable emphasis is laid on the reproduction of existing patterns and 'ways of life', and the slow pace of change within communities. Where major changes are observed to occur, they tend to be interpreted as posing a threat to the community's integrity and viability.

Communities of this kind provide settings within which people experience continually repeated contacts with the same personnel, or at least with the same kinds of persons. At their heart, therefore, such communities appear to be built around groups of family, friends, neighbours and fellow workers or economic partners who are in regular, perhaps daily, and often face-to-face contact with one another. This gives rise to a central idea of the linked multiple relationships which develop inside communities, tying people together in such a way that 'each kind of bond implies another social context in which the same parties are co-actors' (Calhoun 1982: 158). This multiplicity of contacts creates what Frankenberg (1966) referred to as the 'redundancy' of close-knit community: there are many pathways linking members together, so that the failure or breakdown of any one relationship need not weaken the overall unity. Rather, there is a pressure to maintain, or reinstate, cooperation. Thus arguments which arise in one sphere of action may threaten effective collaboration in another, so that there is a propensity either to restore good relations, or for disagreement to spread out from its original source and widen into social schism, or feud. The classic community studies sought to reveal the workings of such dense social networks, and show what consequences they had for those who were caught up in them. Such communities approximated to social groups, in that they were relatively bounded, and set apart from the rest of society, and so able to confer upon individuals a definite sense of membership and collective identity. Where they were small, it was likely that most of the local population were connected to, and knew, one another. The cliched expression of this is a comment along the lines that 'everybody knows (or knew) everybody else – and their business'. This made it plausible to imagine that research could produce an all-encompassing portrait of the entire set of social relationships, just as those who were actually implicated in them would be able to form a complete impression of how they were related to everyone else.

A number of such studies became extremely well known, and helped popularize the practice of social research, partly because their concern with documenting everyday social interaction at a local level made them approachable by the general reader, as well as by those educated in social science. It has been said that the community study provided a sociological substitute for the novel (Glass 1966: 148). Indeed, there is also a popular genre of writing about particular communities, often semi-autobiographical, which commands a large audience (examples would include Roberts 1971; McCourt 1996; Thompson 2000; Woodruff 2002). Fictional reconstructions of different kinds of local community are also commonplace, and trade heavily on assumptions that their audience will be willing and able to compare and contrast the created images with their own experiences of actual communities. Television soap operas are an obvious case in point (Cohen 1997); many are set in what purport to be community-like milieu, such as Coronation Street, Albert Square, Emmerdale, Ramsay Street, or (on radio) Ambridge, where a limited cast of characters continually meet one another, in a setting where home, work and leisure intersect.

Unlike many other areas of social investigation, then, 'community' seems to be quite accessible, not closed off to the few, nor demanding any particularly esoteric knowledge. At the same time, the nature of the specific communities in question may prove to be surprisingly different, and special methods and techniques may be required to gain access to them. The researcher therefore can offer insights into 'secret' worlds, appealing to the voyeur in us all, while at the same time showing how the issues and problems dealt with are entirely familiar and 'ordinary'. Even if community studies no longer represent a major form of social scientific reportage, it is still the case that studies of 'community' provide sociology with some of its more readable and entertaining material, enabling us to participate vicariously in other people's lives. However, as Glass' comments were intended to show, closeness to fiction and the everyday is not seen as an unmitigated virtue in social science. A common criticism of the community studies is that they remain too close to ordinary life, lacking any penetrating theoretical insight, or ultimate seriousness. At worst, they lend weight to an accusation that sociologists merely trade in 'common sense', telling us what we already know.

The actual meaning of 'community' in these studies is controversial, and sooner or later, most discussions get embroiled in a definitional tangle. At its most rudimentary level, and probably that resorted to most frequently in everyday speech, 'community' is simply a label for a specific unit or object of study. Nothing more is intended by it than that some particular set of people or institutions can be grouped together, in order to comment upon them – hence 'the community' can take a wide variety of shapes, including at the present time, for instance, as well as local or geographical communities, a variety of 'faith' communities, ethnic or minority groups, communities defined by sexual proclivity, the seafaring community, deaf community, and so on. These categories may share nothing except the fact that they all represent some kind of aggregate, or grouping, around which a boundary has been drawn. A large part of the 'community study' method consists of setting out to describe and explain whatever internal relationships and organization can be found to exist in such groupings. According to Rose (1996: 332), the approach seeks to render communities knowable by making them into zones to be 'investigated, mapped, classified, documented, interpreted' and explained to others. In their 1971 textbook, Bell and Newby abandoned the attempt to pin down any precise meaning for 'community', leaving it to be decided by whatever those who did community studies chose to make of it. It is not unusual to find that a study of community has been brought to an end without this fundamental question ever really being answered.

Once it goes beyond the classificatory level, however, the concept of community tends to become more significant sociologically, because of what it assumes or implies about the internal structuring of the unit. Usually it refers to a bundle of characteristics that are expected to go together. As is evident from our examination of the conceptual debates surrounding the term, 'community' signifies both an entity and a quality. A community is a place, or setting, displaying certain social characteristics, that can be identified and described; but community is also something that is felt, and which has an emotional or affective impact. Often the two aspects are brought together, since it is commonly supposed that the features typical of a community will generate and sustain the appropriate attitudes and sentiments among those who belong to it: that is, the 'objective' aspects will produce the corresponding 'subjective' response. A large part of the early work in the field of community studies was concerned with establishing that such a correlation existed, specifying its various features, and asking how and why sometimes it failed to materialize. Almost always, there was a further evaluative dimension to community research, so that descriptive accounts frequently became entangled with various kinds of value judgements. The theoretical interpretation of community, and the empirical investigation and comparison of actual examples, was intended by many to yield practical results, in terms of 'policies' or planning rules, for the preservation, construction and improvement of communities. Consequently, as Bell and Newby put it, 'below the surface of many community studies lurk value judgements, of varying degrees of explicitness, about what is the good life' (1971: 16). Farrar (2001) discusses the persistent conflation of the actual and 'metaphorical' uses of 'community', or the objective and subjective dimensions, and the confusions which this produces. Many of the problems in the field stem from the compounding of the two, as in the belief that certain subjective outcomes flow 'naturally' from given conditions: for example, that planners can design community through perfecting the layout of the built environment, or that social engineers can fabricate community feeling by ensuring the right mixture of social types and functions in a given area. When value judgements are thrown into the equation as well, no wonder many find discussions of community to be riddled with ambiguity or evasiveness!

Language itself makes it difficult to keep these various dimensions apart, because it is all too easy to slip from talking about the real social structure and interactional dynamics of particular communities into voicing views which belong more in the abstract moral or emotional realm. References to 'our' community very often elide would-be descriptive/factual references with evocative, and normative, sentiments. This lends strength to what Cohen refers to as the 'community romance', the readiness to imagine community as the way in which society was bound together in 'some golden age of unmediated exchange' (Cohen 1997: 39). Cohen suggests that although community of this kind probably never actually existed in its pure form, nevertheless it represents a situation which, in a whole variety of ways, people strive to retrieve or recreate. There is a strongly romantic (or some would say, sentimental) tone to a good deal of the writing about traditional communities, and 'old' models of community cast a profound shadow over contemporary manifestations and debates. A voluminous literature about their decay and disappearance leads almost inexorably into expressions of nostalgia and lament for everything that is thought to have been lost with their going. It is not only among social commentators that such sentiments exist; they pervade popular culture and attitudes, and fuel a host of social and political responses. Intentionally or not, the backward-looking tendency associated with much discussion of community glamourizes the past, while often denigrating the present.

This owes much to the selective principle through which certain sorts of community have been treated as exemplary, or idealized as the closest approximation we know to true realizations of community. As a body of social research, therefore, the whole approach to community studies displays a certain circularity. Places are singled out for study because they appear to constitute viable communities, and once they are investigated and documented, the findings are read as showing precisely what a real community is like. Accordingly, small towns and villages have often seemed the most appropriate locations for community studies because they were *expected* to have the necessary community character. City sprawl, and areas of social disorganization, on the other hand, seemed inappropriate settings for genuine community, while also presenting greater research problems; therefore they were filtered out from consideration.

Although these decisions might seem to be simply pragmatic, they were also driven by at least semi-theorized underlying assumptions – about the nature of communities as coherent functioning wholes, relatively autonomous, and capable of being looked at separately from the surrounding society. This was most explicit in the studies of small towns with which such research began. The small town often presents itself as a self-sufficient, inward-looking milieu, capable of commanding the commitment and loyalty of its inhabitants, and meeting the majority of their needs, fiercely independent, and distinctive, and this representation has carried over rather too easily into the minds of social investigators. From the start, they were in danger of absorbing and projecting the self-images of community that were prevalent in the places they studied.

Small town sociology

In the foreword to the American study of Muncie, Indiana, published in 1929 under the pseudonym *Middletown*, it is stated that between the psychological/biographical study of the individual and the statistical/analytical investigation of social trends, there is a need to examine real-life community, because 'the masses of individuals concerned live and function in communities, and . . . the picture will not be complete until these communities are made objects of study' (Lynd and Lynd 1929: vi). This assumption that 'community' formed the natural or normal unit of social existence was part of the thinking behind what became the tradition of community studies. It was argued that anthropological science had made considerable progress by comparing and contrasting human communities across the world, and the time had come now to turn the anthropological lens onto communities closer to home, 'to study ourselves as through the eyes of an outsider . . . by approaching an American community as an anthropologist does a primitive tribe' (1929: vi). The aim was to produce an account of ordinary, everyday life through systematic and detailed observation, so revealing 'the interwoven trends that are the life of a small American city' in what was termed a 'total-situation study' (1929: 3). An organizational device borrowed from cultural anthropology enabled the classification of these 'trends' under what purported to be a comprehensive set of headings: getting a living; making a home; training the young; using leisure; engaging in religious practices;

engaging in community activities. The activities listed are so basic that everyone could be expected to participate in them, as part of their routine of social life; but the added twist which made this a matter of 'community' was that the people being studied could do all or most of them within the context of the town itself. When investigated together, over some 500 pages of sociological description, they would provide a thorough impression of the *totality* of life in this particular community. This does not necessarily mean that the enterprise was successful: the Lynds expressed some of their own doubts when they concluded that

> The attempt to reveal interrelations in the maze of interlocked, often contradictory, institutional habits that constitute living in Middletown has led to few general conclusions save as to the inchoate condition of this one small modern community, and the extent and complexity of the task confronting social science.
>
> (Lynd and Lynd 1929: 496)

Critics would contend that later studies in the same vein were no more successful.

As the name 'Middletown' implies, Muncie was chosen to be representative of American life; and yet, in order to be manageable in research terms, it was also selected to be compact and homogeneous. Among other things, the choice was restricted to populations of no more than 30,000 (even in the 1930s, quite a modest size). More seriously, it also meant the exclusion from consideration of certain kinds of social divisions or differences – for instance, between racial or ethnically varied sub-groups. Small town 'middle' America was thus defined as having a single dominant pattern of social organization and culture. It was tempting for later researchers to use this as a standard of the 'normal' against which to measure deviations of various kinds. A similar effect was produced when another research group adopted the name 'Yankee City' for their study site (Newburyport, Massachusetts). The authors claimed that the town could be thought of as a microscopic whole representing the total American community. Yet the same selective principle had been at work, since they deliberately sought out a place which had developed over a long period of time under the domination of 'a single group with a coherent tradition', and avoided areas of conflict and disorganization. Yankee City was also viewed as a working whole in which each part had definite functions which had to be performed or substitutes acquired if the whole society were to maintain itself.

(Warner and Lunt 1941: 12)

This framework is borrowed from the anthropological investigation of small 'tribal' groups and isolated societies, which focusses on the functional integration of the whole (Malinowski 1944). Applied to Newburyport, it presupposed that the town could exist in splendid isolation from the rest of America, a position that played down the extent to which its culture and behaviour patterns relied upon materials and ideas absorbed from the wider society. Instead, it encouraged a reverse view, that wider society itself was built up from adding together the contributions made by many such small, independent, local social worlds. To demonstrate this, Warner and his colleagues embarked on an exhaustive effort to collect a mass of information and observations about life in Newburyport, putting themselves as far as possible in the position of the anthropological outsider. Their findings were spread across five published volumes, plus an abridged summary. A later critical assessment is scathing: 'never in the history of community studies has so much effort been expended by so many people with such wrongheaded assumptions and with such inappropriate concepts and techniques' (Bell and Newby 1971: 110). However, this is written with the benefit of considerable hindsight, and from the perspective of a methodologically and theoretically more informed standpoint. It is not entirely fair to condemn pioneering researchers for making the mistakes from which their successors have been able to learn.

For better or worse, the Yankee City studies established a style of working, and a framework for analysis, which exerted a considerable influence over investigations of community for the next thirty years. Thus, if we jump forward by some years, we find a very similar approach being adopted in Stacey's classic (1960) study of the small market town of Banbury in Oxfordshire, population 20,000. Although she does not make the same wide-ranging claims about the generalizability of her findings, concentrating instead on an in-depth examination of this particular location, Stacey is also concerned to 'relate the parts to the whole'. This time, however, Bell and Newby (who worked with Stacey on a follow-up study, Stacey *et al.* 1975) describe it far more positively, as 'an unparalleled analysis of the local interconnections of social institutions', and a convincing portrayal of a close-knit social structure (1971: 182). Actually there are many resemblances between Stacey's account of Banbury and the Yankee City project, including the attempt to map out distinctive patterns of local social stratification by getting townspeople to evaluate one another, and describe their relative status positions. At about the same time, the Derbyshire town of Glossop, adjacent to Manchester, was chosen for study because it was 'sufficiently isolated and self-contained to have a distinct community life of its own', forming a 'well-integrated and largely independent community' whose population had been stable for many years (Birch 1959: 4–5). Writing in 1982, Calhoun uses the nearby town of Haslingden as a representative example of such small outlying population centres. Whereas Manchester exploded from almost nothing into a world industrial centre during the nineteenth century, the population of Haslingden grew only from 4,040 in 1841 to some 16,000 in the 1980s. When Calhoun (1982) studied it, its inhabitants continued to be known by name, rather than anonymous address, and visiting strangers were a topic of general interest.

There is a tradition, then, of singling out such small, integrated, local populations in order to trace their social characteristics and inter-actions. Treating them as social wholes implied adopting a certain methodological approach, in which fieldworkers were expected to pro-vide 'a full and clear account of at least the main lines of economy, social structure, political organisation, ritual and ideology . . . (and) the con-sistent functional interrelations of all these aspects of a society's culture' (Dennis *et al.* 1969: 246). The idea of the community as a functioning whole, or system of interdependent parts, came to be widely adopted. According to Redfield (1955: 11), in a typically circular formulation, a community was something that could provide for 'all of life's needs for all kinds of people needed to keep that way of life going'. Many others offered similar definitions, making reference to the meeting of needs over a period of time – daily life, a normal year, or even an entire life cycle. A community was a place in which the whole of one's life could be lived (MacIver and Page 1961). The problematic nature of this con-ception can be seen if one contrasts the expectation that such needs could be met within a relatively restricted bounded system, or space, with Harvey's observation that today, even tracing the ingredients for an average breakfast might take one into connections of global proportions (Harvey 1993). It appears to confine community research to the analysis of situations in which people rarely, if ever, leave this delimited space, or look beyond it for significant elements of their material or cultural consumption; that is, to situations which are vanishingly rare.

In one of the most thorough and theoretically informed discussions of the time, Warren (1963: 9) reiterated this view. Echoing Parsons (1951), he defines community as 'that combination of social units and systems that perform the major social functions having locality relevance' and goes on to say that by community 'we mean the organization of social activities to afford people daily local access to those broad areas of activity that are necessary to day to day living' (Warren 1963: 9). Matching the Lynds' anthropological framework, he lists these functions as: production, distribution, consumption, socialization, social control, participation and mutual support. The inclusion of 'locality relevance' in the definition ensures that the link between function and place is retained. Indeed, the starting point for Warren's analysis is a statement of 'the inescapable fact that people's clustering together in space has important influences on their daily activities'. At the time of writing, Warren was confident enough to assert that

> It is in his or her own locality, characteristically, that throughout most of human history and to a very great extent today, the individual confronts society's institutions ... services at the local church, a source of employment, organizations to which to belong, friends and relatives with whom to visit – all these and many other basic ingredients of everyday life remain largely a function of the local arena, and the way people organize themselves to procure them in locality groups is the special subject matter of the study of community.
>
> (Warren 1963: 21)

The claim that this is how most people have lived historically puts 'community' firmly on the sociological map, even if there is a hint that this is no longer quite so certain.

Warren's view that the study of community deals with how people form themselves into locality groups to procure their essential needs corresponds to what has been probably the most frequent version of what community means, sociologically. It conforms to one of Lee and

Newby's defining aspects of community (1983: 57) as 'a set of social relationships which take place wholly, or mostly, within a locality'. The majority of definitions take it for granted the community has such connection with a certain place. Writing about a contemporary rural Australian community, with a population of approximately 2,500, Dempsey states that

> [i]n contrast to the 'typical' large urban settlement, Smalltown is a context in which most social ties and day-to-day activities of most members are bounded by the immediate locality: work, play, shopping, religious, kinship and friendship activity are all conducted in one small physical setting.
>
> (Dempsey 1990: 7)

As a result, these various institutions are tightly bound together with one another. However, Dempsey concedes that this is now a minority situation, since the great majority of Australians live in large urban settings.

From this point of departure, we can deduce quite a lot about 'real' communities, or what is expected of them. The keynote is *integration*, with different aspects of life connecting to, and reinforcing one another. By implication, this means that the people involved will have multiple reasons for coming into contact. Their social world therefore will tend to revolve around a particular place, and its set of social relationships. Others in the locality will be familiar to them, and they will know at least something (sometimes, a lot) about them. One might assume that they will have a firm sense of *belonging* to both place and people; their identity will be wrapped up within their community. In this way, we can make connections between the *institutions* which constitute the local social system; the *personal relationships* in which people are involved; and their accompanying *feelings and sentiments*. 'Community' begins to look like an all-purpose expression encapsulating all these dimensions: it is a totalizing phenomenon. As with the conventional anthropological conception (Amit and Rapport 2002), there is a holism which anticipates the mutual constitution of place, identity, culture and social relations. Community represents the most seamless of webs.

Stacey's description of Banbury as 'bound together by common history and tradition, with a recognised social structure and having certain common values . . . conformity, stability, and conservation of established institutions' (1960: 169) fits this framework well, as does the ensuing claim that 'the family, together with place of origin and associations . . . was the test by which people "recognised" or "placed" each other' (1960: 186). These are things known only to those who share the same community, and who have similar bodies of knowledge or experience. Those who belong to the community can do this 'placing', whereas strangers and outsiders cannot; consequently, this provides a vital criterion of who is a member, and who is not. Writing about the small Welsh slate-mining settlement of Blaenau Ffestiniog, Emmett says

> those who have grown up in the town have such a wealth of knowledge of each other as to make each encounter densely elaborate. Men and women are known as parents, as drinkers or non-drinkers, as singers and speakers, in some version of their work records and in some version of their record as lovers.
>
> (Emmett 1982: 207)

In other words, Blaenau is a paradigm case of Williams' 'knowable community' (Williams 1989). The peculiar depth and intensity of such knowledge rests on a lifetime of contact, interaction and dialogue with one another. Although viewed locally as a relatively substantial settlement, Blaenau Ffestiniog contrives to be village-like, just as Calhoun (1982: 184) found that local social relations in Haslingden 'still retained a decidedly village flavour'.

Village life

Of all the familiar settings for traditional community, it is the village which provides the most archetypal, to the extent that at times the two become almost synonymous. Certainly the widely held conception of the 'rural idyll' equates genuine community with life in the country village (Newby 1979; 1987). In part, this is a question of scale, since the village is the smallest and perhaps most self-contained of common spatial units; but a number of other facets also contribute towards the formation of strong local bonds and feelings of interdependence. The key underlying connection is to agriculture and the rural economy, which historically have provided villages with their *raison d'être*, and given their inhabitants a common purpose and set of shared preoccupations. As places in which agricultural work is done, villages tend to be looked upon as long established, slow growing, close to nature, and in harmony with their environment, surely the most 'organic' of human contexts. This means that they have been regarded very favourably by the majority of urban commentators (although by no means all), as offering rewards and virtues that are missing from more modern and artificial situations.

As early research conducted in rural settings would seem to suggest, the village type of social setting epitomizes the social wholeness many expect from community. Indeed, the presumption comes through in surprising ways even in comparatively modern texts. A collection of papers on *Mobilizing the Community* is prefaced by an introduction which contends that in the modern era, 'global processes have disordered people's conception of who they are, and to whom they are related, and have undermined their bearings as to the nature of the social spaces in which their daily lives are grounded'. The antithesis of this predicament is said to be found in the village, because

> Village signifies a place where there are few disruptions of the routines of living, few surprises and few threats. In the village, strangers are rare, and, if everyone does not quite know everyone else, people at least recognise most of the faces they pass in the street. It is a metaphor for the closeness of people and the reassuring familiarity and durability of the day to day.
>
> (Fisher and Kling 1993: xi)

It is obvious that this statement does not refer to an actual village so much as a mythic village, a village of the imagination, or one that for purposes of analysis has been turned into an ideal type. Once accomplished, this intellectual transformation allows the attribution of certain 'village-type' properties even to places which lack some of the key features of real villages, such as certain urban neighbourhoods, where although the population is large, and physical boundaries ill-defined, social relationships remain close enough for the formation of an 'urban village' (Gans 1962; Taylor 1973).

So far as the scientific understanding of village life is concerned, there is a direct line of descent from the Yankee City study, and work done in the rural southwest of Ireland by Arensberg and Kimball (1940), and through that into the British community study tradition. This is well documented by Frankenberg (1966). This intellectual bond carried with it the conception that local society should be studied as 'a system of mutually interrelated and functionally interdependent parts' (Arensberg and Kimball 1940: xxx). It was particularly easy to imagine that the various aspects of rural life pulled together, in a consistent direction, since normally they would have had plenty of time to become adapted to the demands of the local climate, terrain, and system of agricultural production. For example, rural ways of life would be strongly influenced by the cycles of seasonal activity, and the particular problems involved in managing different crops and forms of livestock. Arensberg and Kimball's depiction of remote rural Ireland as an ageless, unchanging social world rooted in dim and distant Celtic origins inspired similar sentiments among other students of rural life and 'folk' cultures.

Separated from one another usually by considerable distances, agricultural villages could be represented as comparatively isolated and self-contained, each with its own customs and traditions, able to attract strong local loyalties and create a clear sense of identity, place and order, that could be recognized and accepted almost as natural and unchanging facts of life (Newby 1987: 79). A series of well known investigations of village life seemed to confirm this general impression (Rees 1950; Williams 1956; Davies and Rees 1960), and there can be little doubt that the populations of many rural villages themselves share this perspective, celebrating in ritual and custom their difference from others, and their unity as a group. The focus on such places brought accusations, however, that sociologists used the term community in a highly subjective way, to refer only to 'societies which are finite and remote' (Taylor 1973: 193). Frankenberg was taxed for choosing to describe as communities 'so many unrepresentative villages', though the choice was hardly his, but the result of decisions made by those whose work he was reviewing. Their preferences, and theoretical orientations, took them to places which could be designated as 'truly rural', and in which they could find just the sort of community they were looking for. In Britain, said Frankenberg, this attracted them to the peripheral areas of upland countryside, in Wales, Scotland and Cumbria. Elsewhere, equivalent studies were carried out by social anthropologists and rural geographers across Europe, often in places where agriculture was still relatively undeveloped and the majority of inhabitants were part of a peasant way of life (Wylie 1957; Maraspini 1968; Fox 1978). Faced with the proliferation of such studies, one anthropologist accused his colleagues of taking refuge in their villages from complex forces of change, and thereby 'tribalizing' Europe into a host of isolated self-contained units (Boissevain 1975).

In such contexts, they could identify settlements consisting of small numbers of people, who shared a background of close family connections extending back into the indefinite past, growing up together, and often forming all their social relationships from within a very narrowly circumscribed geographical area. The strength of common connections, and the range of shared interests and concerns among such people placed them close to Durkheim's state of 'mechanical solidarity', and seemed to provide the necessary empirical confirmation for Tonnies' rural *Gemeinschaft*. Again, the farming community of Ireland's County Clare, where family relationships, economic cooperation, leisure and worship all embraced the same few scores of individuals, seemed to provide an exemplary case. According to Bell and Newby (1971: 140), while each of these studies added something to sociology, they contributed little to one another, amounting only to a series of one-off cases, interesting for what they revealed about the details and idiosyncrasies of life in particular places, but unable to furnish cumulative and systematic knowledge. However, to the contrary, they have also been widely criticized subsequently (Harper 1989; Wright 1992; Rapport 1993) for imposing a theoretically stultifying framework over the analysis of community, precisely because they had so much in common, namely the tendency to disregard history, and to treat each community as a self-maintaining, functionally integrated, whole. This suggested that, despite all the observable differences between them, rural communities worked in pretty much the same way, to preserve a steady, customary or 'traditional' pattern of life over long periods of time, and across the generations. Indeed, for some, the meaning of rural community could be identified with the struggle to resist change and maintain a given 'way of life' (Harris 1990: 189).

This is an assumption Newby challenged, when he argued that as a result of changes in land-ownership and farming practices during the course of the nineteenth century, English lowland communities in fact became more 'rural' and agricultural than they had been before, losing some of their diversity of trades and economic statuses. In response to these developments, the social organization of English villages had evolved, leading Newby to conclude that the idea of the 'traditional' village community hardly existed except as some kind of folk memory (Newby 1987: 78). Similarly Gibbon (1973) and Brody (1974) provided devastating critiques of Arensberg and Kimball's work in Ireland, showing that, far from timeless inevitabilities of the rural landscape, many of the characteristics described were fairly recent adaptations to the effects of the potato famine of the 1840s. Without a historical dimension to the analysis, there was a constant danger of mistaking ephemeral patterns for permanent features. Similarly, what constituted 'community' in such contexts was shown to depend greatly upon subjective assessment, reflecting the preferences and values of both those studied and those doing the studying. The same social arrangements looked very different when viewed from the perspective of women rather than men, or of the young rather than the elderly. There had been a great deal of mythologizing of rural life, and its stability, and harmony, as well as an uncritical acceptance of the legitimacy of its established order. Newby's work on rural history helped retrieve the record of agrarian unrest and rebellion, while his sociological contribution highlighted questions of inequality, power, and oppression in the countryside, and how they had been handled through ideological frameworks of local order and control (Newby *et al.* 1978). For example, he pointed to the importance of 'deference' as a marked feature of local situations in which the imbalance of power was so great that it was pointless to try to challenge it head-on (Newby 1979).

In many other rural situations across the world, community relationships are equally dominated by the bonds of patronage, dependency and fatalism, and should not be mistaken for relations that are embraced voluntarily, or with enthusiasm (Williams 1975; Long 1977). In such cases, one ought to treat with suspicion any claims that there is a warm and unified community in which everyone participates on the same terms. Observers might come to such a conclusion only because they were looking at the community in isolation from its larger social context, and being seduced into accepting its own verdict upon itself as an accurate reflection of reality. Newby was able to break with the conventional interpretation when he put the evidence of rural community studies into the framework of a broader analysis of social class relationships and class divisions, which could not have been developed on the basis of work done at the level of community alone. This led him to ask how it was conceivable that the analysis of life in rural villages could ignore the impact of such forces, to the extent that village communities were made to seem as if they stood outside mainstream patterns of social change and development.

WHOLENESS AND PARTICULARITY IN TRADITIONAL COMMUNITY

Critics of the community studies approach would find vindication in Newby's position for their view that conclusions taken from such researches are partial at best, and may be thoroughly misleading, because they are too preoccupied with internal processes and mechanisms. This suggests that it is not enough to build up our understanding of society simply through the accumulation of local studies, because by definition communities are no more than part-societies within a larger whole. At the same time, this is not to deny that there may be enough variation between communities to make their study interesting and worthwhile (Harris 1990: 189). If they are not simply to vanish into society as a whole, communities must maintain their distinctiveness, and somehow protect their boundaries. Behind the community studies there lies a basic presupposition that it is the particularities of life in a given place, whether it is a small rural village or a giant global city, which give it a 'character' of its own. Without appreciating these particularities, no account of society will be complete. Nevertheless, although interesting, these differences need not be of crucial social importance, and some-times they may be just parochial. Important though it may be to the residents of a particular village that they observe a certain tradition or ritual – say, rolling a cheese down hill, or burning a barrel of tar – in the general order of things these are not terribly significant facts. Indeed, they may seem merely 'quaint'.

The impression gained of life in a typical village, according to these studies, was that inhabitants were deeply embroiled in a set of close-knit and complicated personal relationships, within which they met one another as whole persons. That is, the woman who served you in the local shop would also be familiar as a member of the local religious con-gregation, a performer in the village choir, and a parent of pupils in the local school. Her produce would be on display at the village show, her skills and advice might be called upon in times of need, and further-more, one would know a considerable amount about her family connec-tions, their history and reputation. There might even be some direct ties of kinship with her. If not, there were bonds of neighbourliness and an accumulation of shared memories and experiences. Compared to the depth and intimacy of these relationships within the community, con-tacts with outsiders and strangers would be cold and impersonal, and lacking in subtlety. Only those who took the time and care to learn about them could appreciate the fine nuances of social relationships within such a community. In appropriately rural idioms, local intercon-nections could be described as 'like a pig's entrails' or in terms of how if you trod on someone's tail in one part of the village, a dog would bark at the other end (Rees 1950). Lacking the knowledge available to those who belonged, the stranger would be prone perpetually to committing social gaffes, speaking badly of someone who would turn out to be the interlocutor's distant cousin or friend. Put into more sociological termi-nology, the overall pattern of social relationships would be dense, multi-plex, bounded, and encompassing, providing a total framework within which the individual was embedded. This produces the conventional understanding of community referred to by Frazer when she writes that

> There is a strong conceptual implication in usage and analyses of community that individuals are related to each other in multiple and complex ways. This multiplexity and complexity enhance the 'entity' status of the whole and accentuates the sense in which to be related to each is to be related to the whole.
>
> (Frazer 1999: 241)

In other words, a community of this kind takes on a strong, objective reality. It consists of a definite set of interconnections, which can be traced out in detail through observation and study, and whose strength is reinforced by the fact that they involve multiple contacts among a limited group of individuals. These connections carry various forms of information, experience and values, which are shared by those who are implicated and encourage certain types of expected behaviour. Through repetition and confirmation, strong norms of community life can be enforced, along with certain routine social practices. These may differ from those found elsewhere, in detail, if not in general pattern. Part of knowing the community is to appreciate that 'this is the way we do things round here'.

Community studies produce example after example of this sort of typical activity and behaviour, and the associated expectations. For instance, people in County Clare were not expected to pay off their debts to one another in full, because this would signify a rupturing of their social relationships (Arensberg 1939). In rural Wales, those who held positions of prominence in the chapel tended to be viewed as the most important members of the community, and vice-versa (Davies and Rees 1960). Comments made by people in a recent study of Welsh villages confirm that these types of social relationship still exist. As one informant puts it,

> This is my village. It's where I grew up. It's where my family has lived for years. This is the place I know best, it's part of me . . . I feel that I have a claim on it in some way.
>
> (James 2003: 54)

When an incomer from elsewhere expressed her sense of surprise and bafflement that, following a bereavement, neighbours called to leave 'gifts of food, cakes and flowers', a local explained that 'this was their way of demonstrating that they were sympathizing with her; that they shared her pain. It is the way that the village shows that we know that you are in trouble' (James 2003: 63). As another informant commented, 'in the village, people value each other, and what everyone gives to the community. Some work really hard, whilst others do small things – but it's all appreciated'. Such comments immediately inspire thoughts of closeness, belonging and inclusion. In the words of a seminal study of a small American community, 'It is as if people in a deeply felt communion bring themselves together for the purposes of mutual self-help and protection. To this end the community is organized for friendliness and neighbourliness' (Vidich and Bensman 1958: 34). What they do not reveal is how people are regarded if they choose not to 'contribute', or if in times of trouble they prefer to be left alone. What strings are attached to membership of such a community? Closer attention to what actually goes on often shows that not everyone is equally deeply attached to, or valued in, such arrangements, while there may be those who are systematically marginalized or even excluded from sharing the warmth and comforts of participation (Dempsey 1990; Cloke *et al.* 1997).

THE CRITIQUE OF COMMUNITY STUDIES

On the basis of work done in the community studies tradition, Frazer (1999: 67) determines that sociologists conceive of community as 'a locality with settled denizens, a stable social structure consisting of dense networks of multiplex relations, and a relatively high boundary to the outside'. Such a definition presents a number of significant hostages to fortune, and might prove to be quite unduly restrictive, since the vast majority of prevailing social situations will not fit its criteria. Following MacIver and Page (1961), Frankenberg (1966: 15) offered a slightly more relaxed definition, as 'an area of social living marked by some degree of social coherence. The bases of community are locality and community sentiment'. However, the thrust of the various examples he considers still conveys that community has its 'true' basis in the existence of a particular pattern of social living, a social structure of interlocking relationships that are materially dense, and from which flow the other features that make up traditional 'community'. Locality may be relevant because it defines the space within which these relationships are contained, and community requires some outer boundary. Sentiments are important because they are generated by the social structure. So, when people are caught up in this close pattern of shared life, they are hard pressed to avoid sentiments of reciprocity; a favour done now must be returned later, although perhaps the timing and form of the exchange are left unspecified. Failure to reciprocate will lead to isolation and exclusion, which are hard to bear in the context of the small and bounded community. In some circumstances, it may even put the individual's survival at risk. Accounts provide examples of the extreme aggravation which may be required before individuals are cut off from social contact, and show that this is a sanction which can be used to enforce the social discipline and order of the community. Exclusion from the community may mean severing ties of kinship, as well as neighbourly obligations. The social structure therefore exerts a pressure towards mutuality and 'fair' exchange, and these are needed to sustain the shape of the structure itself. The functional unity of the whole arrangement depends upon the realization of these mutually constitutive processes. Hence traditional models of community tend to emit a strong flavour of sociological functionalism, a perspective which derives in turn from the examination of self-sustaining organisms able to exist in relative separation from the world around them (Giddens 1984). This encourages students of community to look for comparable 'closure' in their examples, and to take an 'organic' or 'natural' view of community. This has attracted a great deal of criticism.

It has been said that the genre of sociological community studies has come to be 'much-maligned and excessively criticised' (Cohen 2002: 324). Wright (1992) claims that such criticism briefly became a 'major academic industry'. An accumulation of hostile commentary led to the virtual demise of the approach from the 1970s onwards, rather ironically perhaps following the publication of Bell and Newby's classic textbook survey (1971). Their criticism of the unsystematic and impressionistic quality of the reported findings is reiterated in similar vein by Savage and Warde (1993: 25), who offer a verdict that 'much good work was done but it was relatively little appreciated, typically being criticised from a positivist viewpoint for being non-cumulative, unverifiable and parochial'. Part of the emergent critique was internal to the genre, and came from those who found it frustratingly difficult to achieve the goal of providing the complete and consistent account of a social world that the approach promised (Stacey 1969; Stacey *et al.* 1975). Others were driven more by larger changes in sociology and social theory, which were challenging the reign of functionalist ideas and frameworks, and bringing greater awareness of conflict, division and change as key features of social life. The impact of Weberian and Marxist 'conflict' sociologies of the 1960s and 1970s left little room for warm and sympathetic readings of 'community'. Indeed, many now adopted an adversarial stance towards the concept itself, since it was so redolent of consensus and what they considered to be 'false consciousness'.

On the basis of the small town and village studies, it was easy to equate community with closed social worlds, characterized by homogeneity, cooperation and the absence of change. They were the last places from which one could expect any impulse for social transformation. In the light of the newer sociological approaches, the community literature displayed a quite extraordinary neglect of differences and contrasts which ought to have been self-evident: not only between occupants of different economic and social class positions, but also between generations, and between women and men. Many of the studies treated communities as if they were completely undifferentiated in these respects, with all individuals, no matter what their age, gender, or economic position, equally active and respected in the life of their community, or equally ready to defer to local leaders and authority figures. Critical assessment of the neglect of women's views, and the extent to which the subordination of some members of communities to the wishes of others was overlooked, helped bring the notion of community into general disrepute. Indeed, oddly enough for a sociology which claimed to be operating so close to the details of everyday life, the actual voices and perceptions of those living in such communities had been almost wholly suppressed from the published accounts, being replaced instead by the more lofty and analytical language of the social scientists. Those voices which were attended to often proved to be confined to certain 'community leaders', or so-called key informants, invariably men who were well-positioned in the local social structure, and whose version of things might turn out to be self-serving, or deliberately intended to convey a positive impression.

For example, within the daily life of most such communities there were clear differences in the 'contribution' expected from men and women, not only because there seemed always to be a strongly marked sexual division of labour, but also in the sheer quantity of effort required – with women working longer hours, and enjoying less 'free' time, than their male companions. Yet this was mostly taken for granted as a background 'fact'. Similarly, young people rarely got much attention in the studies, but when they did appear, they seemed to be entirely happy following the path laid down for them by local traditions and the authority of their elders. Dissatisfaction and discontent seemed almost non-existent, along with deviance and disorder. From the perspective of functional analysis, all those belonging to the community had their appropriate place within the social structure, and made equivalent and complementary contributions to it. The concept of community fell by the wayside, to a considerable degree, along with the entire socially complacent standpoint most sociologists had adopted in the period immediately following the Second World War. With increasing awareness of social differences and divisions, it became impossible to imagine that communities could continue to provide oases of calm, in which social life was fundamentally harmonious, integrated and stagnant. More critical studies sought to break open the accepted view, to show that in reality communities were riddled with conflict and division.

As Savage and Warde note, one of the consequences of the loss of enthusiasm for community studies, doubtless unintended, was that for an appreciable time thereafter sociologists showed relatively little interest in getting to grips with detailed investigations of the varied everyday life of different social groups. The readiness to do so shifted back into social anthropology, and was taken on as well by those working in the fields of cultural studies and human geography, where an interest in the topic of 'community' was maintained principally by those engaged in the study of 'subcultures' and 'localities'. But on the whole, as sociologists lost confidence in the theoretical frameworks that had underpinned their studies, so 'research into communities became bogged down in a series of intractable problems of a conceptual and methodological character' (Savage and Warde 1993:105). This weakened the sociological appreciation of how different social activities were embedded in the fabric of daily life, and it became difficult to sustain anything like a rounded understanding of how people lived. Sociological knowledge fragmented into an expanding range of specialisms. However, there were many who argued that this was not a problem of method, but rather a reflection of the direction in which society itself was heading, which meant that sites like small towns and rural villages were becoming increasingly marginal settings from which to make any meaningful social observation. These shifts are well represented in the career of Margaret Stacey as a prominent researcher into community.

THE DEATH OF COMMUNITY STUDIES?

When Stacey first wrote about Banbury (1960), she was able to present a coherent picture of its traditional social structure. This included an analysis of the way in which the entire local population could be positioned within a pattern of local social stratification consisting of several layers, in which people were placed according to their personal attributes, social backgrounds, and styles of behaviour. This system of evaluation appeared to be accepted by everyone who was 'local' to the town and its surrounding area. Already, however, there was a problem in assimilating into this framework new influences arising from the intro-

duction into the town of a substantial industrial employer, an aluminium works. Whereas the traditional Banbury community rested on
a diverse occupational structure of small businesses, reflecting its role as
a rural market town, this development brought with it new, large-scale
industrial relationships, which were formal and bureaucratic. Many of
those employed by the company were new to the town, and could not be
fitted into the old status hierarchy; nor indeed were they prepared to
take up a place within it. Hence Banbury became split between 'traditionalists' and 'non-traditionalists', with different attitudes, values and
lifestyles. By the time Stacey returned to the town some twenty years
later, its social structure had fragmented still further, into a 'kaleido-
scope' of many different groups and networks; the status hierarchy had
lost its shape; and the pattern of social inequalities had become 'surprisingly formless'. By now Stacey had to concede that 'identifiable local
social relations [were] not discernible in any local holistic sense' (Stacey
et al. 1975: 4). This left her rather at a loss as to how the social organization of the town should be described, and what kind of theoretical apparatus could be used to make sense of it. It was problematic whether
Banbury could continue to be referred to as a 'community' in any meaningful sense. The feeling that its distinctive reality was dissolving
rapidly in the face of social change was confirmed by another study
which concluded that Banbury was in the throes of transformation from
a market town into 'part of the low-density, light industry dominated
trend of urbanization reaching out from the conurbations to engulf most
of the prosperous areas of Britain' (Mann 1973: 196). Consequently, its
physical and social boundaries were losing their significance. Banbury
was disappearing as a recognizable entity into the general amorphousness of British society.

   Inadvertently perhaps, Stacey had touched upon some of the major
themes of later research: the impact of 'newcomers' settling into established centres of population; the disassociation between place and patterns of social organization; and the impact of wider forces, such as
economic development and reorganization, at local level. Her own sense
of confusion in interpreting these processes arose from the inability of
conventional models of 'community' to comprehend them fully. As a
result, she seemed to be trapped into repeating the standard narrative of
the collapse of community. Over a remarkably short period of time, it
seemed, this town, with its long-established and well integrated pattern

of social life, had been disrupted by unexpected change, with consequences that were inexplicable from its own point of view as a community. It was simply unable to cope with the social divisions and differences
introduced by industrial development. Yet there are severe problems
with the analysis. Stacey's use of the term 'traditional' as a central part
of her theoretical explanation was misleading, because it blurred two
distinct points of reference: to a particular type of social structure, supposedly characteristic of 'community', and to a continuity of historical
patterns. Reading between the lines of her own description, this was not
the first time Banbury had confronted change; closer attention to its history might have revealed change to be a regular occurrence. But change
and adjustment did not figure as prominent themes in the way in which
the town, or those who spoke for it, saw themselves, and in this and other
respects their versions of the situation may have prejudiced Stacey's
understanding.

More than any other contributor to the field of community studies,
it was Stacey who dealt the approach a mortal blow, in her paper on 'the
myth' of community studies (Stacey 1969), when she subjected the concept of community to an unusually rigorous examination. Rather than
simply assuming that there was a coherent and integrated social whole
to be investigated at local level, she suggested that sociologists ought to
make this a matter for inquiry – to what extent did the various social
institutions connect with one another locally, and how were they tied
into the relationships of the wider society? These were questions which
had been asked earlier by Warren (1963) and which Stacey believed
were becoming more pressing, as the grip of 'national' economic, political and social relationships upon local life tightened. Examination of the
evidence from studies carried out in even the most remote circumstances
confirmed that they were connected to the outside world in a wide variety of ways, and that this connection was increasing. For example, the
rural studies showed how the commercialization of agriculture entailed
the sale and purchase of agricultural commodities through the market,
while at the same time the state intervened to regulate and manage
some of the impact of these economic processes. Thus whether they were
aware of this or not, both 'market' and 'state' constituted forces which
had important effects at local level, helping to shape the everyday life of
community members. Any analysis which ignored these influences, or
treated them as no more than unwarranted 'interferences' with the

smooth running of internal relationships, would be seriously inadequate. Stacey argued that only when there was evidence for a strong set of local interconnections might one conclude that there existed a 'local social system' of the type which might engender corresponding feelings of community. She concluded that this was becoming a rare occurrence, and therefore that it was doubtful whether the concept of community referred any longer to a useful abstraction (1969: 134). Put more simply, the fact of occupying the same space would not always result in the formation of significant social relationships, or attitudes. In these terms, her own Banbury restudy could be interpreted as demonstrating how easily a local social system could disintegrate, when put under pressure. In establishing some distance between place and patterns of social relationships, Stacey challenged the 'holistic' bias which had pervaded community studies.

An even more dramatic denial of the usefulness of the approach was made by Pahl (1966: 328) when, on the basis of his own research into changes in rural villages, he asserted that attempting to tie patterns of social relationships to particular geographical milieux was a 'singularly fruitless exercise'. In other words, there was no basis on which to assume that every village, or all small towns, would display similar 'community' features merely because they were the same sort of settlement, or had the same physical shape. What mattered instead was the nature of the wider society to which they belonged. In the context of different prevailing social relations, and at different historical periods, villages would play differing roles. So far as Pahl was concerned, a better understanding would be achieved by going directly to an examination of the social groups involved, and their position in social structure, bypassing the idea of 'community' altogether. Because others drew similar conclusions, the community study fell out of favour (see Newby 1987).

Even in the face of such sustained criticism, it would be wrong to dismiss out of hand everything produced within the framework of community studies. First, because they do provide rich insights into some of the details and complications of everyday life in social worlds which now have largely vanished. Second, because despite the overwhelming influence upon them of theoretical ideas that have since been discredited, there are always possibilities for learning alternative lessons from them. Even where they give the greatest impression of closeness and harmony, one can detect evidence that animosities and disagreements may lurk beneath the surface, as well as more structural tensions (Day 1998). Revisiting the work done by Arensberg and Kimball, Brody's study of Inishkillane (1974) showed how the transition of control within the community from one generation to the next was by no means as smooth and consensual as they had implied, but riddled with anger and hostility. Judging by occasional remarks and footnotes in their own reports, the same could be said of relations between the sexes. Reflecting on his own research experiences, Frankenberg notes that 'indifference, unshared values and neutral silence are the enemies of community. Love, hatred and gossip are its raw material' (in Davies and Jones 2003: xvi). In similar vein, Williams observed that the people of his 'border' community did not necessarily like one another, and often played dirty tricks; but they were also prepared to perform 'acts of kindness beyond calculation' (1989: 114). It would be wrong therefore to suppose that a well integrated pattern of shared life necessarily creates feelings of warmth and affection, or eliminates bad behaviour; after all, we are dealing with *human* communities. An important aspect of community may be that people matter enough to dislike.

Within the genre there are some more systematic explorations of the resulting complexities and contradictions of actual communities. Building on the tenets of Manchester anthropology, Frankenberg (1957) describes how during his fieldwork in north Wales he observed a recurrent process of creating the means of village cooperation, only to see it dissolve into conflict. Outsiders like himself played an invaluable role, as scapegoats who could be blamed for the problems which villagers contended would not have arisen without their interference. In this way the illusion of unity was maintained against ample evidence to the contrary. Frankenberg earns praise from later scholars (Jedrej and Nuttall 1996: 11) for his ability to go beyond simply reproducing the rhetoric used by members of the community, to show how it is produced and deployed by the actors themselves. Emmett (1964) also depicts a Welsh community bound together by its hostility to outside forces, of officialdom and 'ruling England', belonging fully to which consisted in part of 'not knowing' some of the salient facts of its everyday life. Such studies show how membership of a community is not something merely given by social position, but which has to be worked at, in terms of meeting local definitions and conforming to expectations of conduct, which can change over time. These were insights that were taken up and developed fruitfully in later studies. Williams (1963) demonstrated that the apparent stability of a long established rural community actually consisted of many overlapping processes of change, including assimilation and loss of families and their connections; it did not mean stagnation, or require a fixed population.

More recent research has confirmed that many apparently static communities prove on closer examination to be peopled by 'incomers' and others whose life histories show considerable mobility (Jedrej and Nuttall 1996). Littlejohn (1963) showed how the internal relationships of a small community were compelled to adapt to changing class divisions in the wider society, around which local variations were elaborated. In the process, the village became 'less an area of common life than an area within which the individual chooses his associations subject to such barriers as are imposed by social class or physical distance' (1963: 155). All these studies drew attention to ways in which local life had to respond to bigger changes occurring elsewhere, including changing forms of employment, and state intervention. Many other examples could be adduced, in which the strength of the detailed ethnographic observation, and the intelligence of the researcher, pushed the analysis beyond the limitations of dominant theories, encouraging innovations in both theory and methods, and showing how community was a considerably more complex and problematic business than it at first appeared.

However, because such studies occupied a position at the disciplinary boundaries between sociology, anthropology and geography, their findings were never easy to integrate into the main body of received sociological opinion. They seemed of interest mainly to the specialist, and therefore as well as suffering from the limitations of their theoretical stance, they lent themselves to being dismissed, rather glibly, as no more than quaint investigations akin to 'folk' studies, or the work of amateur enthusiasts for local history. Glass (1955) attacked the vogue for 'sporadic detailed evidence' about personal relationships within small communities as a form of 'vicarious neighbouring'. The claim that they were unable to yield cumulative knowledge (Newby 1987: 258) arose partly from the desire to uncover more reliable causal connections, and partly because the sheer amount of detailed observation in the studies tended to obscure the underlying outlines of the analysis. Thus community studies were caught in the tension between being true to the observed phenomena, and making worthwhile additions to generalized sociological knowledge. They were also accused of romantically idealizing the situations they were describing.

It was not particularly surprising that work in rural sociology should be infused with nostalgia and defensiveness towards the values and traditions it observed. For most early sociologists, life in the countryside represented an older, more settled, and often more attractive prospect than an urban/industrial existence. Small towns could also be viewed as the acme of social stability and quietness, and those who were drawn to their study very often wanted to celebrate these qualities. Among American intellectuals of the 'progressive' movement, for example, it could be said that the small community was the *sine qua non* of a humane social order; and they idealized the small town as a place imbued with 'a sense of community . . . an intimacy of face-to-face personal contact and easy neighbourliness' (Berry 1973: 17; Putnam 2000). It was more surprising that so many of the theoretical and methodological problems of community analysis came to be reproduced in studies of urban districts and working class communities, especially when the impetus behind their investigation was often very different, reflecting more avowedly critical, sometimes even radical, social perspectives. Nevertheless, studies of working class community attracted similar accusations of being prone to glamourize what were often fairly miserable and deprived ways of life, whilst overlooking the darker underside of community existence. This meant that eventually they too fell foul of the same kind of critical onslaught.

3

THE RISE AND FALL OF 'WORKING CLASS COMMUNITY'

For a long while, studies of the nature of the working class in industrial societies were close to the centre of the development of empirical sociology. This includes investigations of the organization of working class communities, for which there is extensive documentation. According to one commentary, such studies form sociology's 'single most massive encounter with the located experiences of working class people' and the major accredited source of qualitative accounts of working class culture (Brook and Finn 1978: 131). Like accounts of rural community, these studies have obvious historical, as well as spatial dimensions, and certain accounts of 'the ways things were' (Crow and Allen 1994; Crow 2001) have been constructed more or less exclusively on their basis. Although the classic studies reach back now some fifty years, and the communities they refer to have long gone, the impact they made on sociological awareness is engrained so deeply that they still provide vibrant points of reference.

Communities can be defined as working class in the sense that they consist substantially of populations of workers, or with the more active connotation that they are forms of community created by workers themselves, therefore representing their distinctive attitudes, ambitions, and world-outlook. That is, as with other types of community, differing emphases can be placed upon the objective or subjective aspects of 'community in itself', and 'community for itself'. However, an underlying theme to most accounts is that such communities come about because they are subject to a set of distinct economic, social and political conditions that 'often unknowingly bind working people in a shared experience of commonality' (Charlesworth 2000: 154). The same view is expressed concisely by an interviewee about the West Yorkshire mining settlement of 'Ashby': it is 'a real working class town, always has been, always will be, and will never be anything else' (Warwick and Littlejohn 1992: 77). Referring to the steel-making town of Rotherham, Charlesworth comments that 'living in Rotherham one cannot help but be struck by an underlying coherence to the life of the place' (2000: 150), which generates a strong and distinct sense of common living conditions and shared everyday, collective experience. The *local* nature of this experience is also characteristic: nowhere else is quite the same as Rotherham.

As with the other varieties of community, therefore, a problem arises with regard to the extent to which we can generalize legitimately across different cases. Crow and Allen warn that

> [t]o speak in abstract terms of the traditional working class community, constructing a composite picture out of the findings of the various community studies of the 1950s, loses sight of the diversity of these communities with regard to the industries on which they were based, regional variations, difference in the degree to which women were employed, and more generally the evolving variations of their 'traditions'.
>
> (Crow and Allen 1994: 26)

Nevertheless, such a composite impression of the characteristics of working class community has been adopted pretty generally within sociology, to act as a yardstick against which subsequent changes have been measured and weighed (for examples, see Rose 1968; Roberts 1978; 2001). Whether or not this does serious damage to our appreciation of what such communities were like, or constitutes a 'wilful' neglect of difference, as Crow and Allen suggest, rather depends on the level of specificity at which we are aiming. After all, to categorize a set of communities as 'working class' at all presupposes that, whatever their differences, they have important things in common.

As Crow and Allen indicate, the broad contours were made familiar by the work of Young and Willmott and other 'classic' studies produced during the 1950s and 1960s, a period during which the life of the working class was not only regarded as a topic of exceptional social and political importance, but also considered to be undergoing some decisive changes. While this means that such work could be dismissed now as being of merely historical interest, the fact that it has provided a gold standard for so many discussions of the nature of community lends it continuing relevance.

COMMUNITY LIFE IN BETHNAL GREEN

In Britain, the Institute of Community Studies, founded in 1954, and located in Bethnal Green in the East End of London, produced a stream of books and articles dealing with issues of community and community change, largely centred on the working class. The stated aim of the institute was to bring some of the strengths of social anthropology into sociology, and for a time it developed into what was probably the best known British social research unit, doing much to form the general conception of sociology amongst the reading public, at a time when the discipline was still relatively new (Platt 1971). A cool appraisal of this body of work by Jennifer Platt rated it highly for its contribution to planning and social welfare, but expressed severe reservations about its sociological value. In doing so, Platt set out some of the theoretical and methodological arguments which increasingly came to undermine intellectual support not only for the Bethnal Green studies, but for the entire community studies approach.

A good deal of the work undertaken by members of the institute focussed on Bethnal Green itself, including what became recognized as the classic study of working class community, and the impact upon it of post-war rehousing and relocation, *Family and Kinship in East London* (Young and Willmott 1957). This was not a thorough-going community study of the sort that had been attempted in Middletown and Yankee City, or even in Banbury, but primarily an investigation of patterns of working class family organization and their contemporary transformation. On these grounds, Bell and Newby (1971) say little about Young and Willmott's contribution, because the focus on a single institution (the family) does not conform to the strict definition of a 'community study', namely that it should be concerned with the *interrelationships* of social institutions within a given locality. For the same reason Critcher (1979) dismisses the study as a prime example of sociology's tendency to 'appropriate' working class culture by reducing it to a discrete sociological variable, so ending up with only a fragmentary representation. Yet, because it traces the inter-connections of family, kin and neighbours within the daily life of Bethnal Green, Young and Willmott's text neither amounts to a fully developed study of the family as an institution, nor is confined to the family alone. In its own words, it examines the social implications and value of 'a highly articulated network of kinship relations' within a particular territory; and from this there emerges a strong, if incomplete, picture of a certain kind of community way of life.

Platt's summary of this reproduces many of the characteristics which, rightly or wrongly, came to be identified as typical of working class communities of the time:

> The working class way of life is seen as involving the extended family embedded in a stable and predominantly working class community with great neighbourliness and communal solidarity, expressed in networks of social relations and mutual aid and strong attachment to the local area and its primary groups. In this context people are known and judged as individuals with multiple characteristics rather than as holders of certain jobs or owners of certain possessions. Because they are so well known, and because of the basic homogeneity of the area, pretensions to higher status get little credit and are rarely made; anyone who seriously aspires to other standards is liable to leave the community.
>
> (Platt 1971: 112)

Typically, this description brings together assertions about structural patterns ('networks of social relations'), characteristic values and mindsets, and forms of behaviour, and associates them all with a certain 'way of life'. For the working class at least, it seems, class and community belong together. However, as Platt notes, the extraordinarily influential depiction of this pattern in Young and Willmott's sociological bestseller was derived from a quite limited amount of survey and observational data, much of it descriptive, impressionistic, and at times anecdotal. Memorable vignettes of local social relationships, and vivid interview fragments gave life to the description, and probably lodged better in readers' memories than the fairly simple statistical analyses which accompanied them. Further studies of old people (Townsend 1957) and adolescents (Willmott 1966) in the same district did little to challenge this basic account. At the same time, there are many missing dimensions to the Bethnal Green studies. For instance, there is little information about local political organization, little real detail about gender relations, or behaviour within the home, and above all, a surprising neglect of work. In the context of studies of working class life, this is strange, since usually they revolve around the nature of work and employment, and the ways in which communities are compelled to adapt to its demands. Young and Willmott take for granted the fundamental determination of the patterns they describe by economic forces, and the organization of manual labour, the very things that make this a 'class' community. They devote no more than a few pages to 'the family in the economy'.

London's East End has long been known as an area predominantly inhabited by the poor. According to Young and Willmott (1986: ix), its boundaries were 'almost as strongly marked as those of some countries'. Much earlier, some of the first social 'explorers' to venture into the unknown world of the working classes (Mayhew 1861; Booth 1902) had pointed to the peculiarities of this vast area, and huge population, lacking all the resources of a 'superior' culture: libraries, colleges, concert halls, and cathedrals. They referred to working class people as living in 'urban tribes' (compare Collins 2004). When Young and Willmott did their study, in the mid-1950s, little had changed. Bethnal Green had a population of some 54,000, and 82 per cent of the employed male population were manual workers. The small minority of non-working class people residing in the borough were shopkeepers and publicans, serving the needs of a working class clientele. Most professionals working in the area travelled from homes outside it. Hence, unlike the multi-class communities found in the small towns of Britain and America, Bethnal Green was characterized by an essential homogeneity of circumstances and social situation; its inhabitants could be said to be 'all in the same boat'. The pervading impression is of a one-class community of people doing similar jobs, with similar education, and similar life expectations. Most Bethnal Greeners appear to have had little contact with people who were unlike themselves, and when this happened, it was in strictly controlled circumstances – in encounters with employers, teachers, doctors, or local government officials. Like the archetypal rural villager, they inhabited a world free of 'threats and surprises', with little to challenge their sense of identity or social expectations. They were securely working class, or 'ordinary', and local in their orientations, and their knowledge of the world beyond 'the borough' seemed minimal.

Young and Willmott present some of their strongest impressions of Bethnal Green in the section of their book which contrasts it with the new estate of 'Greenleigh' to which eventually many of its people were rehoused:

> In Bethnal Green, people commonly belong to a close network of personal relationships. They know intimately dozens of other local people living near at hand, their school-friends, their work-mates, their pub-friends and above all their relatives. They know them well because they have known them over a long period of time. . . . They have the security of belonging to a series of small and overlapping groups.
>
> (Young and Willmott 1957: 161)

Despite the district's size therefore, people existed within the narrow sphere of their immediate street or neighbourhood. The description is backed up with telling examples of the extent to which local society is shaped by 'geography plus genealogy'. A sample of forty-five married couples had between them almost 1,700 close relatives, of whom 34 per cent lived locally, and another 20 per cent in adjoining boroughs. On average, each couple had thirteen near relatives living close by. Among such people, there was constant personal contact. Recording those she met in the course of a single week, one woman was able to list sixty-three known individuals, often encountered several times, of whom thirty-eight were related to at least one of the others. For women, these contacts focussed especially closely on the family, with married daughters visiting their mothers on a daily basis, and female neighbours continually exchanging small services. Male relationships centred more on work and the pub, but were no less close: witness 'Mr Aves', who worked all week with his two brothers and a brother-in-law, went to football on Saturdays with one of them, and gathered with the whole family in the public house on Sunday mornings. In other words, the area supported the same kind of 'manifold immediate connections among people' (Calhoun 1982: 155) that could be found in more restricted spatial settings. This is because it was delimited by strong boundaries of social class which narrowed down individual horizons. Despite their urban location, the people of Bethnal Green were not lonely people; they knew the faces in the crowd, and, according to Young and Wilmott, 'familiarity breeds content' (1957: 92).

Before long, sociologists and others were using the expression 'urban village' to refer to this sort of community (Gans 1962; Taylor 1973), the apparent oxymoron drawing attention to the fact that even within cities, it was possible to find supposedly 'rural' social features, just as Young and Willmott's observations seemed also to confound prevailing expectations that extended family connections would be incompatible with modern urban life. On such grounds, the findings from the Bethnal Green studies made a major contribution to undermining attempts to establish the urban/rural distinction as a central tenet of social analysis, and helped detach the concept of community from an undue association with country life. Evidently, there were forms of community which could flourish in urban environments, and which were well adapted to industrialized conditions.

The implications of strong network ties for local values and beliefs were felt to be self-evident. For instance, we learn that, when evaluating others, what matters is personal characteristics and detailed personal knowledge: people are known 'in the round'. 'Reputation' is important, and this is not so much individual as familial. More generally, looking back on their study a few years later, Young and Willmott say that life in Bethnal Green was marked by 'a sense of family, community and class solidarity, by a generosity towards others like themselves, by a wide range of attachments, by pride in themselves, their community and country, and by an overflowing vitality' (1986: xi). It would not be too unfair to say that the impression conveyed is of people who are 'poor but happy'. Throughout the discussion there is a sense of positive endorsement being given to a particular way of life, and its virtues, accompanied by an argument that this was now in the throes of being broken up by the intervention of new forces: most dramatically, by the decisions of planners, welfare agencies and other 'do gooders' that such communities needed to be lifted out of deprivation through deliberate and radical change.

During the late 1950s and 1960s masses of people from such working class districts were relocated into new housing estates, and tower blocks, while the streets they had occupied were demolished, or at least drastically refurbished, and often repopulated. Despite the improved physical surroundings, Young and Willmott contended that this was eradicating the valuable social bonds built up over several generations, and thereby undermining the values and collective solidarity of the working classes. Measures designed to raise living standards were doing so at the cost of a sacrifice of communal strengths and loyalties. In the long run, it could be argued, this would erode the very way of life which gave the working class its identity, and enabled it to organize politically.

SENTIMENTS AND STEREOTYPES

Clearly, as noted earlier, reliance on the example of Bethnal Green alone posed a very great risk of stereotyping the working class, losing sight of whatever distinctive features and variations might attach to other particular working class communities. It is generally acknowledged that London is a special case, in all kinds of ways; nowhere else in Britain could one find such an extensive, and economically varied, working class environment as that of the East End. As early as 1966 Frankenberg raised the issue of the representativeness of the account, claiming that the study had rarity value, because there were so few comparable studies of working class neighbourhoods; therefore, we could not know how valid it was as a general description of working class life. However, Young and Willmott's researches in Bethnal Green formed just part of a much wider swathe of description and analysis of the working class and its fate at around the same time, which for the most part lent reasonable confirmation to their empirical and ethical claims. Although it took a variety of forms, such writing was grounded more or less firmly in examinations and recollections of life in different working class communities: it included Hoggart (1957) on Hunslet, in Leeds; Mogey (1956) on St Ebbes, Oxford; Jackson and Marsden (1962) on Huddersfield; Willmott (1963) on Dagenham; and Jackson (1968) on various working class institutions in northern England. Support was also forthcoming from Bott's analysis of family and social networks (1957) and Rosser and Harris' follow-up study of family and community relations in Swansea (1965). Although the latter highlighted a number of specifically Welsh features absent from Bethnal Green, it presented a similar impression of close-knit, family-centred, and neighbourhood-based living, which also appeared to be poised on the point of disruption by economic and social change. Critcher (1979) lists twenty-four key studies of the condition of the British working class produced between 1956 and 1971, of which some fifteen made extensive use of material to do with aspects of community. Although he feels this does not constitute a true research genre, more a 'rather vague bibliography', the way in which he describes Hoggart's approach to Leeds would fit most of the other studies reasonably well: 'the mode of recognition is to observe working class activities, trace their interconnections, and frame them within the fixed horizons of everyday life' (Critcher 1979: 20). Not all of these studies were intended to focus directly on the analysis of community, but invariably it provided an important background resource and point of reference for the examination of more specific themes and issues in working class life, such as education, family, or recreational habits.

Whether or not these examples were truly 'representative' of the working class as a whole, it was from such sources that the concept of the 'traditional working class' was constructed as a general sociological category (Lockwood 1966). Notions of communal solidarity, collectivism and traditionalism were used to capture the essence of the distinctive working class world view. Jackson summed this up in terms of

> The deeply grained habit of cooperation, the habit of valuing people rather than concepts, and the directness of emotional response [along with] a suspicion of the new and strange.
>
> (Jackson 1968: 169)

These social studies had their contemporary fictional counterparts in the work of authors like Alan Sillitoe, John Braine, Keith Waterhouse and David Storey, who represented a new wave of writers able to articulate and comment sympathetically upon working class sensibilities. The context for their production was the post-war social revolution introduced by the 1945 Labour government, and the welfare state, and the changed economic climate which had come about with 'affluence' and full employment. The literature is suffused with a consciousness that the period represents a turning point in the history of class relations, and that it was important to document working class cultures and their social foundations before they were lost; hence the work has aspects of both celebration and lamentation. As Platt stated (1971: 13) apropos the Bethnal Green studies, 'a preference is implied for the social atmosphere of the working class communities, and this preference is obviously linked with or derived from a general egalitarianism'. Most of the researchers and writers concerned had explicit political commitments to the labour movement, and to the project of social democratic reform; they were not only observers of, but also advocates for working class community, and very often deployed its virtues as part of an attack on alternative, 'middle-class' habits and aspirations. At times, this resulted in a one-sided, uncritical depiction of its characteristics. Reference to 'community' and community values became a way of praising the working class, and talking about those positive aspects of working class life which socialism/labour politics would seek to defend and uphold – to the extent that the writers could be accused of simply confusing community with class (Platt 1971: 63), and giving way to unbridled sentiment.

The cumulative impression produced was that working class people naturally and inevitably lived in communities of this kind. As a later writer comments (Collins 2004: 11), 'it would be impossible to attempt a biography of the urban working class without focusing on a particular landscape, as this class more than any other is inextricably linked with the concept of home, a street, a neighbourhood, a community'. Little was said about those elements of the working class for whom there was no such strong local or collective allegiance, or who might have found drawbacks to living in such conditions. Instead, the rival values and lifestyles of the middle classes provided a constant implicit counterpoint to the discussion. In some of the key artistic representations of the period, in fiction and film, the main theme addressed was the painful transition from one to the other (for example, *Saturday Night and Sunday Morning*; *The Loneliness of the Long Distance Runner*; *The Likely Lads*), and how this entailed a loss of spontaneous, unpretentious, social intimacy. Revealingly, all these accounts centre on the male experience. In a caustic comment on this whole genre of writing and representation, Taylor notes how sociologists and planners 'applauded enthusiastically at a distance the gritty working class togetherness that they would not be seen dead living in themselves' (1973: 188). Platt likewise drew attention to the inconsistency which led well educated, middle-class commentators, albeit often themselves from working class backgrounds, to suspend their critical judgement when it came to commenting upon the opinions of members of such communities. Despite their own commitment to educational achievement, and its value for the working class, for example, they appeared ready to defend attitudes which were hostile to learning, and to 'getting ahead'. Thus the people of Bethnal Green were described as 'indifferent to education and hostile to ambition' (Marris 1967). Young and Willmott themselves conceded that the moral code of kinship could be 'sometimes harsh, imprisoning the human spirit and stunting growth and self-expression' (1957: 162). Even the newer settlement of Dagenham, established as part of the outward spread of London in the 1930s, was criticized for denying stimulus or encouragement to those who had intellectual or cultural aspirations or who did not fit the conventional mould (Willmott 1963: 116–17). That there evidently was a down-side to the ethos of solidarity and readiness to cooperate cast at least some doubt on the overall value of 'community' for all those who were involved in it. According to Platt (1971: 17), this defect was general, in that '[a] closely integrated local community is never likely to provide a milieu in which diversity and individual idiosyncrasy can flourish and be regarded with toleration'. Those who were 'different', a term which might be used to refer to their sexuality, or intellectual enthusiasms or other interests, were unlikely to feel comfortable in such a place. However, the readiness to conceptualize community as an entity, a complete whole, meant that in these studies it was treated as something above, and greater than, the individual, whose needs and aspirations occupied a poor second place (Ennew 1980).

The tension between collectivism and individual expression and diversity, which runs through the very idea of community, took on a new significance from the 1960s onwards, when rejection of, and rebellion against, the suffocating limits of such working class consensus began to drive the formation of various youth cultures. In their different ways, and at different times, teddy boys and mods, skinheads and punks, hippies and new romantics were to distance themselves from or directly challenge many of the traditional mores and values of the working class, especially its attitudes to work, to ostentatious display, to definitions of gender boundaries, and notions of 'respectability' (Cohen 1972; Hall and Jefferson 1976). In so doing, they sapped the authority of an older generation of male manual workers. Yet again, this could be interpreted as part of the break-down of traditional community, and evidence of its transition into something different. Roberts (2001) is not alone in noting how sociologists began to describe and analyse working class ways of life in depth only when they appeared to be under threat.

As Blackwell and Seabrook (1985: 109) put it, 'the prominence of community arose at the very moment of the dissolution of certain aspects of its reality', with the break-up of established working class communities.

The combination of a backward glance at such apparently vanishing social worlds, from the perspective of those who now stood outside or beyond them, helps explain the tone of nostalgia and sentimentality which so many critics detect. In some cases, commentators were looking back at, and reconstructing, their own childhood and youth (Hoggart 1957; Roberts 1971). Roberts seeks to qualify the over-enthusiastic tone of some of the ensuing descriptions:

> It was never really like that. . . . The close-knit working-class communities could be claustrophobic; there was no privacy; it was difficult to prevent everyone knowing one's most intimate business. There were neighbourhood feuds; children (and sometimes adults) fought in the streets. These were risky places.
>
> (Roberts 2001: 88)

The retrospective gaze may see excitement and emotional rawness in these features of working class life. The daily struggle with adversity meant that life was not boring, and this comes across well in many of the reconstructions of working class communities, especially those situated towards the lower and less respectable edges of the class (White 1986; Damer 1989). Even the more negative aspects and relationships seemed to demonstrate that people were interested in, and involved with, rather than indifferent to those who lived around them. Often they could not avoid being so, because a high proportion of the life of such places was led in the open, in the street, or communal spaces of various kinds. An obvious reason for this was that much of the housing was poor, and frequently overcrowded. Descriptions of working class community are forever associated with images of back-to-back, terraced, accommodation or tenement apartments, and conversations conducted over garden fences or on the doorstep.

We have seen how the tendency to conflate a set of structural characteristics with the sentiments that were alleged to flow from them was rife in community studies. Yet to do so carries major risks. As with the other contributions we have considered, the pull is towards treating the community as a seamless, unified entity. It becomes tempting then to attribute characteristics which might pertain at the individual level to the community as a whole, treating its members as if they were identical, and equally representative of the collective norm; or, arguing in the opposite direction, to expect the 'collective' attributes of the community to dictate what individuals are like. This confusion between distinct levels of analysis, known as the ecological fallacy, would lead one to assume, for example, that because a given local authority ward votes heavily for a particular political party, anyone coming from that place must be a party supporter. The effect is to play down, or ignore, the presence of minority opinion and those who are in any way unusual. An example of such argument is provided by Roberts, when he writes in general terms of how

> Within such a milieux, a sense of community is virtually inescapable. Residents feel a consciousness of kind. They share an awareness of facing common problems and mix with an effortless sociability. Neighbourliness becomes natural and is continuously cemented in pubs, streets, corner shops, workplaces and homes.
>
> (Roberts 1978: 73)

In the space of a few sentences, this comment moves effortlessly from the sense that community is something imposed by external pressures and constraints, into its embrace as a voluntary commitment. Those who are suspicious of the notion of community might well see this as exemplifying how it works, to swallow up disagreement and suppress variation. If people are put into a situation where they cannot opt out, or where doing so is difficult and perhaps personally costly, they may well give the impression of having chosen freely to go along with the prevailing norms. Hoggart (1957: 92) commented that when people feel they cannot do much about the main elements of their social situation, they will adopt attitudes which allow them to lead a 'liveable life', including treating those elements as simply external givens, 'facts of life'. Yet, should a chance arise to get out, they will leap at it. In a later discussion, Roberts (2001) notes how delighted many residents of such communities were to be offered the chance to be rehoused in places with bathrooms, hot water and gardens. When 'right to buy' legislation in the 1980s gave local authority tenants the opportunity to become home-owners (admittedly on very favourable financial terms), they rushed to do so, abandoning any pretence that it was wrong to put private interests before the collective good. The ability to penetrate the fog of sentiment surrounding working class lifestyles, and see within them the underlying potential for individualism and ambition, proved to be one of Thatcherism's most effective political weapons. Ideas and ideals of community proved unable to withstand the lure of material improvement and greater individual choice, lending further strength to the contention that, whatever its merits, 'community' has become an antiquated phenomenon.

DIVERSITY AND VARIATION IN WORKING CLASS COMMUNITY

The preceding discussion has shown how easy it is to proceed from concrete observations about life in specific working-class communities to the construction of general models which then become equated with the circumstances of an entire social class. A vital antidote to this tendency was provided by David Lockwood (1966, reprinted in Bulmer 1975a), when he drew attention to the importance of some key variations within the 'traditional' working class. Lockwood brought together research on differences in work and community situations to show how they combined to create a number of distinctive class perspectives. The main difference, he suggested, was between workers in small town (and small business) contexts, who actually met members of other classes, including their employers, in direct personal contact, and thereby formed an impression of society as differentiated and graded; and those whose experiences were restricted primarily to 'their own kind' and who encountered members of other classes only at a distance, in relationships of distrust or antagonism. He characterized these two kinds of worker as 'deferential' and 'proletarian'. While work factors were central to the formation of these differences, Lockwood argued that their impact was reinforced by the nature of the community surrounding the workplace.

For deferential workers, the boundaries of the community to which they felt they belonged extended to include members of different classes, who were viewed as interdependent, and as making valued contributions to meeting one another's needs. Deferentials looked up to, and respected, their social superiors, from whom they received leadership, authority and sponsorship of various sorts. In Durkheimian terms, we might say that they displayed a form of organic solidarity, organized around differentiation and collaboration. Studies of the kind previously referred to, relating to small market towns and paternalistic capitalism, suggested that such attitudes were associated with 'small, relatively isolated, and economically autonomous communities, particularly those with well differentiated occupational structures and stable populations' (Lockwood 1966: 20). This is where one would expect to find local systems of social status, and widespread consensus about how different people are placed within them, although Lockwood concedes that the evidence base is 'skimpy'. Proletarian attitudes flourished in contexts of closely integrated industrial communities, which concentrated sizeable numbers of workers in relative isolation from the wider society. Lockwood indicates mining, dock work, and shipbuilding as typical examples. Such situations encourage proletarians to view their community as made up exclusively of 'us', people in like situations, who stand for opposite interests from 'them' (the bosses, officials and other wielders of power). Their solidarity is more mechanical, based on the strength of resemblance.

Essentially, this framework elaborates the connection already made between structural foundations and forms of consciousness. Its significance for Lockwood lies in the fact that 'for the most part men [sic] visualise the class structure of their society from the vantage points of their own particular milieux' (1966: 16); that is, how they perceive the larger society varies according to the daily experiences they meet in their more local social settings. This implies that, in order to understand their behaviour and beliefs, it is necessary to examine those local settings in some detail, and this makes the analysis of variations in patterns of community sociologically important.

Lockwood is quite explicit that he is constructing a set of ideal typifications, intended to have theoretical and sociological, rather than historical and empirical validity. Both deferential and proletarian types are 'extreme' simplifications of real cases. Similarly the third main type which he sees emerging, the 'privatized' worker, or 'new' working class, is also treated as a limiting case. Such workers are associated with employment in the newer, mass production industries, and with residence in the larger housing estates. They are neither work- nor community-centred, but focussed instead on the 'private' sphere of the home and family. Unlike traditional workers, they are likely to have experienced some degree of mobility, and so lack such strong local social ties. Their view of the class structure is 'de-socialized', revolving around differences of income; their behaviour is competitive and consumption-oriented; and their sense of belonging to a group or collectivity is rudimentary. Altogether they are less firmly embedded socially than the types of workers they seemed to be replacing, for whereas traditional workers were rooted in industries in decline, and places that were fast becoming economic 'backwaters', at the time he was writing Lockwood could depict the privatized worker as representing the new growth sectors, like the car industry, and light engineering. Research in Luton, especially among employees of the Vauxhall motor company, provided empirical substantiation of Lockwood's thesis (Goldthorpe *et al.* 1969). Luton's 'affluent workers' were also held to be an extreme case, but one which was 'prototypical' of future development. Their emergence hinted at the dissolution of community as a central feature of working class existence. Apparently financially secure, and devoted to the improvement of their home environment, such workers seemed to have little interest in associating with one another outside work, and viewed their support for unions and political parties as a merely instrumental commitment, justifiable because it produced tangible results rather than as an expression of intrinsic loyalty rooted in a sense of belonging together.

So far as the established working class was concerned, however, Lockwood was able still to take for granted the existence of strong and coherent communal foundations, which accounted for both the strengths and limitations of traditional working class organization. He portrayed the majority of manual workers of the time as highly integrated into their local societies, with their attitudes and behaviour influenced and controlled by direct face-to-face relationships; as a result, their expectations did not extend much beyond the boundaries of their own community, and they were unlikely to rethink their political allegiances or patterns of consumption. The fact that they were 'encapsulated' in social systems which provided them 'with few alternative conceptions of what is possible, desirable and legitimate' imposed a deep conservatism upon them, captured in the use of the term 'traditional' to describe their perspectives. This was true not only among the deferentials, whose conformity with local status conventions might well go together with political loyalty to their 'betters' (McKenzie and Silver 1968), but even of the more 'radical' proletarians, who voted Labour and joined trade unions, but did so as much to defend what they already had, as to seek to improve upon and transform their conditions. Constructed very largely against adversity, as 'communities of fate', the main patterns of working class existence did not encourage great expectations and aspirations for social change. Very often indeed, the demands of community weighed against the ambitions of class, making people conscious of the risk that challenges to the existing order might pose, by putting in jeopardy those rewards that were actually obtainable in their everyday lives, in terms of work, security and welfare, for the uncertain promise of better things to come. In this way, the forms of accommodation that made a life of hardship and deprivation bearable could impede the more fundamental kinds of action required to escape their effects.

Support for this view comes from Calhoun (1982), whose examination of the development of working class communities during the early period of industrialization shows them to have acquired rapidly a 'moral density', resting on the multiplex nature of their social relations, which closely matched standard descriptions of rural villages. For Calhoun, this communal base was at least as important in explaining popular radicalism as the class features of oppression and injustice, because it enabled powerful outbursts of collective action; but it also set limits to the capacity of the working class to transcend the bounds of local sympathies – so much so that workers were often surprised to find that their particular grievances were not shared by those who lived outside the confines of their own social universe. The tension between the 'parochialism' of local perceptions and solidarities and the universalism expected of class consciousness is commented upon by many of those who have studied working class communities (Brook and Finn 1978), and the inability to overcome it has been seen as one of the major, and possibly insuperable, obstacles to united class action. Searching for evidence of the possibility of a more radical, universalized, working class consciousness, Westergaard (1975: 254) notes how daily life for many workers is 'circumscribed in a very concrete way by parochial limitations, by local boundaries and by boundaries of kinship, by poverty, insecurity and deprivation'. Likewise Parkin (1971: 90) attributes the characteristics of working class communities to the similarity of the conditions under which they are formed; he argues that this leads them to arrive independently at similar sets of values, representing 'a design for living based upon localised social knowledge and face-to-face relationships'; however, the meaning system they generate is of purely parochial significance.

Arguably, therefore, the solidarity which held actual working class communities together had more to do with identification with occupation and place than with class *per se*. The 'traditional' communities identified by Lockwood centred on very distinctive kinds of work situations, whose influence was powerful enough to create a virtually self-enclosed world of overlapping work, family and leisure ties. The industries concerned were predominantly those of early industrialization, founded in the nineteenth century, or even earlier, and capable of absorbing employees for their entire working lives. The development around them of 'traditional' community relations was posited on a stable workforce, and the growth of effective local occupational cultures, into which successive generations could be socialized (Bulmer 1975a; Salaman 1974). Following Lockwood's lead, others pointed out how exceptional it was to find fully developed situations of this kind; the peculiar closeness of homogeneous single-occupation communities was rare enough to be referred to as 'quaint' and vestigial (Salaman 1975). While it was arguable that many manual occupations gave rise to their own distinctive ideologies, cultures and identities, in most cases these did not involve the formation around them of geographically contained communities of the kind discussed by Lockwood; for instance, there were no such spatially fixed communities of carpenters, plumbers or lorry-drivers (Hollowell 1968). Even where occupations stimulated especially powerful work-centred bonds among the actual workforce, as in printing (Cannon 1967; Cockburn 1983), this did not necessarily lead to the incorporation of relationships of family and friendship, let alone wider kin, into an integrated pattern of social connections. Only certain industries, formed during given historical periods, seemed to have this capacity.

Quite apart from all the other problems associated with the idea of community, which drove one industrial sociologist to question it as 'highly value laden, vague and abstract, irrelevant and useless in a contemporary situation' (Salaman 1975: 221), this meant that the majority of manual workers seemed to be excluded from experiencing anything approximating to 'real' community, as described in the community studies. On the other hand, some degree of attachment to a local area, and to those who occupied a similar social and economic situation within it, appeared to be commonplace. Even those who were sceptical of the community studies style of analysis were prepared to accept that

> localism in a looser sense has been a pervasive mode of working-class culture. A class culture has often been identified with specifically local experiences, relationships and practices; it has been articulated around specifically local points of reference, contact and conflict.
>
> (Clarke 1979: 242)

Such cultures took much of their character from the clustering of particular types of work in certain areas, often with a single dominant industry, or a predominant employer. Examples in industrial Britain would include the five towns of the Staffordshire potteries, the steel industry of the Don valley, textile communities in Lancashire and the Pennines and the various coalfield communities. Large industrial regions could be made up of similar types of communities, with common economic foundations. The 'Black Country' of the English Midlands formed one such 'industrial district', with its craft industries centred on metalworking and engineering. Its range of skills, and pattern of work organizations, differed considerably from those found in regions of heavier industry, like shipbuilding and engine building, as in the northeast of England, or Clydeside. The majority of discussions of working class community therefore pay attention to the specific requirements and imperatives of particular industries, and their histories, and there is a wealth of sociological writing exploring aspects of the interaction between community, work and employment. Examples would include Brown and Brannen (1970) on shipbuilders; Hill (1976) on the dockers; Tunstall (1962) on fishermen; and Samuel (1977) on mineral workers.

These studies demonstrated how distinctive types of communities grew up around work, and its demands and constraints, but also how the social organization of the workplace in turn was imbued with myriad influences from the wider community; neither work nor non-work made sense in isolation. In the case of the fishermen, for instance, their periodic absences at sea and the explosive nature of their relaxation and enjoyment while at home, set the tempo of life in fishing communities like Hull. The local organization of domestic and family life could not avoid bearing the marks of the occupation pursued by the menfolk. As in other 'extreme' cases, like mining, whole populations were bound together by shared encounters with disaster and tragedies. In situations like these, work was thoroughly integrated into the life of the community, indeed often at its very centre, and its needs dictated the rhythms of time, as well as the uses of space. While the same could be said of iron- and steel-producing communities, the range of skills they required and the dynamics of their industrial growth and decline made for a very different type of individual and generational experience from that met by miners or trawler men (Harris 1987; Fevre 1989).

The extent to which work and community relationships were shaped jointly is underlined by historical accounts of the development of particular industries (Joyce 1980; Sabel 1982; Whipp 1985). The idea that a sharp break occurred at the factory gates between the social relationships of the workplace and those which prevailed outside, encouraged sometimes by the argument that industrialization had brought about an unprecedented separation between work and home, was never entirely convincing. Prolonged interactions between employers and their workforces helped define the nature of local labour markets. Populations that had been assembled or expanded for the purpose of working in specific industries quickly acquired the experience, knowledge and skills suited to the available forms of work. Even though economic conditions might leave them ultimately vulnerable and dependent, industrial communities helped in the preparation and recruitment of labour, and exercised some element of control over access to jobs, and promotion prospects. The interconnections between employment and local social relations took many forms. Whipp's researches into the pottery industry in the early twentieth century demonstrated how the family often provided the social basis and cohesive glue for workgroups (1985: 779). In ports like Liverpool and London, dock work was amongst many occupations in which work roles were inherited down the family; and daily life within the home had to adapt to the uncertainties of casual employment, with consequences for attitudes towards work, risk and career in the wider community (Hill 1976). People living near to large employing companies formed strong attachments to them, and expected special treatment in return. A 'moral economy' of mutual obligation between workers and managers tempered the divisions of interest which otherwise might have split labour from capital. Employers benefited from access to a socialized and possibly skilled workforce, with the 'correct' attitudes and values. In the town of St Helens, for example, the Pilkington glass company earned the reputation of a 'family' enterprise, not just because it was owned by a single dominant family, but also because it gave preferential treatment to those who were relatives of existing employees (Lane and Roberts 1971). Membership of a local family gave access to worthwhile jobs, but also added an extra layer of control, since misbehaviour at work not only went against the wishes of management, but could tarnish the reputation of one's kin, including those one worked with.

Bearing these considerations in mind, the extent to which any given working class community ever actually conformed to the terms of the above discussion must remain a topic for detailed empirical investigation. Predictably enough, the more closely particular examples are looked at, the more variations and divergences tend to be revealed. No actual community ever corresponds wholly to the simplifying assumptions that have been built into the generalizations, and this makes it hard to sustain the distinction Lockwood and others have sought to make between the 'sociological' and the historical or empirical. This is true even where the basic conditions appear to be met most fully, as a consideration of the communities associated with an 'extreme' industry like mining will show.

THE CLASSIC SITE? COAL-MINING COMMUNITIES

Conventional assertions about working class community reach an apotheosis in accounts of mining communities, especially those associated with coal-mining, of which there are enough to constitute a substantial sub-literature. Described as 'ideal-typical repositories of working class life' (Strangleman 2001: 265), such communities have exerted a fascination for sociologists, because while they seem to provide quintessential cases of class communities, they also exemplify political and industrial behaviours that are quite exceptional, and often very dramatic. The conditions of working class existence appear to be concentrated in ways that produce some remarkable effects. Thus the intensity of industrial conflict in coal-mining has long been notorious, and sustained a claim that miners were at the forefront of proletarian class consciousness and action (Kerr and Siegel 1954; Allen 1981). This has included engagement in struggles of epic proportions, such as the 1926 General Strike, and the 1984/5 confrontation with the government of

Margaret Thatcher. The endurance and passion shown by the protagonists in these struggles has added to the mystique of their situation, so that

> To outsiders, mining communities are still objects of legend, mystery and even awe . . . the pit and the type of work done there dominate lives in a way that few other jobs do . . . the very act of going underground into a world that most outsiders cannot understand or comprehend, adds to the social isolation of mining communities.
>
> (Hall 1981: 45)

Consequently miners assume a kind of mythic status, as working class heroes, and their fortunes have been regarded as emblematic of wider developments in class relations and prospects. Even given the historic significance of their industry, the amount of attention paid to it has been disproportionate, and has tended to distort the general perception of working class existence. The 1984/5 strike alone generated a sizeable volume of sociological work, mainly documenting the death throes of the 'traditional' mining community, paralleling what amounted to the virtual demise of the British coal-mining industry itself. Many also saw it as signalling the end of the proletariat, in anything resembling its conventional guise.

There are a number of useful reviews of the literature about mining communities (Bulmer 1975b; 1978; Crow 2002; Dicks 2000; Warwick and Littlejohn 1992). Bulmer assembles many of the features which have been referred to already as characteristic aspects of working class life in his summation of the ideal type mining community, which presents a particularly stark combination of elements, including: relative isolation; domination by one industry; work which places very specific and demanding requirements on those who do it; social homogeneity; and a 'gregarious communal sociability'. These attributes are said to form a whole in which 'meaningful social interaction is confined largely to the locality' (Bulmer 1975b: 88). As participants in close-knit collectivities with a shared sense of history, miners evince unusually high levels of solidarity and readiness to engage in struggle to protect their perceived interests. Like Lockwood's models of traditional workers, this typification is a theoretical construct intended to aid empirical analysis; its formal purpose is to enable researchers to test out the relationships, and pinpoint where the expected patterns and associations do not hold.

Warwick and Littlejohn (1992: 129) comment that there has been no systematic attempt to revise this model, though it is not clear exactly how they think this ought to be done; unless something vital is missing altogether, or some aspect included which never can be found in any actual case, then we should expect that different empirical examples will measure up to the model in varying degrees. Their own testing of the model, by converting it into a series of hypothetical claims, shows that it does indeed apply variably to different mining communities, although their overall conclusion is that by the time of their research it was not an adequate guide to contemporary reality, and needed updating.

The main danger with such a construct is that it encourages those who use it to extrapolate too freely across its component parts. Something very like Bulmer's model has been adopted as the standard description of real mining communities. As one commentator puts it, 'a degree of shorthand has come to characterise these ontological discussions, and coalmining communities have been conceptualized holistically' (Parry 2003: 230). Invariably miners are listed among 'those actual working class communities . . . which were the very paradigm of "organic" solidarity' (Cohen 1997: 30). In fact, the skeletal account provided by Bulmer is very close to one of the earliest and most influential analyses, the study of 'Ashton' (Featherstone) undertaken by Dennis *et al.* (1969). Originally published in 1956, and hailed as the classic social scientific account (Warwick and Littlejohn 1992: 27), it is widely celebrated for the clarity with which it handled the economic dimensions of mining (Critcher 1979). Written at about the same time as Young and Willmott were researching Bethnal Green, it adopted a much more analytical approach to dissecting the underlying conditions of manual labour, and its relationship with the capital which employs it. In other words, it utilized a more sophisticated, essentially Marxist, conception of class than the majority of other studies of the period. Miners are presented as wage-labourers, who sell their labour in the same way as any other workers subjected to capitalist relations of production; but they work in an industry with its own very distinctive properties, history and patterns of organization. Furthermore, they live in places which confront them with sets of unique conditions, including the peculiarities of the pit, its proximity to and distance from other centres of population, and the availability or lack of alternative labour market opportunities. Whereas Young and Willmott focus mainly on the working class family and its relationships with wider kin, and are content to describe rather than explain its composition, Dennis *et al.* set their appreciation of the family's role within the framework of its location in the total set of economic and social relations of the miners, at both local and national level. In their view, 'basic features of family structure and family life derive their character from the large-scale framework of Ashton's social relations' (1969: 171). They see the wider pattern of community life in similar terms, as shaped by the impact of economic forces and relations that mostly are beyond local control or determination.

In this way, community is treated as a dependent variable, with only a very limited scope to make a difference. Unlike many other studies of working class community, the focus is not turned inwards. Although distinctive in certain respects, the local way of life is said to add 'no new quality to the characteristics of the miner. . . . But the participation in and sharing of a common set of community relations and experiences through time gives confirmation to those characteristics, considerably strengthening them' (1969: 83). Thus involvement in a set of densely local social relations, persisting over time, serves to reinforce the solidarity and awareness of collective interests which anyway would have developed from the shared experience of working underground, as wage-labourers. However, a little room is left for community life to show some autonomy from these economic forces. Like other working class communities, it is implied, Ashton mediates between employees as individuals, and their full exposure to the exploitative and alienating effects of the economic relationships in which they are caught up. Relations of kinship and friendship allow the mobilization of collective support, which gives miners and their families greater ability to withstand times of hardship; and the 'frivolous' round of social enjoyment in which most of the miners appear to engage compensates them for the daily pressures and dangers of the work. But the community is also obliged to meet demands put upon it by the industry; for example, families have to produce the 'social personalities' it needs. This is achieved because most of the young men growing up in the town expect to follow their fathers into the pit, and are socialized within the family to know what to expect when they get there. The status of miner is also respected and valued by everyone around, so that it is seen as a worthy position to achieve. So despite the Marxian perspective, the argument retains a streak of functionalism. As with other working class settings, the domination exerted by work ensures that there is 'an interpenetration of work and non-work spheres which conditions expectations among the community, and through these linkages the workplace becomes known and understandable' (Strangleman 2001: 258).

As viewed by Dennis *et al.*, therefore, community is a mechanism for the reproduction of existing patterns of life and work, not for the creation of things that are new. In fact, the account leaves a strong impression that, in many ways, Ashton is too local, and too well adapted to the exigencies of the industry; its inward-looking nature inhibits change, just as the fact that many of its working population spend their leisure time in the pubs and clubs means that they do not do the 'serious' work of education and political organization needed if they were to develop a more complete consciousness of class. In this way, the attributes of community laid out by Dennis *et al.* help explain why, although miners have been categorized so often as 'militant' and bloody-minded, and their reputation has sometimes led them to be feared as 'the enemy within', mostly they have not pursued especially radical, let alone revolutionary, aims. Measured against the criterion of an advanced, or 'true', Marxist class consciousness, Ashton seems to have produced a 'failed' culture, which disabled it from providing the necessary cutting edge into the deprivations and inequalities of class society (Warwick and Littlejohn 1992: 24). Its social organization is more oriented to getting by, and meeting the ordinary problems of everyday life, than challenging them. That this should be the case for a supposed vanguard group within the working class gives some backing to broader criticisms of the sectional, hermetically sealed forms of consciousness such communities support. The 'particularistic' strengths of community that were carried into the labour movement from occupations like mining lent it much of its organizational effectiveness, but at the same time inhibited the formation of more universalistic values and sympathies (Anderson 1965; Beynon and Austrin 1994; Westergaard 1975). The collective power of community, which made it such a bulwark against the demands of employers and bosses, also insulated it against assimilation into larger, class, identities; the obverse of solidarity within was suspicion towards those on the outside, even when they had essential interests in common.

To some extent, this was because mining was actually far from typical of all, or even most, working class situations; in some ways, it was rather peripheral to the norm. Other analyses of mining recognize this dualism of community, its capacity to unify and to separate, to amplify local solidarity while putting up barriers against the outside world. In their study of four West Yorkshire mining settlements, for example, Warwick and Littlejohn state that

> For close observers, as well as members of mining households, the experience of living and working in mining villages can take the form of a 'manifest community', creating identities and consciousness, which can be markedly different from those in other parts of the same society.

> (Warwick and Littlejohn 1992: 17)

Beynon and Austrin (1994) point to the 'double exceptionalism' of the miners, in that their way of life showed strong continuities with rural, and in the case of the Durham coalfield, even feudal origins, while simultaneously they occupied a position at the forefront of an emerging working class. The rural influence is acknowledged in the use of the term 'pit village' to refer to settlements built around collieries. Even the largest pits rarely required a workforce of more than a few thousand; 'Ashton' was a place of 14,000 population, and the majority of mining communities reported on are even smaller. Quite reasonably, even apart from their physical nearness to the countryside, such places possessed many village-like qualities. Beynon and Austrin note the bucolic nature of miners' recreations and pastimes – including pigeon fancying, dog-breeding, and competitive sports like running and wrestling. These provided respectable ways in which members of such intensely solidary communities could differentiate themselves from one another. More structured divisions developed around different work roles and skills, political disagreements and religious beliefs. The contrast between those displaying the 'serious' and 'frivolous' attitudes to life mentioned by Dennis *et al.* corresponds to many other versions of the 'rough' and 'respectable' distinction which regularly crops up in examinations of the working class (Mogey 1956; Elias and Scotson 1965; Wight 1993). These internal variations, which tend to get lost behind the imagery of a united and single-minded community, add considerable complexity to the picture. To those who knew them well, mining communities could always be disaggregated into diverse families and households, and a mixture of differing social groupings, whose attitudes and behaviour were far from uniform. This helps explain why accounts of community life from the inside often stress issues of privacy, intolerance, and the need to keep the community 'at arm's length'. Due concern for one's neighbour had to be balanced by watchfulness, and care not to be too nosy (Warwick and Littlejohn 1992: 78). As one participant says 'You knew everybody in the street to talk to, you saw them every day, but you couldn't say you were very close to them . . . neighbours didn't go in and out of people's houses' (Beynon and Austrin 1994: 188).

If these points can be made about occupational communities of a kind that are usually deemed to be about as solid as is imaginable, then they are even more likely to have applied elsewhere, where conditions were more variable, and the range of jobs, occupations, and family backgrounds wider. Similarly, we find ample evidence that mining communities differed in numerous respects, and could not be reduced to simple copies of one another. Even within a single coalfield there could be marked contrasts, for example between situations of paternalism, where not only housing and household provisions were supplied by or through the employer, but also medical care, and schooling that was received with some gratitude, and those 'Little Moscows' which were known to be exceptionally militant and obstreperous (Beynon and Austrin 1994; Macintyre 1980). Some miners espoused Leninism, whereas others were shaped more by the influence of religiosity and associated values of responsibility and sobriety (Moore 1974). The traditions of the various British coalfields themselves reveal similar contrasts. The Durham coalfield has a history of deep paternalism and domination by coal-owner, church and state, which produced a culture of moderation and respectable Labourism (Beynon and Austrin 1994: xvi) that contrasts with the more volatile and aggressive collectivism of Scotland, Yorkshire and South Wales. According to Gilbert (1992: 249), the latter displayed an exemplary depth of solidarity which arose from 'the complete character of the local formation and the way in which local communal interests and class interests were fused'. Such a formulation suggests, however, that mining communities in Durham were somehow 'incomplete', whereas the evidence points to sound reasons why they were different, representing their own solutions to unique sets of circumstances. Reactions to the 1984/5 strike brought out the significance of such differences: far from reactions being uniform and automatic, different groups of miners, and different mining communities, took up contrasting stances towards the struggle; such divisiveness was one reason why it ended in defeat.

As research in mining communities during the latter half of the twentieth century documents (Sewel 1975; Coulter *et al.* 1984; Gibbon 1988), the strike, and its eventual defeat, was the culmination of a long-drawn out industrial collapse, which has left most of these communities devoid of their original purpose. Apart from the natural cycle of development and exhaustion afflicting any community based on production of a primary raw material, other changes driven by economic, political and strategic considerations resulted in the gradual transformation of mining communities into something different. As the industry modernized and contracted, increasing numbers of miners were forced to move between pits, and coalfields. Thus 'the older close knit communities were destroyed, expanded, reduced or diluted but they were no longer the same. With this restructuring died old traditions and consciousness' (Coulter *et al.* 1984: 175). In fact, few pit villages consisted solely of miners and their families, and this introduced into them extra distinctions of class, education and lifestyle, so that they were altogether more variegated than the ideal type would suggest. When the time came to face up to the challenge to their future, differences in their social composition meant that they positioned themselves differently (Waddington *et al.* 1991). While some conformed to the image of stubborn resistance and unity, others broke apart along dividing lines which had always been implicit in them.

More recent studies highlight nevertheless some important continuities with earlier work. Warwick and Littlejohn (1992: 131) found that social networks linking households with kin, friends and neighbours 'provide resources and constraints in a manner not unlike those of earlier communities, and a basis around which community identity is still maintained'. In conversation, people still proclaim the sense of belonging to a 'friendly' village or town. In a study of three communities close to Sheffield, Waddington *et al.* (1991: 99) observed that all contained dense networks of families, friends and workmates, which 'seemed to have as their fixed points the mining industry and the family. Over generations, these have become intertwined in the fabric of community life'. Such attributes can persist long after mining has vanished from the local economic scene. Wight (1993) describes the ex-mining village of 'Cauldmoss' in central Scotland as a place where social contacts are built largely around kinship networks, and people are preoccupied with exchanging information about 'personally known individuals', in order to place them within a subtle gradation of respectability, and conformity with local standards of behaviour and material lifestyle. Recognition as a member of the 'local' population gives access to support networks, and facilities, and also creates expectations of certain 'rights' to local housing and other benefits, especially when compared to 'outsiders' and incomers. Values and behaviour are shaped mostly by such parochial relationships, and far less attention is paid to events elsewhere. Cauldmoss presents a front of unity and homogeneity towards the outside world, even if internally it is riven with divisions, chiefly to do with how well individuals and families succeed in maintaining expected standards of 'niceness'. Hence despite the many complexities and variations his analysis reveals, Wight concludes that Cauldmoss exhibits a 'Durkheimian' social cohesion 'founded on a common past', and 'reproduced through a common interpretation of the fundamental cognitive categories' that make up its social world (Wight 1993: 232). This would support Warwick and Littlejohn's view (1992: 84) that, unlike the great mass of urban neighbourhoods which form the majority of community spaces in the contemporary world, mining localities continue to function as social entities. While it could be argued that this level of closeness and interdependence exposes those involved to new forms of risk and exploitation, for instance by making them immobile and unadventurous, studies of such communities 'post-mining' show how these well established social networks can go on providing support, and emotional security, and mobilize valuable resources within a context of limited possibilities. In that sense, they continue to provide important forms of local social and cultural capital (Strangleman 2001; Rees and Thomas 1991).

THE DISINTEGRATION OF WORKING CLASS COMMUNITIES

In an extreme way, mining communities exemplify the loss of the occupational foundations which once held working class communities together. Today it is difficult, if not impossible, to find comparable situations where very substantial numbers of employees continue to work, as well as live, together. The disintegration of communities so strongly focussed around work has helped to undermine the potency of working class identities, and by contrast with the fascination it attracted in the earlier period, Savage *et al.* (2005: 97) note that it is difficult now to detect much sustained interest among sociologists in the nature of working class culture. Likewise, local studies are thought by many to be outdated. Many convincing arguments have been advanced to suggest that the old working class has fragmented, and/or been assimilated into an expanded 'middle mass' which encompasses the bulk of the contemporary population, blurring former boundaries between manual and non-manual workers (Pahl 1984; Saunders 1990; Crompton 1998) and reducing local distinctiveness. Hence, as Scott (2000: 45) puts it, subordinate manual workers no longer *live* class in the same way as their counterparts in traditional working class communities. Analyses of modern working class ways of life tend to bifurcate accordingly. The mass of manual workers appear to live in ways that are barely distinguishable from most members of other social classes. Their life patterns were foreshadowed by accounts of the 'privatized' affluent workers who came to inhabit the private estates and 'suburban' locations which grew up around modern manufacturing industries (Goldthorpe *et al.* 1969; Devine 1992), and they have shown resilience in the face of major technological and employment changes, including the relative decline of manufacturing jobs. Savage *et al.* (2005) point to the distinct spatial clustering of numbers of people with modest incomes, and backgrounds in hard manual labour, who continue to be embedded in and emotionally identified with their place of residence. In such neighbourhoods, there is still a need for supportive social networks of neighbours and family to cushion individuals against the inherent insecurities which still accompany their economic and social positions. The difference from the old-style communities is that relatives and neighbours now may work in a multitude of different jobs and workplaces, and must show considerable flexibility and mobility between jobs. Their patterns of daily interaction with one another are therefore not so dense, and they may not describe their neighbourhood as a community, in anything like the old terms; yet there are definite continuities with earlier forms of working class existence.

A far more negative impression of the fortunes of working class people can be gained from that stream of critical writing that has talked essentially about the degeneration and collapse of working class community. Seabrook (1984) provides a fairly typical analysis of how such organic communities began to fall apart, just as they were being discovered by the sociologists. He claims that the shift of population to outer-city estates and high-rise blocks from the 1950s onwards caused a general deterioration to set in, until by the 1970s many such estates had become 'no go areas covered with graffiti, sites of muggings, drinking and glue-sniffing' (1984: 11). While the vast majority of residents remained 'decent and good' there was a concentration of 'the weaker and more vulnerable – single parents, the disabled, those with few skills and no ability to increase their earning power, the mentally or emotionally disturbed, the less well endowed'; those with the potential to become community leaders opted to move elsewhere. At worst, estates were becoming dumping grounds for 'problem people'. Seabrook argued that the transfer of an ethic of collective solidarity to the state (or 'society' in general) had removed the necessity for communal sentiments at the local level, and therefore was destructive of more intimate forms of community. The argument foreshadows more recent discussions about the need to restore a sense of mutual obligation and responsibility in the face of the 'dependency' generated by a welfare state. A number of those who wrote about and enthused about working class community in the 1960s ended up thirty years later taking this line about the need to recover communal morality, so as to deal with the problems of an emergent 'underclass' and the mass of 'dependent' individuals; calls for a return to community values formed part of the agenda of the right-wing Institute of Economic Affairs, for example (Murray 1990; Dennis and Erdos 1992; Green 1996). Campbell (1993) berates Seabrook for his 'snobbish' attitude towards the working class, but her analysis of the origins and effects of the sporadic urban riots which occurred throughout the 1980s and 1990s provides a similarly dysfunctional image of the criminalization of declining working class neighbourhoods. Following a spate of disturbances in places like Cardiff, Newcastle and Oxford, Campbell examined the condition of the large estates involved. They were places in which large swathes of the working class has lost their economic purpose, leaving young men especially prone to engage in displays of macho aggression and intimidation.

The values and modes of community living had been distorted to serve their interests, imposing codes of silence on those who suffered most from their actions, their own neighbours, and especially the women and members of ethnic minorities among them. Campbell suggested that such areas served as 'local windows on a larger landscape' of economic and social change and disruption during the Thatcher years. Her account of such neighbourhoods as social spaces increasingly regulated by 'organised crime and masculine tyrannies' (1993: 177) conforms to Lash and Urry's (1994) vision of the emergence of poorly integrated 'wild zones', thin in resources and lacking social regulation. They attribute this to the removal, without replacement, of the organizing structures of family networks, industrial labour markets and local welfare institutions. A decade earlier, Harrison investigated the creation of inner city areas with high concentrations of poorly skilled, or de-skilled, workers, usually with a fringe criminal element, subject to continual daily disputes and conflicts, which boiled over from time to time into ugly confrontations, often with a racial or ethnic edge. In such contexts he felt 'the community . . . no longer controls what happens on the street, for it is no longer, in any meaningful sense, a community' (Harrison 1983: 316).

Other accounts tell a similar story. Collins (2004) examines the transformation of the London Borough of Southwark from a neighbourhood dominated by the indigenous 'labouring classes' into an ethnically mixed, multicultural hotspot, increasingly attractive to the more culturally attuned middle classes. There had been an exodus from the area of many of the descendants of the local working class, taking the route of upward social and outward geographical mobility towards the satellite suburbs, leaving what remained of the white working class resembling a beleaguered minority in an area they had thought of as their own. Collins indicates how established norms of trust and sociability were forced to struggle with the growing effects of drugs, crime and antisocial behaviour. Charlesworth (2000: 60) depicts the working class inhabitants of Rotherham as leading lives bereft of their 'usual' sociological coordinates, confronting a social experience 'by its very nature fragmented, dissolute, polysemic, ambiguous, and . . . desolating'. The loss of dependable sources of local employment removed the basis for planning ahead and eroded the continuity which once had fostered a coherent industrial culture. Without the protective framework of community, lives become serialized and episodic (Charlesworth 2000: 162). Each of these versions of the direction taken by members of the working class may correspond to the divided realities of a spatially separated, fragmented class (Byrne 1999). Neither provides room for anything like the traditional working class community.

4

OUT OF THE WRECKAGE
THE RECOVERY OF COMMUNITY

THE DEATH OF COMMUNITY?

After a brief period of popularity, conventional community studies were subjected to two distinct lines of attack, which often became entangled with one another. The first was that the accounts they had provided were invalid, because they left out significant details, or misinterpreted the observed reality. The most insistent version of this criticism was that they neglected to consider crucial gender differences within communities, presenting instead a relentlessly masculine point of view (Frankenberg 1976); but they were also accused of playing down other key social divisions and conflicts, to offer a generally over-optimistic, bland view of community relations. Although damaging, this was a criticism that could be met potentially by more reflective forms of research, showing greater sensitivity to developments in social theory. The second contention was that, regardless of whether or not their descriptive accounts were accurate, investigations carried out in such communities were becoming simply irrelevant. No matter what their historical value might be, they no longer corresponded to contemporary social realities. This was harder to rebut, because apparently it left students of community without anything worthwhile to study.

Communities of the kind described in the preceding chapters were underpinned essentially by the dependence of all those involved in them upon a common mode of existence. Typically this took the form of a concentration of a particular sort of productive activity in a given place. The rural village came into being as part of a system of agrarian production, as a settlement uniting those who provided the necessary workforce, and those who serviced them. In some of the most rural settings for community studies, although there was no village as such, the 'community' consisted instead of farming families bound together in intricate patterns of cooperation and interdependence. working class communities focussed similarly on the occupational clusters associated with a certain industry or form of work (principally manual labour). As well as enabling the fulfilment of key productive functions, these communities also took care of the provision of the essential means of social reproduction, especially family relations, but also social support and exchange of services. The emphasis in the community studies literature was on portraying the mundane practices of daily life which grew up around these tasks: the actions and interactions of residents as they engaged in visiting, socializing, building family connections, worshipping and working together. As the unit which brought all these social dimensions into alignment, the community formed something approaching a self-enclosed world, exercising a determining influence over its members. Indeed, because most of their operative ideas, beliefs and forms of conduct were developed within its boundaries, at times they seemed to have had only the haziest idea of what was happening outside their own limited local world. Not only did this make their own concerns seem somewhat parochial, it also made those who studied them appear to be interested only in the trivial or 'everyday', and therefore unable to make adequate connections with the larger processes shaping society and social life, including the forces which were working, arguably, to destroy the underlying foundations of community life itself. The most important of these involved the long-term transformation or disintegration of the economic functions which had brought the traditional communities into being. Pahl (1970a: 107) suggested that since there was no longer the degree of local autonomy and economic interdependence that it implied, 'community' had become a word that confused more than it illuminated.

Although the analysis of working class communities in urban and industrial contexts helped push back some of the limits of these traditional conceptions, progress in the field was beset by the tendency to keep referring back to the bounded entity of the small local, usually rural, community (Albrow *et al.* 1997: 21), and to the kind of ethos Mitford captured when she referred to the rural village as 'a little world of our own . . . where we know everyone and are known to everyone, interested in everyone, and authorized to hope that everyone feels an interest in us' (1938: 3, originally published in 1824). It is telling, as Mitford's editor notes, that her writing was not all about one village, or even any actual village; it belongs rather to a long line of semi-fictionalized accounts of rural life (see also Evans 1956; Blythe 1969). By the mid-twentieth century it was becoming increasingly apparent that communities of this sort resembled narrow, old-fashioned enclaves in a social universe that was leaving them rapidly behind. As a concept 'community' appeared to be rooted firmly in the conditions of a disappearing social order, and despite many subsequent attempts to reconstruct it, in various guises, this kind of all-embracing, self-contained, social milieu seems totally at odds with modern conditions. Indeed, the destruction of the coherent 'ways of life' involved was a theme inherent in the accounts provided by the social researchers themselves, who ascribed it variously to the forces of 'modernization', urban planning, social integration and state intervention. These were represented as massive external pressures impinging upon life in local settings, undermining their self-sufficiency, and weakening their integrity and distinctiveness. Whether in the context of the most remote of rural environments, or at the heart of major industrial cities, there seemed to be no escaping the overwhelming intrusion of forces hostile to the survival of community. So, although there were many ready to single out aspects of the traditional community for praise, few were willing to express much optimism about its future prospects. At both the conceptual level, and as an empirical reality, many were eager instead to pronounce upon the 'death of community'.

A notorious example was a study of a small American town, 'Springdale' (with a population of fewer than 3000, more deserving the title of a village), which concluded that the controlling conditions of life were centralization, bureaucratization and dominance by large-scale organizations (Vidich and Bensman 1958: x), all means through which the local population were drawn increasingly into the 'central machinery' of American life. The authors comment therefore that, contrary to received opinion about the importance of endogenous determinants, the decisive factors shaping the actions of the rural community originated outside it, including even local conceptions of the idyllic nature of rural life, mainly absorbed from the mass media. Members of the community recycled amongst themselves ideas about rural–urban differences they had learned from elsewhere. This produced an interesting shift of analytical perspective, in which it is stated that the resulting study is not about rural community as such, but rather about 'how some of the major institutions of a society work themselves out in a particular community'(1958: xi). This brought the account more into the framework of community study as a 'method', or form of case study, used to throw light on wider societal developments and dealing chiefly with 'transitional processes' of change (Bell and Newby 1971: 40). Vidich and Bensman examined these primarily with respect to local politics, religion and leadership. The study became controversial because it seemed to expose quite brutally some of the illusions and pretensions of those whose behaviour was being investigated, including the idea that they were just 'plain folk' who all got along very well together. In the muckraking tradition of some early American social investigations, it took the lid off 'community', to lay bare its ideological distortions.

According to Vidich and Bensman, Springdale's self-image was as 'a community of religiously-minded people and a place where "everybody knows everybody" and where "you can say hello to anybody"' (1958: 30). As its moral values it upheld 'honesty, fair play, trustworthiness, good-neighbourliness, helpfulness, sobriety and clean-living'. These values were made to appear real, in part, by ignoring inconvenient facts, about those who either failed to live up to them or chose to live by other standards. When the published study questioned their validity, the affront to the community's view of itself resulted in enormous controversy, including a public hanging-in-effigy of the principal investigator. In fact, the authors gave some credence to the importance of these values, because not only do they describe them as 'traditional' values, typical of the American past 'at its best', but they also regard them as a useful defensive screen behind which local people could conceal, from themselves and others, their lack of real control over the circumstances of their lives. By contrast it is suggested that more urban people, lacking the same shared ideology, were compelled instead to react to their powerlessness by resorting to 'the cultivation of privacy, of leisure, of "style", and of culture' (1958: x). Thus, despite offering a rather negative deconstruction of rural community, Vidich and Bensman still see it as providing a backdrop against which certain agreed cultural and behavioural standards could be maintained, whereas city-dwellers are driven back more onto their individual resources. This makes their verdict on Springdale equivocal, both denying and yet affirming the significance of distinctively 'rural' lifestyles. In making such contrasts between rural and urban reactions to contemporary circumstances, they were tapping into a very extensive literature on urban life and its alleged incompatibility with community.

'URBANISM' VERSUS COMMUNITY

As noted in Chapter 1, the association of city life with experiences of isolation, alienation and social disorganization has been a dominant theme in urban sociology (Simmel 1903; Park *et al.* 1925; Wirth 1938; Riesman 1950). Simmel identified the modern metropolis as the domain of individuals who were reserved, blasé and intellectual in their attitude to one another, as a necessary way of coping with the fragmented and incoherent conditions of life that confronted them. In keeping their distance from one another, inevitably they rejected the bonds of community. Wirth argued that, for reasons of size, density, and social diversity in the population, urban people were thrown into relationships that were superficial, anonymous and transitory. Generally they were devoid of intimate personal ties, and related to one another mainly through formal organizations and bureaucratic devices, rather than informal and spontaneous association. The research programme of the Chicago School sociologists presented a mass of evidence to support such conclusions, and had they known much about contemporary sociological work on the city, the people of Springdale would have found ample backing for their own view of urban life, as typified by 'crime, dirt, filth, immorality, vice, corruption and anti-Americanism' (Vidich and Bensman 1958: 102). Like influential sociological analyses of the time, everyday images of community played off against each other these contrasting understandings of urban and non-urban conditions. Vidich and Bensman themselves stand firmly within this tradition, and their analysis of the leading traits of 'mass society' conjures up the same bleak vision of urbanism and its characteristics. In its supposed 'surrender' to mass society, and its penetration by urban influences, they regard Springdale as a microcosm of the fate of American society; to differing degrees, they contend, all modern communities were suffering from the same processes of assimilation which would absorb them into a uniform, urbanized world. In a later study of a comparably small settlement in rural Australia, we find the same basic narrative. A strong sense of local belonging and attachment to place is matched by a deep-seated conviction that life in the country town is superior to anything that would be possible in the city; yet its survival is held to face constant pressure from external forces tending to undermine such settlements, and their social cohesion (Dempsey 1990). As with Springdale, the local way of life seems more a relic of the past than a secure adaptation to present exigencies.

References to 'mass society' are no longer so commonplace as they were during the 1950s and 1960s, when they provided an alternative way of talking about the social homogeneity, loss of firm identity, and anonymization usually associated with city life and the growth of large organizations (Mills 1956; Kornhauser 1959). However, there are strong continuities between these classic conceptions, formulated early in the twentieth century, and more contemporary accounts of 'postmodern' city life by writers like Bauman (2001b), Harvey (1989a; 1989b), and Wilson (1991). Cultural images of the city and urban life also play their part in highlighting these issues, for example in writings as diverse as those of Charles Dickens, Raymond Chandler, Paul Auster and Tom Wolfe, or in films such as *Metropolis* and *Blade Runner*. The image of city existence they present is encapsulated in a comment by Raban that

> To live in a city is to live in a community of people who are strangers to each other. You have to act on hints and fancies, for they are all the mobile and cellular nature of city life will allow you. You expose yourself in and are exposed to by others, fragments, isolated signals, bare disconnected gestures, jungle cries and whispers that resist all your attempts to unravel their meaning, their consistency.
>
> (Raban 1975: 15)

According to these sources, the urban world is one in which there are no clear boundaries or delineations, but a great deal of diversity, choice and mobility, all of which tend to militate against the formation of strong communities of shared identity. Relationships among strangers, who meet one another in piecemeal and haphazard fashion, are as different as could be from the close personal knowledge and overlapping social ties associated with more traditional social contexts, so that one wonders what Raban could possibly mean by calling this a 'community' of people at all; it is much more like a random mass, or crowd. This is city life as perceived from a distance, when the overall impression is of energetic but chaotic disorder.

In sociological discussions of urbanism and its effects, references to the disorganized, unpredictable and dangerous quality of urban living abound. Cities are seen as conducive to problems in a way that the countryside, with its assumed orderliness and integration, is not. The contrast is very entrenched, and often almost unconscious. When in 1996 a gunman opened fire on pupils at a school in the small Scottish town of Dunblane, the sense of horror and outrage was heightened by a feeling that somehow this was an *inappropriate* place for such a thing to happen. A *Guardian* newspaper editorial (14 March 1996) conveyed this feeling:

> There are some obvious parallels with Hungerford, the English town where Michael Ryan shot dead 16 people in 1987. Both are *the last places* where one would expect random violence to erupt: small attractive country towns with strong community ties and *none of the alienation associated with larger cities*. Both killers lived within the communities they devastated.
>
> (*Guardian*, 14 March 1996, emphasis added)

Apart from begging an obvious question as to where one ought to expect 'random' violence to erupt, this shows very clearly how engrained rural/urban contrasts can be. It is presumed that the small town signifies community, whereas the city brings alienation. The example could be counterposed to an infamous incident in New York City, when a woman was attacked and killed, and it turned out afterwards that dozens of people had heard or seen it happening, without anyone intervening. This has been interpreted as an unsurprising illustration of urban indifference, symptomatic of the absence of communal feeling, for which many other examples could easily be substituted. Harrison (1983: 36) provides a comparable case from Hackney, in east London.

In his definitive contribution to urban sociology, 'Urbanism as a Way of Life', Wirth characterized modern cities as consisting of a 'motley of peoples and cultures' with 'highly differentiated modes of life' between which he suggested there could only be relationships of tolerance, indifference and strife, but always the sharpest contrasts. He argued that this explained the appearance of a long list of urban social problems, including personal disorganization, crime, corruption, delinquency, mental breakdown and suicide (Wirth 1995: 75, 79). Short (1996: 418) proposes more briefly that the anonymous city is a city freed from social constraint and community sanction; within city limits, anything goes. Apparently, then, the absence of community constitutes the central problem of urban life. However, there has always been another strand to social science analysis and writing about the city, at least as strong, which has focussed on grasping more firmly the social implications of fragmentation and differentiation in urban organization, and the impact this has on people's experiences. Raban hints at this with his remarks about the 'cellular' nature of city life and its 'disconnected' character; what is questionable is his conclusion that this renders the city and its meaning impossible to grasp. As well as describing the generally anonymous and segmented form of city life, Wirth also wrote about the city as a 'mosaic of social worlds', and it was very much part of the Chicago School approach to try to convey how differently people lived within their respective social worlds. Through methods of ethnography and participant observation, Chicago sociologists sought to uncover the 'hidden' rules and codes of social life amongst particular social groups and in particular settings (Hannerz 1980). It was out of this background that the work of the symbolic interactionists and other sociologists of everyday life like Blumer, Becker and Goffman sprang, to throw light on the secret universes of such groups as taxi hall dancers (Cressey 1932); marijuana users (Becker 1963); and asylum inmates (Goffman 1961). This interest extended to the close investigation of particular spatial and social locales within the city, both at the generic level and through specific examples (Anderson 1923; Wirth 1928; Zorbaugh 1929; Whyte 1943).

EXPLAINING URBAN DIFFERENTIATION AND SEGREGATION

Chicago urban sociology is known best for the way in which it produced a social map of the city. According to the ecological conception of urban structure developed by Park *et al.* (1925), every city generated a distinct social organization, which was visibly demarcated in space. Different functions, and different social groups or population elements, occupied specific places and spaces within this organization. For example, residential areas tended to be separated from centres of industrial or business activity. Furthermore, different areas accommodated different groups separated according to variations in class, ethnic origin, and cultural background and propensities. Adopting the template of Chicago itself as a model, these were given descriptive labels like 'Little Sicily', 'Chinatown', 'Deutschland' and the 'zone of working men's homes'. The origins of such districts were attributed to a variety of 'sifting and sorting' mechanisms, which broke the urban population down into its distinct sub-groups. According to Burgess (1925), this arose from a natural process of competition for urban space, equivalent to the ecological battle for living space among plant life and animals. The significance for a sociological understanding is that although the city in its entirety might present a confusing arena of seemingly random variations and contacts, the vast majority of people were not actually moving freely throughout the city, but inclined instead to remain within their particular place. This might be as small as a street corner (Whyte 1943) or as large as a substantial urban neighbourhood or district (Gans 1962). Whichever it might be, it constituted a more bounded, effective social world than the 'metropolis' as a whole.

Chicago ecological theory has been criticized heavily for its misleading analogy with plant life and its tendency to biological reductionism (Saunders 1986; Dickens 1990). The approach was also accused of overgeneralizing a description of urban structure too closely fitted to the particular experiences of the city of Chicago during the 1930s. Nevertheless it contained a central truth, that urban contexts were differentiated socially into quite distinctive types of neighbourhoods, containing population groupings between which there were divergent patterns of social organization and lifestyle; in other words, that there was the basis for the formation of a variety of urban communities. It was a major contribution of the Chicago School to document how at least some of these groups lived. The attempt to formulate this into a general theory came rather late in the school's history, and had precedents in the efforts of many others, from Engels onwards, to map urban social patterns according to their physical and geographical layout (Engels 1845; Fried and Elman 1974). Most observers of large cities, especially after the Industrial Revolution, had noted that there appeared to be a definite spatial arrangement of different types of residents and activities. Even though they were formed under conditions very unlike those pertaining to Chicago, many British and European cities showed something like the 'concentric zone' pattern identified by Burgess (Dickinson 1964; Perkin 1969). Writing about London, for example, Booth described how one could trace different elements in the population 'ring by ring', moving outwards from the centre.

Closer inspection might prove that the exact configuration of districts within a town reflected the historical circumstances of its growth, and the types of specialization it contained; for example, historic towns like Oxford or Bristol were bound to take shape differently from new towns like Telford or Milton Keynes, where planners had a relatively free hand. This does not undermine the essential point that there are significant divisions and separations within the urban landscape, and that this can give rise to the occurrence of distinctive local patterns of community life. Indeed, this forms the commonsense starting point for a large body of writing about urban situations. Whilst the attempt to find a causal explanation for this patterning in terms of unconscious biological forces may have been misconceived, it left the door open for later, more adequate, social explanations. These were developed through critical engagement with the Chicago tradition by writers like Gans (1968), Pahl (1970a; 1970b), Robson (1969) and Rex and Moore (1967).

CHOICE, CONSTRAINT AND COMMUNITY FORMATION

Studies of so-called 'natural areas' within cities have been pursued by geographers employing increasingly sophisticated means of data gathering and analysis to define the relevant spatial boundaries and measure variations within and between them (Carter 1972; Badcock 1984). This entails bringing together information about a range of urban characteristics, including aspects of local demography (such as age, family structure, health and morbidity), the built environment (housing types, distributions of amenities) and evidence of social behaviour and organization (school catchments, crime rates, numbers of voluntary bodies, and so on). It was quickly established that areas defined in terms of these common objective characteristics were not necessarily the same thing as territorial groupings with shared social contacts and common institutions (Glass 1953). In fact, it was altogether more difficult to uncover the prevalent social relationships within a population than it was to create indices of external facts about them. Despite its statistical refinement, there was mounting dissatisfaction with the quantitative search for empirical regularities in the spatial geometry of cities; its lack of explanatory power led to its dismissal by some as 'low level science' dealing with a lightweight problematic, typically mistaking measurement for explanation (Badcock 1984).

The underlying objection was that the spatial order of the city reflected its social order, rather than the reverse. Consequently, describing how cities were laid out in space did not bring one any nearer to understanding why this was the case; to do so demanded a more social and historical approach (Gregory and Urry 1985). In fact, because spatial variations did not coincide directly with more sociological phenomena, critics argued that the quest for positivist rigour in measurement could easily lead away from meaningful social explanation; it was not possible to reach conclusions about the social nature of an urban district on the basis of measurable facts alone. For example, locations with very similar physical features could elicit different responses from people according to how they were perceived, and what those people brought to them in terms of hopes, expectations and values. Urban amenities which some viewed as the fulfilment of their dreams would fall far short of the aspirations of others, while areas which seemed indistinguishable to most outsiders could acquire very different reputations amongst those who lived in them. Over time, the same area could undergo processes, such as gentrification and urban degeneration, that transformed its meaning and reputation, without the physical structure altering greatly, and quite arbitrary differences could assume surprising social significance; in one study, the colour of high-rise apartment blocks became the basis of a major cleavage between residents who were otherwise indistinguishable (Suttles 1972: 28). Hence the social significance of an urban district could not be understood fully without examining the interaction between objective and subjective factors. This provided a way in for those who wanted to build on the legacy of the Chicago School, without reproducing its over-deterministic emphasis on non-social influences. It also enabled some sociologists to respond to the criticism, expressed by Saunders (1985: 71), that even though some community study-type monographs continued to appear, the collapse of the ecological framework had deprived community research of any coherent theoretical rationale.

We have seen how the work of Young and Willmott in London was conducted against the grain of conventional expectations of urban amorphousness and isolation; they 'discovered' community where it was least expected. Their examination of working class community was premised on its relative separation and insulation from the surrounding urban mass by invisible social barriers of class, occupation and economic hardship, which created an unexpectedly homogeneous milieu within which people could develop their own modes of belief and conduct. Their work was paralleled in the United States by Gans' study of the working class Italian-Americans of Boston's West End (Gans 1962). Again Gans was able to show how, contrary to external perceptions, this was not a disorganized urban slum, but an area possessing a well defined social order, reflecting a combination of class and ethnic influences. The visible, external signs of physical dilapidation were not a trustworthy guide to how people felt about the area, nor to their behaviour. As he puts it, it was 'a run-down area of people struggling with problems of low income, poor education, and related difficulties. Even so, it was by and large a good place to live' (Gans 1962: 16), a sentiment repeated almost word-for-word in other studies of communities in deprived areas (Suttles 1968; Coates and Silburne 1973; Gill 1977; Damer 1989). Indeed, the discrepancy between evaluations made from an external perspective and the view from within has become one of the most common themes of community research. In the same way, areas of good quality housing and high living standards can be found to contain impoverished lifestyles of loneliness and conformity, of the sort which have given 'suburbia' a bad name (Whyte 1957).

At the same time, of course, it would be foolish to go to the opposite extreme, and assume that areas of poor quality housing and limited amenities always conceal warmth and solidarity. Referring to the St Ann's district of Nottingham, Coates and Silburne emphasize that long-established housing does not necessarily generate a sense of fellow feeling among those who occupy it: 'this one sometimes does, and sometimes does not' (1973: 111). The unpredictability comes about because processes of social meaning and interpretation intervene between the physical environment and behavioural and attitudinal outcomes in ways that complicate straightforward causal explanations. The value people attribute to their local environment depends upon what they want, and expect, from it. Gans found that in the 'urban village' of the West End, as in Bethnal Green, the majority of inhabitants formed part of an extensive network of peer groups, through which they experienced regular, often life-long interaction with a small circle of relatives and peers who shared the same basic class, age, sex and often ethnic identity. Ties of family and kinship were at the centre of this rather loose-knit social structure, which was bound together into a more formalized 'community' by a limited number of institutions and voluntary bodies, such as those linked to the churches, which asked from most people only a minimal level of individual involvement. External influences were refracted through the localized attitudes and relationships of the peer group, and it was a measure of the enclosed nature of the district that Gans refers to those crossing its boundaries as 'missionaries' and 'ambassadors'.

Within this framework of common circumstances, there was room for a diversity of styles of living, as well as a range of incomes, ethnic backgrounds and population sub-groups; Gans lists at least ten major groupings sharing the neighbourhood, varying from first- and second-generation Italians to artistic, bohemian and 'pathological' households. He also notes a number of remarkably close parallels with observations made about working class lifestyles in Britain, including the distinction between 'rough' and 'respectable' patterns of behaviour, organized respectively around a search for action and excitement, or the maintenance of a comfortable routine. The prevailing values, including egalitarianism, reciprocity, and readiness to put the interests of the group ahead of those of the individual, were much as described in other accounts of working class community.

The main point Gans makes is that this was a population brought together primarily by its need for cheap housing. It happened also to possess some strong ethnic bonds, and in this respect it formed part of a succession of similar groups which had moved through the area over time. Until threatened by urban redevelopment, the majority of those studied did not identify themselves strongly with the West End as a territorial unit; their sense of belonging derived more from their personal social bonds, and their enjoyment of the everyday friendliness and sociability they met in its streets. Shortly after Gans completed his fieldwork, the West End was thoroughly redeveloped, and as happened in Bethnal Green, most of those he had studied were dispersed elsewhere.

Only when this threat materialized did people begin to mobilize around their sense of belonging together, but the highly personalized, informal and habitual pattern of life to which they were accustomed did not equip them with the necessary skills or confidence to mount an effective resistance to the plans of outside developers and political agencies. Their interests and perceptions carried little weight in the considerations of those who had stigmatized the area as a social problem, and valued it more for its development potential than for its social integration.

In a formulation strikingly similar to that of Pahl (1966: 328) referred to previously, Gans drew on these Boston findings to declare that ways of life do not coincide with settlement patterns, but should be seen instead as the outcomes of processes of social choice and constraint acting upon distinct social groups and their members (Gans 1968). The choices they make reflect their social values and aspirations, but can be put into effect only within whatever limits are set by the material and other restrictions on their actions. Explanations in terms of straightforward ecological adaptation to the environment would arise therefore only where people lacked any effective choice. Otherwise their behaviour would be governed by their social characteristics, of which Gans suggests two, social class and life-cycle stage, are paramount. These work to assemble people together into groupings which reflect their shared situations. In that sense, values and constraints could be viewed as fundamental determinants of community, giving shape to its outer limits. Work done in the field of spatial modelling had helped to establish this. According to one expert, when measures of social status and family or household composition were superimposed on one another, they produced a grid-like pattern in which 'the resulting cells will contain neighbourhoods remarkably uniform in . . . social and economic characteristics' (Berry 1965: 116). The same author explained how this followed from individual efforts to come to terms with urban circumstances:

> The whole is too large for the individual to comprehend. In the search for self-identity in mass society, he seeks to minimise disorder by living in a neighbourhood in which life is comprehensible and social relations predictable. . . . He seeks an enclave of relative homogeneity.
> (Berry 1973: 51)

The resulting homogeneous niches are 'exquisitely reticulated in geographic space' and generate a repetitive pattern of smaller-scale communities, offering coherent lifestyles. On this basis, Gans looked forward to a reinvigorated urban sociology, and a revival in community studies.

In Britain, Pahl argued along the same lines. Focussing on the need to analyse systems of urban power and inequality, he believed that sociology should concentrate on clarifying the nature of the constraints surrounding the social actors, while letting the choices 'take care of themselves' (1970b: 156). This was because planners and others who were responsible for making decisions about urban development were more likely to be able to exert some control over factors which limited people's choices and channelled their decisions – for example, the provision of urban amenities such as school and hospitals, and the allocation of housing stock. By doing so, a variety of 'urban managers' intervened in ways which framed the parameters within which others were compelled to live. Major public housing schemes were the most obvious example: both Bethnal Green and the West End of Boston were on the receiving end of massive redevelopment projects, which took place with minimal consultation, and in disregard of prominent local interests, because planning experts and other powerful figures thought they knew best. The new housing developments which replaced the older slum districts imposed constraints of their own – for instance, high rise living, and a lack of provision for leisure and entertainment, or even shops and other basic facilities. Of course, values could not be wholly set to one side in such an analysis; a complete understanding would have to take into account the role of both subjective and objective determinants in shaping the life chances and lifestyles of different groups. As Dickens notes (1990: 54–5), sociology cannot afford to lose sight of people's own understandings of the social world, because to do so would seriously jeopardize our ability to understand how 'people are not only constrained by, but also through their actions change, the deeper structure in which they are caught up'. This is well illustrated in the outcomes of planning processes, in which often there is a fundamental clash of perspectives, representing differences in values, between local interests and those of various kinds of outsiders (Goodman 1972; Wates 1976; Gill 1977; Foster 1999).

NEIGHBOURHOODS AND SOCIAL COMPOSITION

Both Gans and Pahl illustrate how the framework they propose would enable the analysis of the specific combinations of social types who come to occupy different areas. Gans deals with the population of the inner city, and Pahl with the changing make-up of English rural villages. In the former, we find living side-by-side for example those who are extremely deprived, and without choice, such as destitute occupants of rooming houses, and others who find the inner city a desirable place in which to satisfy their needs, like well-to-do 'cosmopolites' and students (Gans 1968). In the latter, alongside the older established groupings of traditional rural employees and owners of large country houses, we meet various kinds of commuters, and people who have retired from the towns (Pahl 1970b); some choose to be there, others are forced. Although these might seem to represent unusually complex and varied assemblages of groups into one place, it is worth remembering that in their study of 'Springdale', despite its smallness and supposedly traditional characteristics, Vidich and Bensman comment on its 'profusion of lifestyles and life plans' (1958: 52). On the basis of distinctive social and economic ways of living, they claimed to distinguish no fewer than five main 'classes', with even more class subdivisions. As an American settlement, Springdale also contained people with varied ethnic backgrounds; hence its composition anticipated Pahl's statement that 'paradoxically, there is no village population as such; rather there are specific populations which for various but identifiable reasons find themselves in a village' (1970a: 68). This might appear to make the idea of community redundant; certainly it blows apart any lingering assumption that people in communities are homogeneous clones of one another. Yet it also encourages a reconceptualization of community, away from the notion of a tightly integrated entity in which everyone is the same, towards a consideration of the relationships which can develop among such different groupings, within a relatively confined space; which indeed is what many would take 'community relations' to mean, in the modern era. In more theoretical terms, the emphasis has shifted from a Durkheimian consensualism towards a more Weberian concern with how groups with different interests and frameworks of social meaning orient themselves towards one another 'communally'.

A version of this approach was developed by Rex and Moore (1967) in an influential study of race relations and community in the inner city district of Sparkbrook, in Birmingham, England. In this they consciously sought to salvage urban sociology from its state of malaise, suggesting that to do so required the development of a convincing new general hypothesis. In line with the rising prominence of sociological conflict theories derived from Weber and Marx, they proposed as a suitable starting point the thesis that the structure of social relations in modern urban industrial societies is determined by a 'pattern of conflicting interests set up by the differential control by different groups of men [sic] of material facilities' (1967: 36). In urban contexts, they contended, the key disputes arose over the ownership of domestic property, or housing, access to which divided the population into a series of distinct segments, according to the type of property they possessed, and their means of access to it. Patterns of choice and constraint came into play to distribute the urban population into these groupings, depending on the supply of different kinds of housing, and other valued aspects of the built environment. Whereas some had the means to purchase the most desirable housing, in the very best locations, others were forced into taking whatever was available, which meant rented accommodation in run-down areas. Where the market failed to supply suitable and affordable homes, agencies of the state were forced to step in to provide forms of public housing. On this basis, Rex and Moore initially identified a number of distinct 'housing classes' in Birmingham. Moreover, they believed that, despite their differences, these groups were bound together into a single competitive system, because they were motivated by a common set of underlying values, which made the most desirable end-position the ownership of substantial housing assets in or close to the countryside. For most people, in practice this meant getting as far away as possible from city centre, into the leafy and spacious suburbs. According to Rex and Moore, even immigrant groups new to Britain were drawn into this system, and could be said to be at the end of the queue for the best housing. Drawing on their work, Pahl refers to the game of 'urban leapfrog' which ensues, as groups battle to get an advantage over one another. In this way, an idea originally put forward by the Chicago sociologists, that during their development cities underwent processes of 'invasion and succession' by different groups, was revived, but with a better understanding of its underlying social dynamic.

Thus out of the debris of the Chicago School there emerged a perspective on urban (and rural) differentiation which identified a number of significant social influences relevant to understanding community. Pahl summarized the position by saying that 'the meaningful social area which people inhabit depends on class, life-cycle characteristics, length of residence, career pattern, type of social network, and many other factors' (Pahl 1970a: 106). Following Gans, and Rex and Moore, ethnic origin must be included as well. Although complicated, this results in a distribution of people across urban space which is far from random. While the groupings which develop are not in themselves communities, they lay important foundations for their construction. It is vital therefore to understand how certain social characteristics come to be clustered into space, to such an extent that 'place' can often serve as both a geographical and a social expression. For example, we are accustomed to the everyday use of terms such as inner city, suburbia, ghetto, trailer park, slum and estate to convey simultaneously a sense of location, and of the social character and reputation of those who inhabit it. To those familiar with particular cities, actual place names perform the same function; whether correctly or incorrectly, most British people can probably picture to themselves the physical character and social nature of areas such as Moss Side, Brixton, Cheltenham and Surbiton, and out of their knowledge or experience of such areas, form more general impressions of the nature of the inner city, and suburbia. A more codified understanding is shown by references to the 'postcode lottery', whereby particular services, such as health care or education, are assigned to different social groups by means of a system of geographical designations. Market researchers routinely utilize such socio-spatial categories to target relevant sub-sections of the population, knowing that they serve to encapsulate important variations in attitudes, aspirations and lifestyles.

Whether driven together by circumstances, or brought there by choice, the spatial allocation of people in this way provides the basis on which distinctive communities can be formed, with their own specific properties. The congregating together of numbers of people whose social situation is broadly similar makes it likely that they will react to circumstances and events in similar ways, and find common cause together. Occupancy of a shared space reinforces this tendency. As Harvey (1989a: 118) explains, 'residential areas provide distinctive milieus for social interaction from which individuals to a considerable degree derive their values, expectations, consumption habits, market capacities and states of consciousness'. Not only are people shaped to some extent by the neighbourhoods they inhabit, they also actively select those areas which hold most appeal for them, and because households 'tend to seek out compatible neighbours who share essentially the same views and attitudes, relatively homogeneous social areas ("communities") are created within cities' (Badcock 1984: 14). Like a number of other writers (Byrne 1999; Farrar 2001), Badcock places inverted commas around the word 'community', presumably because he does not wish to foreclose debate on some of the other issues surrounding the term. For our purposes, it is enough to have established that there is no irrefutable reason to anticipate the complete disappearance of communities from urban settings. Rather, as has been evident from the beginnings of systematic urban analysis, it remains the case that an urban mosaic exists, even if it may have become more complicated over time (Jarvis *et al.* 2001). Short highlights why this is significant for studies of community and urban sociology:

> The residential mosaic is fracturing the city into distinct areas. At certain times and in some places where conditions are favourable, these areas are the basis for identifiable communities of shared attitudes and common interests in which broad value systems are shaped to local needs. The identification of these communities and their creation and restructuring is one of the more important topics of a renewed urban geography, combining as it does the important issues of place and space, economy and culture, global and local.
>
> (Short 1996: 204)

If correct, this offers scope to reinstate much of earlier interest in examining how such communities come about, and how they function to develop and maintain their distinctive local values and attitudes.

SOME INNER CITY EXAMPLES

That a distinctive communal social order can grow up under the right conditions even in areas with the worst of reputations was confirmed by a study of Chicago's West Side, a district renowned for crime and disorder since the era of Al Capone. A closely observed account of the 'Addams' district (Suttles 1968) demonstrated that, no matter how unstable and frightening it looked from outside, seen from within it possessed a complex pattern of social organization with its own moral standards and disciplinary rules, ably enforced by its residents. Suttles found that the population of the area was subdivided, following a principle of 'ordered segmentation', into a lattice-like social structure of blocks defined by age, sex, ethnic identity and territory. Each sub-section constituted something like a small self-sufficient world, but with the ability to come together with other similar groupings when faced by a common threat or enemy. Overcrowding and lack of privacy accentuated the pressure on residents to control and limit their differences; as Suttles notes, it makes no sense to fall out too definitively with those who you are bound to meet again, and again, especially when doing so will make enemies of their whole social circle. Nor is it easy for those who routinely occupy the same space to simply ignore one another, and certainly not when the bulk of their life is lived out publicly, on the street, as it was in the Addams neighbourhood. Instead the district's public spaces became the venue for the formation of chains of interlocking peer groups, formed largely within the confines of the area's four main ethnic divisions (Italians, black Americans, Mexicans and Puerto Ricans). These groups were the setting for intensely personalized relationships of trust, in which people had extensive knowledge of one another, and were prepared to exchange the most intimate information. The street became a 'total communication network' for the fast transmission of news, rumour and gossip, and this flow of information helped cement a common moral order throughout the neighbourhood. True to his Chicago School roots, Suttles says that it was this ethos of 'provincialism', the creation of a local moral order, which staved off what would otherwise have been the most likely alternative, 'a pervasive anonymity, distrust and isolation' (1968: 225). Rather than alienated isolates, exposed to the full urban blast, it allowed residents to remain 'heavily engrossed in their local neighborhood as a separate and rather distinct moral world' (1968: 4–5), whose conventions and practices afforded them the necessary security to lead quite ordinary, decent lives. Only a minority engaged in the disorderly and criminal activities which brought the whole area into disrepute.

Despite the complexity of its internal boundaries and subdivisions, the attributes of localism, moral integration, shared knowledge and personalized trust would seem amply to qualify the Addams district as an integrated community. Divided within, nevertheless when necessary it was able to present a united front against outsiders. Suttles notes that this level of solidarity develops only when individuals have time and occasion to become really familiar with each other's past history and future intentions (1968: 229); therefore it requires a core of stability to be sustained, even if it is surrounded by change. Integration was assisted also by the inhabitants' assumption, or perhaps recognition, that residential unity implied a readiness to collaborate socially; in this way, Suttles suggests, inner city residents 'help create the situation they imagine' (1968: 34), namely one in which they form a distinct and orderly community. From his work he took the lesson that in any distinct locality probably there would be similar processes, ensuring the development of such a moral code, through which residents who were in frequent and continuous contact would be able to decipher and evaluate one another's behaviour. In other words, community was not an exceptional phenomenon. At the same time, he was able to show how an underlying agreement about key social norms and values could be dressed up in a wide variety of ethnic styles, including forms of language, clothing, gesture and dance. Although this diversity sometimes impeded clear communication between groups, gossip, slander and invective provided the 'informational content' that kept their different ethnic identities alive (1968: 105), whilst enabling them to coexist in a reasonably stable mutual accommodation. A prominent University of Chicago professor asserted that this study not only helped put the Chicago approach back on its feet, with stronger theoretical and methodological foundations, it also proved that the community study remained a valid vehicle 'for holistic and comprehensive understanding of the metropolitan condition' (Janowitz, in Suttles 1968: vii).

Not everyone working in an area like Chicago's West Side would choose to refer to it as a 'community'. Certainly it lacked the homogeneity and peaceableness traditionally associated with the term. The social world described by Suttles is abrasive, divisive, and sometimes threatening. The same might be said of inner city Birmingham. John Rex has claimed that the word 'community' was inserted into the title of his (1967) book about Sparkbrook to lend its contents a more optimistic gloss (Farrer 2001: 120; Rex and Tomlinson 1979: 241). However, while the term does not feature as an entry in the index, it is scattered liberally throughout the text. Parts of Sparkbrook were said to exhibit the remnants of working class community, its physical and social features described as 'mean, drab streets of terraced housing, small shops and corner pubs, indefinitely awaiting the bulldozer', where 'women can be seen popping in and out of their neighbours' houses and in the warm evenings people sit on the front steps and call across the road to one another' (Rex and Moore 1967: 44–5). When studied, the area was undergoing the transitional processes associated with recent inmigration of ethnic minority populations, from the Caribbean and Pakistan. There was already a substantial Irish population. Birmingham's ethnic minorities are said to form a 'mosaic of tiny primary communities' engaged in interaction with a 'host community'. Towards the end of the book, the question is raised explicitly as to whether the people of Sparkbrook constitute a community, but no definitive answer is given. Instead Rex reviews the differing orientations of the groups occupying the area, showing how their commitments vary according to whether or not they are trapped in it or expect to leave. In this way he aims to clarify the 'structure of community' within a zone of transition, by describing the different orientations and expectations among its social groups.

Like other such inner city zones, Sparkbrook contained a mixed population in the throes of significant change. Established residents who wanted to uphold what they regarded as its traditional standards were faced by a disorienting assortment of newcomers whose situations, backgrounds and values differed greatly; inevitably, there were conflicting interests, which revolved largely around the changing uses of properties, especially large houses converted into rented accommodation, and the general upkeep and reputation of the area. Rex concluded that the future of Sparkbrook as a community depended upon the ability of these groups, working with their local associations and leaders, to find ways of reconciling their interests and damping down their disagreements. In other words, rather than a fixed entity, frozen in time, community is represented here as a process through which group interests could be mediated, and attention paid to those issues which arose because the groups were placed in daily contact with one another in the same space. In Weber's terms, they were oriented to one another because their interests converged onto the same set of social and material conditions – not just housing, but other everyday resources like shops, playgrounds, schools and churches. Either they had to establish a *modus vivendi*, a way of sharing and cooperating in the use of their local environment, or they would be left grappling with irreconcilable hostilities. In the same way as Pahl describes modern villages as places in which different and competing social groups and classes actually connect with one another in daily life, the neighbourhood of Sparkbrook had become a meeting point at which key social forces and pressures were expressed thorough actual interaction and confrontation among groups.

Commenting a few years later, Rex observed that what he and Moore witnessed in Sparkbrook was the emergence of 'ethnic sub-cultures and communities of a fairly lasting kind which were going to make Birmingham a multi-racial city' (Rex 1988: 53). These were taking shape through the formation of various ethnic associations, providing groups with the means to advance their particular interests, but also offering them broader social frameworks within which to conduct their lives. Their level of local organization was influenced by their different social and cultural characteristics. Irish people in Sparkbrook enjoyed a 'kind of community life' in its streets, shops, pubs, clubs and cafes, as well as churches, where they met their own kind and encountered familiar cultural signals. Other population sub-groups had their equivalent meeting places. In reality, when examined more closely, the Pakistani and 'West Indian' groups, like the Irish, were heterogeneous, containing people with different origins, backgrounds and traditions. West Indians were the least well organized as a group, because they were keenest to integrate with the local population; but they experienced extensive racial discrimination and exclusion. Pakistanis were set apart from the rest of the population by strongly marked cultural and religious features, and yet themselves were split into a multitude of different factions. Perhaps because much of the immigration was comparatively recent, the arrangement of these different population subdivisions in Sparkbrook did not exhibit the same structured orderliness as Suttles found in Chicago; Rex and Moore carried out their research at a time when patterns of race relations and community ties in British cities were complex, and their future open-ended.

A frustrating aspect of the literature on community is the lack of cross-referencing between studies of settings which have much in common; for example, the work of Gans (1962) is ignored by Suttles (1968), as well as by Rex and Moore (1967). Similarly, Pryce's study of the St Paul's neighbourhood of Bristol, which appeared twelve years after the Sparkbrook study, reproduces many of the same elements, yet is written with remarkably little reference to other comparable sociological work.

Apart from sources on race relations and the West Indies, Pryce admits that his only preparation for conducting fieldwork and lifestyle analysis in Bristol was a single reading of a Chicago-style study of community and ghetto culture in the United States (Hannerz 1969). St Paul's is also an 'area of disrepute' seemingly decaying into a slum. Insiders register its ambiguous nature; they refer to it as 'the village', as well as 'Shanty Town' and 'the jungle'. Given its low social esteem, the area has served as place of first settlement for migrant groups, and also attracts various socially undesirable and illicit activities, including prostitution, drug-dealing, gambling and crime; but at the same time, it provides its population with more legitimate commercial and business services. Like other inner city quarters, it is home to 'many honest, stable, hard-working people, students and intellectuals and some deviant types' (Pryce 1986: 25). Pryce strikes a note of realism, warning that life in the area should not be romanticized – no automatic spirit of conformity, consensus or agreed standards flows from its experiences of deprivation and external disapproval. Its groups are often unable to communicate, and prepared to exploit one another. Nevertheless, his immersion in the daily life of the district revealed how a number of very different ways of living were brought continually into contact with one another, so that their adherents had to take note of, and make adjustments to, each other's existence.

The main focus of Pryce's observation is the life of those residents whose origins could be traced back to Jamaica, and he depicts half a dozen distinct styles of life, ranging from 'hustler' to 'saint', to be found among them. These lifestyles correspond to differences in attitudes towards work, sexuality, religion, family and respectability, and can be grouped into two predominant orientations or walks of life, which he terms expressive-disreputable, and stable law-abiding. In other words, with due modification to allow for the absorption of various 'ethnic' elements derived from a West Indian background, St Paul's exhibited a familiar division between 'rough' and 'respectable' lifestyles. Of course, as Pryce reminds us, these patterns did not emanate from St Paul's alone. His explanation for them is referenced to the wider 'West Indian' population of Britain, as well as to an even larger British black community, whose characteristics have to be related in turn to the history of racism, and colonialism, as well as to relationships between social classes. However, the major insight he can offer, through his own participation and observation, has to do with the way in which these very large-scale, historical forces play themselves out in the arena of everyday interaction within this particular district. Many aspects of life in St Paul's would be reproduced in other similar places, where Afro-Caribbean and white British populations have been brought into everyday contact, yet no other community is quite the same. In this context, it is surprising that Pryce does not make more of the very specific nature of Bristol as a place, especially its historic connections with the slave trade. Still, his interpretative approach enables him to produce a close-textured understanding of key aspects of daily life in St Paul's, illuminated by vivid vignettes and extracts from life-histories, including insights into the 'small, congested, socially compressed community' inhabited by some of its low-life inhabitants (1986: 33). In this way, his work conforms well with the traditions of Chicago School sociology.

CONCLUSION: BRINGING ORDER OUT OF DISORDER?

Drawing together some of the threads of this style of research, Suttles (1972) notes that areas such as have just been described inevitably fall well short of the expectations of those who look to community for complete social integration, harmony and stability. There is no single bounded unit, which persists unchanged through time, and absorbs the full commitment of its members; boundaries are variable, relationships are episodic, and loyalties are qualified and provisional. This encourages talk of the absence or 'loss' of community from urban districts. Yet we have seen how, despite this, village-like social structures can take shape deep within city limits, and provide their occupants with a meaningful, ordered, social existence. In some situations, Suttles suggests, the accumulation of local practices and understandings adds up to the development of a subculture where a 'private existential world' takes hold (1972: 36). In part, this reflects the need felt by urban residents to simplify and manage what otherwise could be a chaotic and dangerous environment. They do so by establishing boundaries, and constructing myths and stereotypes about what is to be found inside them. As Byrne notes (1999: 110), a 'detailed knowledge of the socio-spatial divisions of an industrial city forms a crucial part of the repertoire of everyday knowledge of those who live in that city' and is put to use in the practices of everyday life. Other, external agencies do the same, until certain areas acquire precise and persistent identities of their own, which can be transferred easily onto those who inhabit them. Through such labelling processes, community becomes a social reality. Things are done to areas, and to their people, or by them, because they are perceived as forming particular types of community; for example, some areas are policed heavily, whereas others are left alone or permitted to provide for their own regulation and control. Some communities are listened to closely by politicians and officials, where others fail to achieve a collective voice. On the basis of their knowledge, or beliefs, about such communities, a host of decisions are made by individuals and groups, including judgements about which places are safe and rewarding, and which are best avoided. To this extent, community grows out of the accumulated decision-making processes of many social actors. But more than simply the aggregate of individual choices is involved, first because community reflects the impact of the forces and pressures which structure those choices, and second because as people are brought together, their proximity encourages them to form new kinds of social bonds and interests. Even in the most varied parts of the inner city, it is possible for people to manage their anonymity and separation by developing overlapping social ties and cohesive groupings of various sorts. These might include gangs, vigilante groups, community associations, or informal social circles. In so doing, they help to construct their different communities. Suttles comments that while this may involve considerable simplification and exaggeration of their actual attributes and traits, such constructs are rarely complete fictions.

5

THE DIVIDED COMMUNITY

COMMUNITY AS AN ARENA OF CONFLICT

The studies examined in the preceding chapter go some way towards rescuing the concept of community from being confined to its conventional interpretation, as 'a static, bounded, cultural space of being where personal meanings are produced, cohesive cultural values are articulated, and traditional ways of life are enunciated and lived' (Smith 2002: 109). By questioning these presumed equivalences between community, tradition, cohesion and fixed boundaries, they open up the analysis of social life at local level to the examination of complex patterns of change, diversity, and conflict; yet without discarding altogether the possibility that they may display nevertheless some overall level of coherence and integration. Indeed, we could be even more positive about them, since they help draw our attention to the importance of social differentiation, segregation and exclusion as key aspects of social organization, not only with regard to the interactions which take place within communities, between class positions, ethnic groupings, locals, migrants, and others, but also to the way in which boundaries are drawn so as to include some and leave out others. Far from being a homogeneous, unified entity, they depict community as a focal point of social division, conflict and competition – not a thing, so much as a dynamic process.

Reformulating the idea of community to encompass a set of interactions among a number of coinciding social interests, groupings and institutions brings the use of the term closer to that found in other, non-spatial, contexts, such as in references to the 'policy community' which surrounds government decision making, or the 'communities of faith' centred on major religions. These also are made up from a combination of elements of many different kinds, having a common focus, yet not necessarily solidly in agreement with one another. As complex configurations, it would be foolish to expect them to display total consensus, or remain immune to change. This meaning resonates better with contemporary concerns to do with community cohesion, 'development', and regeneration, rather than maintenance and preservation of an existing state of affairs. It also suggests, contrary to the views of Stacey (1969), that often there will be some version of a 'local social system' bringing the component parts together, although perhaps this will rarely be complete enough to contain all the salient relationships. Similarly, while it is unlikely that all the groups involved in this system will adopt a uniform position on any local issue, there will be some element of working together among them, whether voluntary or compelled. For instance, when there is a threat which touches on their interests, there is a capacity to mobilize collective opposition, as in the case of 'NIMBYism' ('Not In My Back Yard'). Proposals to open a site for travellers or 'asylum seekers' near a rural village, or to drive a new road or position a waste incinerator close to urban locations, invariably energize such action. So will efforts to attract some desired resource into a locality – pressures to secure a local supermarket, school, or community centre, for example. On such occasions 'community' comes to the surface as a collectivity, as different groups take up positions on the matter, and the fact that it is prone to do so may justify the use of the term even during times when it is dormant. Interests do not have to be identical to form a community, but they do have to converge with one another around matters of mutual concern. Conversely, when there is no underlying community of interests whatsoever, the possibility of joint action is more restricted, if not impossible. In the absence of community, virtually anything can be done to people, and very little accomplished by them.

THE WEBERIAN CONTRIBUTION TO COMMUNITY SOCIOLOGY

These ideas are not entirely new. Even in the earliest of the community studies, there was ample evidence of division, dissent, and shifting lines of cooperation, among individuals, families and organized groups such as religious denominations, so much so that a readiness to argue with one another might be seen as a plausible criterion of membership (Frankenberg 1957). The more closely you looked inside such communities, the more evident these differences and divisions became. However, these features tended to be suppressed by an overwhelming theoretical bias towards unity. A vision of community as 'an arena in which social divisions are given expression' (Crow and Maclean 2000: 240) or as intrinsically contested among a variety of interests (Hoggett 1997) makes these features more explicit. It has behind it the strengths and weaknesses of the Weberian theoretical perspective (Craib 1997; Holton and Turner 1989), which has been very influential in the developing field of local studies.

Weber conceptualized individuals as coming together into a multiplicity of social groupings, around distinctive sets of interests. These included class interests, where they shared typical chances for 'a supply of goods, external living conditions, and personal life experiences' (Weber 1947: 181). For Weber, class interests were linked intrinsically to the market, and to the ability to dispose of assets for an economic return. In other words, money was the main mechanism adjudicating the disposal of assets among classes. He recognized that although they did not automatically form themselves into communities, class groupings could develop a collective identity, especially when their members found themselves unable to move out of their class positions, due to economic or social barriers. The formation of distinctively working class communities in the past reflected the lifelong confinement of large numbers of people into such positions, making their interests permanent enough to stabilize their social relationships.

Today it is less apparent that members of the working class experience such containment, but we have seen the emergence instead of an increasingly well defined underclass, or excluded population, of the poor and deprived, which tends to be highly concentrated into particular spatial areas, and trapped into such situations for long periods of time, possibly over several generations. Wacquant and Wilson (1989: 25) refer to the 'unprecedented concentration of the most socially excluded and economically marginal members of the dominated racial and economic group'. Such situations are likely to generate distinctive lifestyles and social practices, or what Byrne (1999: 118) refers to as 'the emergent social forms which derive from the common residence of people in excluded space'. This means that at the present time, alongside the disintegration of working class communities, there is potential for the formation of communities of the poor and deprived, which explains why more recent studies of community have tended to focus on life in estates, projects and ghettoes (Parker 1985; Campbell 1993). More generally, there are many local situations in which people have a shared interest in the supply of goods, living conditions and experiences, and therefore have a propensity to form 'classes' in Weber's sense. Weber also identified status groups, which were organized around differences of social esteem and 'honour'. These included groups possessing common ethnic or religious identities, with the associated array of interests. Since ideas of esteem and religious beliefs definitely involve conscious perceptions, status groups are more likely than classes to be aware of what it is that they have in common, and so to form distinct and visible communities. Ethnic groupings are an obvious example.

Class interests focus on the material conditions of people's existence, whereas status touches on more symbolic matters. However, the boundaries between economic and status differences are not hard and fast; they blur into one another, in the way that economic and status (or 'racial') attributes do in Wacquant and Wilson's definition of the underclass. When economic divisions take on status aspects as well, then we are especially likely to see the formation of group 'cultures' and ways of living, or the attributes of distinctive communities of interest. In these terms, studies like Rex and Moore's (1967) are concerned with the identification and analysis of various class and status formations active at a local level, and the extent to which they become organized. Following Weber's lead, they emphasize the struggles in which these groups engage to assert their interests. Farrar (2001) provides a similar account of the 'community' of Chapeltown, Leeds, over a much longer time span, tracing the multiplicity of groupings caught up in the 'competing and violent' politics of community, and their shifting contours and alignments. There is nothing especially harmonious or placid about such local political relationships. Farrar insists that Chapeltown is 'profoundly heterogeneous', and that no assumptions should be made about the unity of any of its component groups and populations; yet there is a continuity in the way in which they have worked, as 'Chapeltown people', to make and remake their community. By virtue of their residential location, their interests converge on the area, and its facilities, and therefore on the relationships they have with all those who inhabit it. Many of their activities are directed towards making a difference to these relationships: gaining relative power and influence, creating alliances, or fighting off opposition.

According to Farrar, during the period he covers, from the 1970s to the present, a number of forces, internal and external, have conspired to make it harder for people to enact a strong affiliation with their neighbourhood. As in Sparkbrook (Rex and Moore 1967: 115) and St Paul's (Pryce 1986), many of the most important forces originate from far beyond the limits of the local area. The very presence of a variety of minority ethnic groups in an English community signals that these include events occurring at the world scale, including diasporas and migrations. It is a virtue of the Weberian approach that it can accommodate such influences quite easily, since it does not operate with a model of a closed system of relationships; interests that are expressed locally do not have to derive from local influences alone. Nor does it presuppose any *necessary* connection between residential location, and the attitudes and behaviours of inhabitants, but it does assume that actors have certain propensities, from which reasonable predictions can be made about their typical modes of conduct. Weber couched these in terms of probabilities and dispositions. Hence, as we have seen, the character of inner city, outer city, suburban and other locales will differ, not because of their spatial positioning or the nature of their physical environment, but because they act as containers for different kinds of people, and accommodate their preferred or enforced styles of life. Looking at different neighbourhoods of contemporary Manchester, Savage *et al.* (2005) observe processes of selection whereby people choose those areas in which they feel 'comfortable' and at home. This leads to similarities of behaviour and lifestyle among such groupings, and makes the case for retaining 'certain elements of "community" studies by recognizing the importance of studying how local belonging is generated or challenged' (2005: 101).

Mobility versus community?

Weberian sociology is probabilistic, rather than deterministic, so that degrees of flexibility and movement are built into its understanding of social action. Action is 'typical', not inevitable. We have seen how, as active social agents, people strive to select their locations, and to exert an influence over their social milieux; but their efforts are filtered through a variety of processes which they cannot control. Since these models were developed in the 1960s, society has become more fluid, and the capacity of most people to move about has increased considerably (Bauman 2001b). This includes both geographical mobility and movement between groups. There is evidence, for example, that increasing numbers of actors now envisage their life-courses as trajectories over time, during which they will move between different residential spaces (Byrne 1999: 110). This can take them through a succession of local communities, with which they may identify temporarily, only to leave them behind as their horizons shift. For instance, the market for housing has changed in ways which allow for greatly expanded choice. Sales of housing from the public sector, where formerly it was allocated according to social criteria of need, have increased substantially the proportion under owner-occupation, thrusting more people into the marketplace, where access to housing is determined primarily by income, and ability to borrow. The majority of people now aspire to being owner-occupiers. Gaining a particular sort of housing becomes a major personal project, underwritten by a good deal of media hype and celebration, on television programmes with names like *Location, Location, Location* or *The Property Ladder*; in magazines like *Homes and Gardens*; and countless weekend newspaper supplements.

Success brings both financial and status rewards. It is not only a house which is being acquired, but an address, with all that signifies, including potential membership of a community. Yet there are still excluded groups, including many young people, single parents, and rural dwellers, as well as the urban poor, who find themselves squeezed into a shrinking provision of affordable and public housing. Consequently some of the fiercest local struggles turn on the question of the accessibility of suitable housing, which serves as a prime point of entry to membership of different kinds of community. The appearance of gated communities, surrounded by physical barriers and systems of surveillance, symbolizes the attempt to regulate access to particular spaces, and ways of living, as do proposals to establish local controls over the ownership of housing in pressurized areas like the Lake District and rural Wales, restricting purchases to those who have established local connections.

Housing figures especially prominently in Weberian urban sociology, as a major item of personal and social consumption, around which different interests take shape (Saunders 1981; 1990), but it is just one element in the total bundle of goods and opportunities associated with particular kinds of social and geographical spaces; at the very least we need then to consider how the formation of groups and interests reflects multiple causations. Parents of young families, for example, will be especially interested in local educational opportunities, and other related issues like safety and childcare provision; as they grow older, these interests will fade, and they will make their location decisions on other grounds. In a society which has become oriented to evaluation by league tables, awareness of disparities between areas in education and health provision has become more acute. The way in which individuals and households respond to such factors fuels overall social patterns, like movements from urban to rural locations, or towards outer city settings (Champion 1989; Boyle and Halfacree 1998), and these have decisive impact on the composition of particular communities. Attempts by parents to position themselves as close as possible to the catchment areas of the most desirable (meaning the most successful) schools impact on urban neighbourhoods, resulting in the desertion of some areas combined with intense competition to enter others. The greater the flow of people between such opportunities, the less appropriate old ideas of solid communities and fixed identities may seem. Individualism, choice, privatization, and the reduction of collective regulation all militate against the maintenance of stability, while at the same time heightening the significance of many of the contests taking place at local level. Rather than being taken for granted, community becomes increasingly fought over, and subject to choice and intention. Paradoxically, then, it may assume even greater importance to those concerned than it did when it seemed to be a more settled phenomenon. Bauman (2001a) among others points to this tendency for community to gain increased attention in conditions where its existence seems less assured.

The limits of Weberianism

The drawback to the Weberian position is that it can go too far in making these consequences seem to emerge only out of a multitude of separate decisions made by individuals and households, without providing enough by way of an account of how they are structured into definite trends. Theories of choice and constraint provide us with some useful middle-level explanations, highlighting factors proximate to the individuals themselves. They are readily intelligible in terms of the kinds of influences we know we have to deal with in the course of our own lives – getting a home, paying the mortgage, finding a decent school for the children. Indeed, these were the kinds of everyday actions and decisions that figured prominently in the classic community studies. However, we also know that much bigger forces and determinants are at work behind these decisions, and they must be brought into the account if answers are to be forthcoming to a range of important questions. Why is it easier to obtain mortgages at some times than at others? Why are some neighbourhoods well supplied with facilities, or blessed with funding for major projects, whereas others are starved of resources? Why do some towns and cities prosper, as others decline? What accounts for the successive phases of depopulation and repopulation the countryside has undergone? Without an understanding of these more distant types of influences, we may feel that we have not succeeded in making all that much headway towards understanding what makes communities tick. If an answer is to be given to recurrent complaints that, by focussing on community, a bigger, and more important, picture will be missed (for example, Dunleavy 1980: 34), then communities have to be located more firmly in the wider context of social arrangements, including relevant aspects of social change. Otherwise, a lot seems to be left dependent upon local variations, like the particular combinations of interests and organized groups that happen to be found from place to place; but it is less clear what brings these specific combinations into being. It is hard to believe that the explanation lies with an accumulation of personal choices alone.

Opponents of Weberianism would argue that this explanatory gap is only to be expected, since Weber does not really offer a theory of social structure; as a result, much is left to chance, and the accidental accumulation of circumstances. Whether and how these eventuate into orderly patterns and processes remains a matter for empirical determination. Weber himself resolutely refused to introduce more structural explanations. However, this can lead to the development of very complicated sets of distinctions and classifications. Weber's model of class, for example, encourages us to identify an almost infinite number of class categories and positions, according to the varying forms of ownership and possession pertaining to many different types of property. Craib (1997: 128–9) warns that relying on such 'surface factors' will yield a 'complex and chaotic definition' that is not helpful in formulating a coherent theory of class. This flaw became apparent in the prolonged debate which followed the introduction of the concept of 'housing classes' as an organizing device for understanding community relations, attacked by critics for just this lack of clarity. Rex and Moore started with the observation that those who were in the same occupational class could be differentiated according to their access to different forms of housing, because whereas some could claim the privilege of being 'local', others could not. Hence housing classes cut across occupational class, to favour established groups against 'outsiders'. In the context of 1960s Birmingham, this conferred advantages on white residents, bringing 'race' and ethnicity into the account as well. More generally, any group able to claim established membership of a given community could argue that they deserved preferential treatment in the allocation of its resources.

Unfortunately, it soon transpired that there was a tendency for the number of housing classes to proliferate uncontrollably, according to whatever additional factors were taken into account (Saunders 1981). The housing market is finely divided by different kinds of property rights in assorted types of housing; in Sparkbrook, there were at least seven distinct 'classes' or housing situations. When we bring into the picture all the other possible cross-cutting influences, including differences of age and gender, which might place the same population into contrasting situations with regard to assets like health, education, and so on, we end up with a multitude of different classes, or sub-groups, and a highly fragmented picture, in which any semblance of common ground has dissolved back into individual or small group differences. While this might represent rather well how it seems to people on the ground, as they attempt to juggle with all their competing interests and differences, it provides little help in clarifying the social characteristics of the world they inhabit. Many would see this as an intractable feature of the 'community' level of analysis: because perhaps it stays too close to the lived realities of people's own experiences, it produces results that are 'empirically rich but theoretically barren' (Hoggett 1997: 7). Another way of putting this is to envisage the local or community level as the realm of contingency, or happenstance, consisting of idiosyncratic combinations of circumstances and events that do not lend themselves to systematic explanation, a residual element left over after the predictable aspects of social structure have been dealt with (Duncan 1989).

FROM ACTIONS TO STRUCTURES: TOWARDS STRUCTURAL EXPLANATIONS OF COMMUNITY

Brook and Finn (1978) observe how, for many sociologists, the impetus behind the exploration of the idea of community had been to get beyond immediate empiricism and statements of the 'obvious', in order to interpret underlying structural relationships, or discover how the parts related to the whole. They believe this was why community held such a pivotal place in the post-war sociology of the working class, because it drew attention to how the different aspects of working class life fitted together to form a distinctive pattern. This promised a better understanding of what it was like to be working class than the statistical analysis of various dimensions of social inequality. Yet they go on to castigate sociology, and community studies in particular, for being unable to envision society as a total structure, and unprepared to probe sufficiently deeply beneath its surface. Instead, they allege, social reality continues to be 'taken as given and giving of itself in immediate experience' (1978: 130–1); attention is too focussed on the everyday realities of life in the community, explanations are limited to appearances, and hidden connections are ignored. In support of this view, they cite an earlier self-criticism by Henriques, that concentrating on community compels sociologists to 'abstract from the societal framework at every level of social life' (Henriques 1969: 7). The argument is that this results in treating communities as if somehow they were excused from participating in national structures of politics or class relations, and as if everything that it was really important to understand emanated from within them – as a 'little world' of their own. This forms part of what Bagguley *et al.* (1990: 7) condemn as an 'unfortunate history' of 'untheorized studies' of communities or 'real places' in sociology and geography. An example would be the disarming admission in Moore (1982) that he was rather at a loss as to what to make theoretically of his findings about the booming oil town of Peterhead, where so many complicated social divisions and categories needed to be considered. Stacey *et al.* (1975) were in a similar position with the second Banbury study, as they got bogged down in a welter of detail about relationships among local social groups. Lacking an appropriate explanatory framework, they could attempt only to describe what they saw. These studies were not able to overcome a classic limitation of community research, the lack of a systematic procedure for connecting ethnographic observations with accounts of society as a whole (Byrne 1989: 28).

It could be argued that these difficulties arose because researchers were looking for their explanations in the wrong place: many of the main forces which needed to be taken into account were societal in nature, and could not be apprehended from the local level. It will not do to suppose that communities are formed simply through the accumulation of a host of independent local decisions and choices, even if this is a comforting perspective for those who believe that they are shaped 'from below', by action at the 'grassroots'. A community created in the context of modern capitalism will differ fundamentally from one that grew up under the dominance of pre-capitalist social relations, because it incorporates basic relationships which came into being only at a later stage of development. Similarly, a community that has experienced the impact of international migration will face different problems and realities from one that has not. In fact, with regard to all the key dimensions of social organization, such as age, class, 'race' and gender, it can be asserted that their impact extends throughout the entire spectrum of social life (Bradley 1996), in a way that leaves only limited scope for independent local variation. Unless they have it as their specific purpose, communities are unlikely to overturn relationships that apply throughout the rest of society. Thus ethnic identities transcend membership of particular geographical communities, and can be carried from one community to another; and though barriers of social exclusion definitely exist at local level, sometimes even to the extent of the erection of walls and fences between different groups (Collison 1953; Harris 1972; Jenkins 1983), no community on its own can give rise to anything resembling an 'underclass'. Ethnic and class phenomena operate at the level of society as a whole.

Likewise, the institutions which govern the majority of people's behaviour within their particular communities are designed and regulated outside them. This would include practices of marriage and family formation, citizenship and property rights, and large parts of systems of belief and culture. While these may be acquired or reinforced locally, through processes of socialization and education, they also are amenable to only limited local freedom of action. Taking the long view historically, we could say that even when they were initiated by specific communities, as customs and practices among particular groups, in the course of the development of regional, national, and now supra-national social arrangements, they have been lifted out of their immediate contexts and generalized far beyond the limits of the local. This limits the extent to which communities can deviate from social norms. Finally, given that they are bound into much larger political frameworks, communities possess strictly limited powers to make, and implement, decisions, and there are strong arguments that power has tended to drift away from the local level. On all these counts, community appears to be much more the product of forces from outside than it is capable of initiating them; that is, communities are more acted upon, than acting.

This implies that communities might be understood best as shaped by the intersection of external structural forms and processes of various kinds. Despite the retrospective reservations expressed by Henriques, the team with whom he worked in 'Ashton' was in no doubt that this applied to the fundamental relationships of social class (Dennis *et al.* 1969). Taking their lead from Marx, they saw these as embedded in the overall nature of capitalism as a social and economic system. This ensured that all communities within a capitalist society would have certain basic conditions in common, relating to the ownership and control of private property, and the powers this conferred over labour. Ashton was no different from other places in this respect, except perhaps in displaying these features so openly. After all, while he learned a great deal from Engels' groundbreaking work on Manchester (1848), Marx himself did not need to engage in any kind of local community investigation to identify these general characteristics. By comparison, those studies which have attempted to document the operations of class, or social stratification, as a local phenomenon have either singularly failed to make the necessary connections between local evaluations of status and prestige and the dominant structures of power and inequality in the wider society, or else have tended to show how local patterns were little more than flourishes hung onto the framework of national distinctions. Consequently, in terms of our knowledge of class structure, it is debatable whether anything uncovered at the local level differs fundamentally from what could have been predicted given a knowledge of the larger context (Bell and Newby 1971: 187–204; Day and Fitton 1975). Westergaard indicated as much when he proclaimed that class phenomena are societal in their sweep, owing little to distinctions of place or 'parochial' solidarities (1965: 107).

Evidence drawn from community studies does enable us to see how members of different social classes have engaged with one another in everyday contexts, and suggests that through this sometimes they may gain a more rounded appreciation of one another's attitudes and lifestyles; this may temper conflicts and divisions with elements of mutual understanding. Such relationships played a part in the formation of attitudes of deference and paternalism as described by Lockwood (1966) and Newby (1977). But, though humanized somewhat by such direct contact, the underlying shape of class relationships remains the same: those with property and wealth are at the top of the hierarchy, and those below them exert less power and influence, and usually command less respect. Others would want to argue the same point for relationships of gender, or patriarchy, and racial discrimination: following the logic of any of these basic social relationships soon takes us out of particular communities, and onto a more abstract plane of theory and observation. However, once it is accepted that the main contours of community are defined externally, by the working of these macro-level factors, questions must arise again as to whether the concept of community retains much explanatory power. Can community research do more than provide confirmation, yet again, that society works in a particular way? If not, then how many local examples do we need to make the point?

There are those who would argue that, given the right sort of theoretical apparatus with which to understand these larger processes, local investigation becomes largely redundant; what happens on the ground, locally, is only what one would expect from a knowledge of these external forces. On these grounds, many who were sympathetic to the direction taken by Weberian analyses grew impatient with local studies. The explanations they provided satisfied neither those who wanted a better understanding of the influence of social structural forces on patterns of community life, nor those who looked in the opposite direction, for more detailed insights into the specific social meanings and practices produced at local level. Even some who had been influential in developing the Weberian position made moves in one or other of these directions. Debates about the significance of 'urban managerialism' drew exponents away from discussions of community, into the realms of corporate governance and the state (see, for example, Pahl and Winkler 1974; Cockburn 1977). This movement conformed with Pahl's aspirations (1970b: 241) for a 'vigorous urban sociology', able to make the connections between urban phenomena and an 'encapsulating social structure', but did so at the cost of relegating local concerns to a position of secondary importance.

Community power, urban managerialism and the state

Unlike earlier approaches to understanding community relations, Weberian analyses centred firmly on questions of power and inequality. The weight they gave to concepts of 'class', interest, and struggle showed that the writers concerned were keen to highlight differences in fortune between urban groups, and the extent to which life within their various urban locations was constrained by problems of unequal access and differential treatment. In no way could it be said, then, that they adhered to misplaced assumptions of natural social harmony and community well-being; for them, conflict was a normal state of affairs. Yet their chosen theoretical stance set definite limits on the extent to which they were able to pursue these issues back to their source. That their attention was focussed mostly on the limited spatial arena of the urban district or neighbourhood made this problem worse, since many of the root explanations seemed to lie outside it.

This was the burden of an increasing swell of criticism directed at the Weberians, that whatever the merits of their approach, they seemed unable to explicate the necessary connections with larger social and political processes. To do so required them to go beyond the individualistic tenets of their theory, but as one commentator put it, 'even in their most holistic formulations, Weberians hold back from any explanation of social development in terms of non-individual entities or structures' (Dunleavy 1980: 41). This weakness can be seen with regard to the progress they made towards analysing local systems of power.

Beginning with the early community studies of 'Middletown' and 'Yankee City', there had been a tradition of argument about the nature of 'community power', in which it was debated whether it was possible to track the networks of influence that existed among powerful local notables, the kind of individuals whose reputations tended to be known and publicly discussed, at least within a local population, and to show how it was that they managed to exercise control over key decisions. Most of the relevant research was carried out in America, seeking to establish whether or not such a local 'power elite' existed in cities like Newburyport, Massachusetts (Warner and Lunt 1941), Atlanta, Georgia (Hunter 1953) and New Haven, Connecticut (Dahl 1961). Some confirmation was found for the existence of close-knit social circles of influential and well-to-do families, holding prominent positions in local business and politics. In Britain, Pahl (1970b) proposed a comparable power-based way of defining those urban areas which he thought mattered for the purposes of sociology, specifying them as spaces within which key decisions affecting people's life chances could be made. He argued that this was done by officials and bureaucrats, who were not a social elite in the American sense, but a set of 'urban managers', mostly located in the offices of local government authorities. This meant that the area over which they exerted some control would coincide more or less with the administrative limits of a local government unit.

Despite marked differences in the way they conceived of power, and the groups exercising it, the underlying thrust of the two approaches was the same, that there was an important arena of independent local action, where decisions were made which helped to define the outer boundaries of the urban community and its concerns (Dunleavy 1980; Short 1984). Pahl contended that urban managers exerted an influence over patterns of inequality that was separate from, and additional to, the activities of economic agents like industrial managers and employers. This created a sphere of urban politics, distinct from the class politics which surrounded industry and employment. Studies of local planning processes (Dennis 1970; Davies 1972) threw light on the part played by various professionals, officials and local representatives in defining and allocating scarce urban resources. This included decisions about the provision of public housing, the creation of large urban estates, and the redevelopment of facilities such as shopping centres. In this way, urban managers could be seen to be responsible for framing many of the basic parameters within which individual and household decisions were made. It was they who set the conditions under which people could gain access to financial or administrative support, who 'red lined' certain districts as unsuitable for development, or who endeavoured to exclude certain social types from particular neighbourhoods. By behaving as urban 'gatekeepers', helping some groups to achieve their aspirations, while blocking others, such authority figures played a major part in defining local communities and their interests, without necessarily always themselves being perceived as forming part of them.

In fact, it was not unusual for people to define themselves as the 'community' in *opposition* to the outcomes of action taken by such 'faceless' authorities, supposedly acting on their behalf. Many of the struggles taking place at local level were therefore oriented towards the policies and decisions enacted by the local state (Cockburn 1977; Saunders 1979). In the USA, Williams (1971) examined how local government agencies sought to regulate the distribution of urban opportunities, and showed how their activities stimulated the formation of interest groups and coalitions engaged in urban politics, especially around the development process. However, he suggested that the main way in which people responded was by exercising their individual capacities to improve their position, by moving between locations. Although he recognized that it was not enough for a sociological analysis to pay attention only to such individual actions (1971: 36), because definite structural processes were involved, his notion of social structure did not reach beyond the workings of local government institutions. Their contribution was summarized by Dunleavy as follows:

> By means of differential zoning laws, the manipulation of local taxes and alterations in the balance of municipal service provision, they seek to exclude categories of households likely to prove a drain on municipal resources or a threat to property values (such as poorer or lower-class people, welfare recipients, blacks and members of other oppressed ethnic minorities) and to attract land uses with high tax-yielding potential (such as upper class residential development and clean industrial or commercial uses).
>
> (Dunleavy 1980: 37)

In other words, these agencies exercised a significant influence over the composition of local populations, bringing about the concentration of certain social types in some areas, and separating them from others, just as Rex and Moore had shown how in Birmingham housing policies and controls contributed to the development of lines of ethnic and racial segregation. Individuals and households responded to the limitations this placed upon them.

The operations of powers of this sort may not be easy to observe. Indeed, as part of the developing commentary around the power elite model, it was asserted that some of the most profound forms of power do not require deliberate or explicit action, but are built instead into the way the world is organized; things are biased so as to favour certain types of action, or interests, while militating against others (Crenson 1971; Lukes 1974). It may be misleading therefore to concentrate too much on the 'middle layers' of power and their agents, as if they were free to decide things for themselves, because their actions are already subject to severe limitations and restraints. Rex (1988) conceded that his approach to these matters, which treated certain kinds of urban gate-keepers as if they were the ultimate decision makers in local affairs, left him open to criticism from those who believed that genuine power lay elsewhere. The accusation that sociologists have been overly concerned with middle-ranking powers has been a hallmark of more radical, or critical, approaches, including of course those influenced by Marxism. Goodwin (1989) notes how the focus on individual urban managers isolates them from their proper context, making them appear responsible for observable variations in local policy. There are echoes of earlier criticisms of community studies in Dunleavy's comment that an emphasis on mediating institutions, like urban gatekeepers, results in a set of noncumulative studies that are 'excessively individualistic and voluntaristic' (1980: 42), allowing larger structural forces to escape from view. It is dangerous to attribute too much influence to local power-holders, when it is evident that the lines of power usually run through and out of the locality, rather than being contained within it.

Indeed, those who exercise the most significant forms of power rarely reside locally themselves, but pull strings from a distance, sometimes from a very long way away. Building society branch managers and estate agents, like managers of local businesses, have to refer major decisions to headquarters. Planners must observe national policy directives and guidelines. Local authorities are hemmed in by central government edicts, and funding. Concentration on the role of local power-holders may hide these larger sets of relationships. No matter what people may believe locally about the exercise of influence, communities generally are not independent actors, but objects of power; and this means that whole systems of power and stratification cannot be defined at the local level. This has become ever more evident with the growth of large and complex organizations, operating across increasing geographical distances. Long-standing claims that this has brought about the 'eclipse' of community have become stronger with recent discussions of the impact of globalization on these relationships. According to Giddens (1990) globalization can be defined as the intensification of worldwide social relations, which link localities in such a way that local happenings are shaped by events occurring many miles away, and vice-versa. This means that the forces structuring local communities have become even more remote, and less transparent.

RETHINKING THE URBAN QUESTION

In a paper on 'Urban Processes and Urban Structure' published in 1975, Pahl questioned whether there really was any justification for a distinctive urban sociology. He suggested it was mistaken to look for the explanation of urban issues only within the context of the city and its social arrangements, because this lost sight of the operation of more fundamental social, economic and political forces. However, rather than abandoning the venture altogether, he proposed the need for a 'new urban sociology', which would develop a clearer sense of these connections to the surrounding social structure. A number of voices were making similar assertions at around this time, especially in Continental Europe, and particularly in France, where there was a strong intellectual current of Marxist and neo-Marxist social theory (see Althusser 1969; Poulantzas 1973; Pickvance 1976). These ideas began to exert a considerable influence over those who were concerned to reconceptualize the questions that had been dealt with conventionally by urban sociologists, including those associated with the significance of 'community' and local social relations, the linkages between patterns of social life and particular kinds of geographical areas, and the wider connections between society and its physical environment. The most significant contribution to these arguments came from the work of Manuel Castells, on the 'urban question' and the role of urban social movements (Castells 1977; 1978; 1983).

Castells acknowledged the undoubted social importance of 'urban' issues and problems in the contemporary world; he even referred to an impending sense of 'urban crisis'. But he contended that previous attempts to grasp their nature had been wholly misconceived, and deeply ideological. This included the persistent tendency to look for explanations of social behaviour in the material environment or urban 'ecology', as with the studies of the Chicago School, and the way in which sociologists had deployed notions of community as a socially integrated, consensual, and well demarcated entity, often as a standard against which to criticize those social relationships they were actually observing. According to Castells, this had led to endlessly oversimplified debates about the qualities of 'urban' versus 'rural', or 'traditional' versus 'modern', ways of life, and encouraged misguided expectations that urban conditions would always, in all circumstances, give rise to similar kinds of social patterns and values. Essentially, Castells argued, this way of thinking wrenched patterns of urban existence out of their proper historical and material context, whereas it should have been obvious that cities would differ greatly at different periods, and when subjected to differing sets of social relations. As a Marxist, he attributed most importance to the impact of prevailing forms of economic relationship, the ways in which a society carried out its productive activities, and the associated relations of social class. Marxist explanations would always begin from the analysis of the economic organization of society.

However, Castells argued that under contemporary circumstances, of advanced capitalism, a significant separation had developed between these crucial productive arrangements and the sphere of everyday life which most people confronted in their urban settings. Certainly at the level of experience there was a strong, and growing, consciousness of the specific problems and difficulties associated with modern urban living. The 'urban ideology' which attributed these to the nature of the city itself, and its physical features, had deep social roots, and filled the heads of ordinary people as well as those of academics and officials; superficially, it seemed to capture very well many of the problems they faced in their daily lives (1977: 86). Yet for Castells it served to divert attention from the real origins of such problems, which lay in the way in which the whole society was structured, and [lay] with the social contradictions that this produced. These had to do with the nature of modern capitalism, the condition of the class struggle, and the role of the state. In line with the structural Marxism expounded by Althusser, Poulantzas and others, Castells argued that to treat urban areas as places in which people were free to make choices, express themselves, exercise their values and so on, rather than looking into the prevalent social and technological relations of production and domination which imposed tight limits on, or even determined, their behaviour, was to ascribe far too much independence of action to individuals, and their social groups. Studies of community power hitherto had oscillated between ideas of voluntary choice and the search for some form of 'occult' hidden powers, whereas, when properly conceived, it should be possible to 'read the underlying structural contradictions' from the positions taken up by different groups, since essentially these would express their objective place in society (1977: 253).

Much of the work that had been accomplished already in community research was reprised by Castells when he accepted that there were indeed scientifically valid questions to be asked about how well defined different social areas were; whether or not they produced significantly different forms of 'local social life', such as patterns of neighbouring; and how various kinds of social and cultural behaviour varied between social classes and types of areas. Like Pahl and Gans, he concluded that it is more useful to think of these kinds of local social patterns as consisting of 'displaced segments of social structure' rather than as 'local collectivities structured in space' (1977: 103). He noted the importance of social homogeneity in stimulating the emergence of particular styles of behaviour. His assertion that the production of racial ghettoes in America resulted from the combined effects of the way in which certain racialized 'subjects' are distributed in the social structure, and how housing and other amenities are allocated, is highly reminiscent of the arguments of John Rex. In other words, a great deal of the substantive content of his analysis seems familiar, and compatible with work already done on communities; so wherein lies the difference? It is in the view that for sociology the principal task is always to determine how these outcomes are produced by the combined operation of certain fundamental social processes – economic, political and ideological – and how these express in turn the underlying relationships of class and power in an advanced capitalist society. The aim is not simply to 'discover' empirically whether or not localized social relationships of certain kinds exist, but to elucidate or 'lay bare' how they are produced by these structural determinants. Castells believes this can be grasped only through the application of a sophisticated Marxist theoretical framework, and that it was the lack of such a structural framework that inhibited the ability of previous students of community to deliver meaningful scientific lessons from their work, leaving them prey instead to ideological delusions.

From this perspective, any connection to be found between different sorts of urban spaces and ways of life is not direct and natural, but an effect of how the two have been brought together or 'articulated', for example through systems of social representation and practice. Representations, or social images, would include the impressionistic ways in which people draw upon their experiences to conceive of certain districts as 'working class' or 'bourgeois', or to characterize some towns as 'soulless' whereas others are 'charming' (1977: 96). While everyday reactions are full of such associations, Castells insists that they must not be accepted at face value, because people's immediate experiences are clouded by all sorts of false conceptions and mythologies. When these experiences are examined in the light of Marxist theory, he contends that one finds there is indeed an underlying unity to the kinds of issues which people label as 'urban'. They centre on the provision of key resources which are distributed around the urban system, such as housing, transport, and major services and amenities like health care, education, recreational facilities, and so on. Urban conflicts revolve around access to, or denial of, these resources to different social groups, and this is often organized spatially, because of the way different assets are positioned between areas. This explains the significance of the concerns people feel about such matters as how easy it is to travel to work, or the shops; how well local housing compares to that found in other districts; the relative performance of local schools; or their distance from the nearest accident and emergency hospital unit. Broadly speaking, these can be characterized as questions of consumption, and the quality of life; they are not directly about the orthodox Marxist problems of production and the struggle between the working and ruling classes.

However, Castells points out that the ability to satisfy consumption demands plays an integral part in the effectiveness of a capitalist system, and one with growing importance. Under modern capitalism it seems indeed that attention has moved away from the politics of the workplace towards these kinds of problem. Furthermore, there has been an increasing involvement of the state in these areas, since most of the key assets are not provided or distributed individually, but collectively, to very large numbers of people. For instance, a decision to invest in a rapid urban transit system inevitably involves the intervention of government, because it affects the life chances of whole populations, as will the implementation of congestion charges to shift the balance of urban transport away from private to more 'public' forms. Hence, says Castells, processes of collective consumption form the real object of the 'urban question'. Accordingly, much of the empirical information in his book *The Urban Question* refers to processes of urban planning, renewal and development, the associated transformations in the social composition of different residential areas, and the territorial struggles in which groups engage to defend or improve their conditions. This provides the substance of urban politics. It should be noted that under this definition urban politics does not take place only in towns and cities; issues of collective consumption will also engage the inhabitants of rural areas.

Urban politics, social movements and community action

Castells notes that the path to the discovery of this field of urban politics has been lengthy, and that it has been reached through 'the successive development of the theoretical contradictions at which community studies have arrived' (1977: 246). In other words, the sociological preoccupation with community has led, by a series of stages, to the uncovering of the significance of collective consumption. To some extent, therefore, his own contribution can be seen as further reworking the meaning of community. By ridding the field of the confusions of 'urban ideology', he claims to enable a clearer understanding of what is at stake. His particular formulation, that urban politics is organized around problems of collective consumption, reflects the growing separation of 'work' from many other aspects of everyday life. It is notable how often, in the various studies of urban communities we have been considering, relatively little information is provided about the work that people do, or about how they engage with questions to do with basic economic relationships, including wages and incomes, working hours, or the distribution of workplace power. There are several reasons for this. Today matters such as these tend to be fought out by trades unions and to some extent political parties, usually at a 'national' level, separately from community relations. This is significantly different from those traditional communities, including agricultural villages and working class communities, where work was integral to, and even dominant over, patterns of daily life. In modern urban contexts it is no longer common to find places built around a particular sort of industry, or the interests of a single employer, or type of employer; instead people are involved with a rich variety of occupations, and employments, and a large proportion of them probably commute to spend parts of the working day outside the area where they live. Consequently there has been a general breakdown of the old-style occupational communities (Lash and Urry 1987) so that many people experience a gap between the problems that concern them at work, and those which preoccupy them while at home. This separation is reflected in the process of 'suburbanization' of location.

Castells endorses this view, when he states that industry (or 'production') tends now to be organized on a regional, national or international scale, and therefore beyond the grasp of local communities, whereas consumption occurs closer to where people live. Furthermore, for large parts of the workforce, experiences of unemployment and economic marginalization have meant the removal of 'organized' production from the centre of their social being (Byrne 1989: 14; Harris 1987). For many others as well, orientations to issues of consumption and reproduction have become more central aspects of individual and collective identity. Following Castells' lead, these patterns could be seen to correspond to a more structural separation that has arisen between the productive domain, and what he calls in Marxist terminology the reproduction, or extended reproduction, of the workforce – all those ways in which its daily needs are met, outside work. These needs are still satisfied mainly in or close to the home, in family life or leisure. This explains the terms in which others have come to define the realm of community life and activity. For instance, Short says that

> Community concerns are expressed by people as residents, as users and consumers, of particular places.... They are concerns with places as *living places*, to be contrasted and distinguished from the concerns of capital with places as markets, sources of profits, and scenes for economic calculation and the concerns of the state with places populated by people as voters.
>
> (Short 1984: 126, emphasis supplied)

In specifying this sphere of 'community concerns', Short has in mind issues to do with the quality of housing and the environment, the availability of facilities, and the maintenance and improvement of existing local social relationships. It is around matters like this that a host of groups engaging in various kinds of 'community action' are likely to form, such as residents groups, amenity associations, social clubs and voluntary organizations. Any of these may become involved at certain points in making claims on behalf of their locality, or in challenging the claims made by others. The result is a mass of small-scale, localized actions which make up the bread-and-butter content of local politics. Very often the issues are confined to a particular community, or entail some level of competition between communities. In most cases they are short-lived, and die away, to be replaced by some other issue, so that there is little overall consistency or continuity of action. But certain issues, like urban redevelopment and renewal, gentrification, or resistance to unwanted innovations or changes of use, will produce more systematic responses. Most large urban redevelopment schemes trigger a degree of organized opposition and resistance, and some of the ensuing battles can attract considerable attention, and grow into major confrontations. Examples from London would include struggles around the redevelopment of Covent Garden (Christenson 1979), Tolmers Square (Wates 1976), Docklands (Foster 1999), and Spitalfields.

Castells felt there was potential in the field of urban politics for these kinds of issues to generate real social transformation, through the intervention of 'urban social movements'. These were movements aimed at altering the terms on which provision for collective consumption was made, and to begin with Castells expected them to link up in some fashion with the wider class struggle, to help shift the balance of power between social classes. In this way, conflicts over consumption would reconnect with struggles around production. Hence his interest lay mainly with large and dramatic movements capable of bringing about substantial changes in urban conditions and policies, because they attacked them at the level of the city as a whole. Examples he gives include the 1915 Glasgow Rent Strike, Citizens Movements in Madrid in the 1970s, and the emergence of San Francisco's gay community (Castells 1983). A more recent British example might be the successful opposition mounted to the Poll Tax, which played a major part in the downfall of the Conservative government in 1997. Despite his earlier dismissal of the term, Castells chooses to reinstate the idea of community when examining the significance of such movements, because such struggles appear to be organized around a social base which represents some form of common understanding and shared identity, usually with a territorial focus. He also notes how important it is to understand the subjective motivations of the actors involved, and how they are grounded in their personal experiences; thus he retrieves a great deal of the ground he attacked so vehemently in his theoretical analysis of the urban problem.

Critics of his position soon pointed out that remarkably few examples met all the demanding criteria he laid down for defining an urban social movement, and Castells himself gradually modified his approach, to widen the range of movements which could be included. According to Lowe (1986: 52), the real importance of Castells' work lay in drawing attention to the significance of local communities as focal points of urban movement activity. Likewise Byrne (2001: 16) notes that 'much urban social politics has its foundation in communal identities and communal interests'. Castells himself says that, in the face of overwhelming national or global pressures, people tend to 'go home' and organize themselves locally, to fight their disputes at a territorial level. This is a theme he has developed extensively in later work (Castells 1983; 1997). Seabrook (1984) provides a relevant example. Inspired by the success of certain local action groups, a system of neighbourhood offices was set up in the town of Walsall, in the English Midlands, to undertake the mobilization of support for regeneration and community-building projects amongst a dispirited working class population. Seabrook interprets this as a reaction against the loss of a valued local social identity, and the sense people had that their lives were being shaped more and more by economic and social forces beyond their, or anyone else's, control. Neighbourhoods constituted knowable spaces, within which individuals remained familiar with many of those around them, aware of the available facilities and the functions they performed, and felt competent to act. For Seabrook, this is what local politics should be about. Bulmer (1986: 95) refers to 'modern neighbourhoodism' as the attempt to *create* such local social worlds through political or quasi-political action. Considerable organizational skill and ingenuity can be devoted to efforts to mobilize residents, in order to 'protect amenities, enhance resources, and to a greater or lesser degree wrench control of the local milieu from outside authorities and vest it in local hands' (1986: 95). In their different ways, all these writers are responding to a resurgence of local action, and community politics, during the 1980s and after. Some would trace this even further back, from the 1960s onwards, and see in it a tendency which contradicts claims that society was moving towards an increasingly national, or even international, homogenization of identities and interests (Goodwin 1989; Warde 1985).

Others endorse this view of the local arena as the setting for various forms of oppositional and resistance politics. Lash and Urry (1987: 224) note the emergence during recent years of a multitude of locality-based campaigning and other social groups, and suggest that they played an especially important part in the rise of the peace movement during the early 1980s, and in the development of the environmental and women's movements. These groupings were 'overwhelmingly local' in their formation, and relied on the ability to develop real social bonds and shared objectives with those who were close by. Similarly Dickens (1988: 167) stresses the importance of 'locally rooted social movements' which do indeed sometimes propose alternatives to the wider social order, yet are the product of specifically local social relations. Not all these movements are organized around collective consumption issues, but they do exhibit certain characteristic features which they share with those that are (Dunleavy 1980: 157). They tend to operate outside conventional party politics, with a low degree of hierarchy and formal organization; they encourage a good deal of direct participation, and engage in forms of direct action and protest. Frequently they claim to speak on behalf of relatively powerless groups. In short, local and community politics typically involves a 'bottom-up' style of local organization. These attributes distinguish such movements from more formally organized voluntary bodies and associations, as well as from established political parties. Like Castells, Dunleavy would prefer to restrict the term 'urban social movement' to actions which go beyond the merely defensive or parochial, in seeking to bring about some change in social institutions, or introduce a new social order. For Lowe (1986: 3) an urban social movement entails the mobilization of a distinct social base, whose activity is directed towards producing a change in policy direction. Pickvance (1999: 354) also writes about social movements in terms of groups which 'advocate ideas and challenge existing policies and practices'. Others employ the term more loosely, to allow for the great variety of ways in which people organize themselves 'on the ground' to contest particular decisions or threats to their environment and living conditions, without necessarily always developing more extensive social ambitions.

There is some agreement that movements concerned with consumption and lifestyle issues are capable of welding together members of different social classes, or building local alliances across other social differences. Consequently 'community cleavages overlap, exacerbate and sometimes contradict class divisions' (Short 1984: 5). Often, however, they follow the lines of particular social interests and identities. Lowe (1986) provides accounts of actions taken by tenants on large working class estates in Sheffield, by middle-class 'ratepayers' in more salubrious neighbourhoods, and by squatters seizing empty properties in London. He notes that effective action by such groupings rests on the ability to mobilize existing networks of association within local social systems, and allows that this finding shows some continuity with the supposedly 'dated' work done in the community studies tradition. Bagguley *et al.* (1990) make a similar observation: the local actions they witnessed in Lancaster also followed existing networks of social relationships. In this case, as well as campaigns by tenants against local authority landlords, they refer to anti-nuclear protests occasioned by the nearby presence of the Heysham and Windscale power stations. Although these linked up with wider national and international movements for peace, and against nuclear energy, they had important foundations in matters of more immediate concern to the local community. This lent support to the view that political mobilizations based on 'local particularities' and organized on a territorial basis were overtaking more traditional class-based, and production-oriented, politics.

Whereas they regard battles over the wage packet as having formed the 'usual object of struggle', Bagguley *et al.* notice how issues like the cost of household essentials and the accessibility of public services become important in the politics of community; also, that neighbourhood, community and friendship networks offer an alternative foundation for political mobilization to that of the workplace (1990: 193). This has a special significance for women, since whereas historically they have been rooted less firmly than men in the politics of production, they have engaged more closely with questions of reproduction and consumption; hence women play a prominent role in community organizations and struggles. For Bagguley *et al.* the growing importance of local politics is evidenced by 'the emergence of local social movements, environmental concerns, issues of local and national identity, along with the sharpening of geographical differences in electoral behaviour' (1990: 218). These are all forms of action in which the nature of particular communities plays a pivotal role. Lash and Urry (1987) concur with this general line of argument, but also want to bring back into the picture those local struggles which are directed more towards the activities of industry and the state, in reshaping the nature of local communities. There is no reason, after all, to exclude altogether from the realm of local politics conflicts to do with economic questions, such as the availability of work, the prospects for career promotion, or the size of the pay packet. Very often what most concerns people is that these opportunities should exist for them at a local level.

There are others who are troubled by the tendency to separate consumption issues from production. Harvey (1989a; 1989b) maintains the orthodox Marxist emphasis on the centrality of processes of the accumulation of capital through production, and of class struggle, against what he regards as the 'defection' of Castells. In his view, urban spaces are shaped and reshaped by the logic of capital accumulation, forces which transcend the wills of individuals, or even social groups. Many of the 'choices' people make within the urban context are therefore predetermined, to a great extent. The areas they inhabit form a mosaic of urban labour markets, whose limits are set by the daily patterns of commuting through which they dispose of their labour power; and urban places compete with one another to provide capital with attractive packages of physical and social infrastructure, labour, lifestyles and environment. For Harvey, the community remains essentially 'the place of reproduction in which labour power suitable for a place of production is reproduced' (1989a: 118), although he accepts that it may also take shape as a distinctive grouping from the viewpoint of consumption as well. This does not mean that what happens in the community is unimportant. Its significance is stressed throughout Harvey's analysis of the urban experience. As well as a locus of social reproduction, community is a distinctive milieu for social interaction, a source for the formation of consciousness, and a basis for action, including processes of active 'community building'. Indeed, Harvey acknowledges that in the modern era consciousness of community tends to outweigh class consciousness. Nevertheless, the urban community is the product of forces emanating from the system of capitalist production, which cannot survive without 'some operative geographical conception of community' (1989a: 148). Elsewhere (2000: 56) Harvey observes that when factories become more mobile, or disappear, and much of the workforce is temporary or casualized, the workplace ceases to provide the natural base for organization, and alternative models must be found. He cites the example of Baltimore, where a city-wide movement for a living wage relied upon an alliance of community institutions (like churches), activist organizations, and student groups. Here, although the organizing took place outside work, its objective was still to have an influence over issues of production.

ECONOMIC RESTRUCTURING, LOCALITIES AND COMMUNITY CHANGE

To see communities as focussed solely upon matters of consumption and living conditions, as Short (1984) does when he defines them simply as 'living places', is to perpetuate the separation between community and some of the main determinants of social existence. His approach implies that it is only 'capital' which has an economic interest in the fate of communities, whereas ordinary people, as 'residents', have a range of non-economic preoccupations. Such a distinction is plainly false, since the way in which capital treats communities obviously bears directly upon the life chances of those who live within them. The removal of economic support and investment from British coal-mining communities was responsible for destroying the livelihoods, and with them much of the infrastructure of communal life, of miners and their families. In their response, the miners explicitly described their struggle as a defence of 'community', and not just a fight about wages (Beynon 1985). Research projects like Stacey's on Banbury (1960; 1975), or the Lynds on 'Middletown' (Lynd and Lynd 1929; 1937), had shown previously how communities could be transformed over time by the repeated impacts of industrial investment and occupational change. Banbury was altered in major ways by the successive influences of an agricultural machine manufacturer, an aluminium company, and a multi-national food processor. According to Stacey, as well as having a direct effect on people's incomes and career prospects, these organizations brought new attitudes and values into the town, along with new kinds of social relations, and introduced crucial social divisions, like the split between 'traditional' and 'non-traditional' styles of life. Banbury's unique character as a place was built up through the addition of residues from each of these stages of development. In this we could see a precursor of Doreen Massey's argument (1984) that local economic and social structures are constituted through the layering effects of different 'rounds of investment'. Each time a new wave of capital investment occurs, replacing existing and worn-out commitments, it adds a further layer of employment opportunities, class positions, and social relations to what is there already. In a dynamic economic environment, most communities will be influenced by such processes; and during certain periods, the depth and pace of such changes will be especially acute.

There is general acceptance that the 1980s were such a period of rapid social change, a phase of extensive economic and social restructuring, necessitated by acute problems confronting capitalist production, especially manufacturing industry. In order to overcome these difficulties, major changes occurred in industrial structures, the organization of firms and enterprises, and the relationships between employers and their labour forces, which left few local communities unaffected. Very importantly, these changes had different consequences for different geographical areas and locations. There was much talk of a growing north–south divide, as well as of shifts in employment between rural and urban districts, and more localized variations in fortunes. This gave rise to a spate of new writings, reflecting a rekindling of interest in understanding what was happening to particular places (Massey 1984; Savage *et al.* 1987; Dickens 1988; Cooke 1989). As the authors of one study put it, 'it suddenly became necessary to pursue detailed investigations of named places' (Bagguley *et al.* 1990: 7). The outcome was a clutch of place-specific studies (for example, Pahl 1984; Urry and Murgatroyd 1985; Boddy *et al.* 1986; Byrne 1989). While this might have presaged a revival in old-style community studies, those concerned claimed that they now had a far better theoretical grasp of what was required to produce reliable knowledge and explanations. For instance, Bagguley *et al.* assert that their standpoint enabled 'insights inaccessible to the empiricism of earlier approaches'. At the same time, they remain fearful that research might be drawn into reproducing the former style of 'descriptivist and parochial case studies' (1990: 211), and they are extremely keen to defend themselves against accusations that they are reviving discarded notions of community. They employ instead the alternative language of 'locality', and locality studies.

'Locality' refers to some kind of identifiable space within which the outcomes of key social and economic processes can be observed. Those examining the restructuring process sought to trace the ways in which a reorganization of production was bringing about a range of distinctive effects at local level. They argued that their understanding of the general processes involved would suffice to ensure that their analyses would achieve greater rigour, and comparability, than previous efforts. That is, rather than conducting their research on an *ad hoc* basis, to see what came out of particular case studies, they could reason more systematically from general tendencies to particular consequences. Alternatively, the 'specificities' of given examples could be explained by relating them to wider causal influences and trends. As expressed by Dickens (1988: 22), it was a case of 'general and nationally-based processes . . . combining with existing local societies to form quite new kinds of local social diversity'. In the same way Massey sought to show how a quite limited number of underlying basic processes were capable of producing highly differentiated outcomes between different places. A funded research programme based on her framework, examining the 'Changing Urban and Regional System' of the UK (CURS), gave further encouragement to sociologists to explore what was happening in distinct localities (Cooke 1989).

Massey's work on the changing spatial division of labour was a formative influence on the restructuring approach. As a social geographer, Massey's prime interest was in the spatial effects of patterns of industrial location, and how they related to changes taking shape at regional, national or international levels; she refers to community organizations as being towards 'the very local end' of the spectrum of changes she aims to explain. Yet her arguments fit very well those developments which were taking place at more local levels as well, within different communities. In keeping with her Marxian inclinations, Massey pays most attention to economic processes, like the reorganization of specific industries, such as clothing and footwear, the changing nature of the employment patterns this produces, and how they impact upon different geographical areas. Principally she was interested in understanding how this created such varying effects at regional level, in a pattern of uneven development. Thus she discusses the contrast between changes in the coalfield areas and the effects in more rural districts, like Cornwall. In the former, she argues, the arrival of new types of employment together with greater integration into the wider society had broken down their previous 'spatial coherence' and social homogeneity, undermining their working class identity and political unity; whereas the small-scale 'industrialization' of rural areas, through the appearance of increased numbers of small firms and craft producers, was diversifying their economies, and challenging the interests of more established local employers. These developments shifted the balance between different social groupings, including social classes, and found expression in new forms of local social and political relations. Different parts of the country were experiencing radically different kinds of social change.

In spatial terms, Massey's account deals mainly with developments taking place in certain kinds of local labour markets, rather than actual communities. The majority of the other studies of locality and restructuring follow suit, identifying the appropriate local area for investigation with the space within which a given local population was able to find work. This use of 'travel to work areas' (TTWAs), or local labour markets, allowed researchers to make extensive use of various kinds of labour market statistics, in order to describe changing employment patterns for different occupations and skills, for men and women, and for various ethnic groups. However, there was an essentially arbitrary aspect to such definitions, in that the 'locality' in question was no more than a ring drawn around a particular set of labour market elements. As a statistical construct, most of the population involved probably would have little subjective awareness of such an area. Yet at the same time, many of these areas were also identified with 'named places' – such as Cheltenham, Swindon, Lancaster – and claims were made about the 'less tangible sense' in which 'most people can know something about many of the significant elements within such a locality' (Bagguley *et al*. 1990: 11). This made it a meaningful unit 'in which subjects can pursue relatively well informed struggles'. In effect, places, and TTWAs, were equated to medium-sized towns, and roughly speaking to local authority districts. Massey recognizes the importance of this local level for ordinary people when she says that 'most people still live their lives locally, their consciousness is formed in a distinct geographical space' (1984: 117), a claim matched by Dickens' assertion that 'for most of us' small-scale localities continue to provide the settings for everyday life, and determine the scale at which we develop and reproduce our social relationships; the 'urban scale' encompasses the major direct experiences of home, paid work, school and other routine activities like shopping (1988: 11).

There was then some ambiguity about the meaning of 'locality', so that adopting it as a substitute did not resolve all the problems associated with 'community'. Instead the debate as to whether it should be seen as an artificial construct designed for analytical purposes, or as a real phenomenon capable of generating genuine social effects, made it for a while one of the more vexed topics in social analysis (Duncan and Goodwin 1988; Duncan 1989). The bias towards the components of economic change among those who used the term also led to accusations of economic determinism, and an excessive debt to Marx. As Byrne puts it (2001: 18), locality was construed as 'an essentially structural concept set in an economically deterministic programme'. Massey responded to these charges, first by emphasizing that the final outcomes of restructuring processes were always unpredictable, because every place was different, and these differences helped shape what occurred. Hence, in an often repeated mantra, 'geography matters'. Second, a complete understanding or explanation of local circumstances would require factors other than the economic to be taken into account. As she states it,

> The social changes in an area, the shifts in prevailing ideology and temperament, are not bound up only with economic changes within that locality. They reflect also broader shifts and in other aspects of society. The layers of history which are sedimented over time are not just economic; there are also cultural, political and ideological strata, layers which also have their local specificities.
>
> (Massey 1984: 120)

Developing this theme, Bagguley *et al.* refer later to places as 'the intersection of a multitude of processes, the sedimentations of the past, the social practices of the present and projects for the future' (1990: 219). An idea of the complexity this presents is conveyed by their listing of some of the wide array of substantive entities and social collectivities which form the content of a given locality. The list includes: households; housing or 'neighbourhood' communities; school catchment areas; ethnic and religious communities; classes at local, regional, national and international scales; political party districts; factory catchment areas; labour markets; the state; voluntary organizations; and social movements (1990: 10–11, 145). For all the sophistication of the theoretical framework, there are some uncanny echoes in this of the methodologically 'primitive' studies carried out in Middletown, and Yankee City, as there are in the claim that focussing on a locality will give access to a more 'rounded' set of processes and interrelations. The catalogue of different elements which go to make up contemporary Lancaster reminds us of Warren's definition of community (1963: 9) as 'that combination of social units and systems that perform the major social functions having locality relevance'. There are also continuities with Stacey's discussion of community, and local social systems, as can be seen from Byrne's summing up, that 'the essence of the idea of locality is the emergence of a specific local system through the spatially delimited interaction of economic and social systems with each other and with the physical geography of a particular place' (Byrne 2001: 73).

COMMUNITY OR LOCALITY?

Introducing some of the fruits of the CURS research programme, Cooke (1989) laid out the case for dispensing with community as a concept, and replacing it with locality. He argued that to speak of 'community' presupposed too much stability and continuity; furthermore it was inward-looking and reactive. By this he meant that the idea of community did not allow for the exercise of effective power by its members; rather, communities are shaped passively by external forces. The same distinction is adopted by others. Byrne (2001: 77) states that 'the idea of locality has a dynamism which is not inherent in the idea of community. On the contrary, community is an idea which implies the absence of transformational change'. Through its link to the restructuring approach, the idea of locality has been used to explore how places change, and also to seek to give places an active role in determining change. Thus Cooke associates the capacity for local mobilization with the possession of citizenship and welfare 'rights' at local level, and the push to protect or extend such rights. Where people do not have rights, then he argues they must fall back on what 'more accurately' could be called their community. He adds that it is not unreasonable to think of such communities as occupying particular locales. He has in mind specifically groups of immigrants, living as aliens within a host territory, but offers no explanation as to why they are unable to draw upon the strengths of their community to exert claims for admission to rights or to make active political interventions. There is then some special pleading for the value of the concept of locality, as an active social force, which relies on perpetuating the idea of community as something intrinsically static, and defensive.

Cooke defines locality as 'the space within which the larger part of most citizens' daily working and consuming lives is lived' (1989: 12), and from which they are able to launch their interventions into the economic, social, political and cultural spheres. He contends that CURS research succeeded in clarifying how such localities functioned internally, and how they were linked to wider national and international processes. It confirmed that localities could play an active part in their own transformation, as 'centres of collective consciousness', representing the combined energies of the various individuals, groups and social interests gathered within them. He refers to the role played in this by local traditions, and local initiatives of various kinds, including distinctive attitudes of 'boosterism' and local chauvinism. Much of this could be expressed equally well in the vocabulary of community and community action. For instance, Cooke's definition of locality resembles Harvey's conception of the urban as 'a community in which daily processes of living and working occur' (1989a: 148). In the case study reports of CURS research, locality and community appear frequently as cross-cutting categories; thus southwest Birmingham is described as 'one locality, several "communities"', whereas the diffuse population of Liverpool's outer estates is termed a 'community under siege'. A shift to the language of 'locality' does not seem to have done away with the need to refer to community, or to community sentiments.

As well as dealing with some of the major structural forces shaping particular places at a given time, the various locality studies strive to give an insight into what it felt like to live in them, in terms of how people perceived change and the nature of their social surroundings. In Swindon, for example, we learn that owing to the number of new people coming in, 'there isn't a community feel'. The picture is one of increasing fragmentation and complexity, as working class solidarity, collectivism and community ties give way to home-centred individualism and social fragmentation (Cooke 1989: 83). By contrast, despite massive economic losses, people in the working class estates of Kirkby and Knowsley were adjusting with considerable resilience and cohesion. They were utilizing family support networks and a strong sense of local identification to develop various bottom-up initiatives, like credit unions, housing cooperatives and women's health action groups, which 'speak volumes for the local sense of community' (1989: 229). In Kent's Isle of Thanet, a cluster of declining seaside resorts had not been able to find a distinctive position within the developing urban and regional system, and consequently lacked the necessary capability and resources to restructure themselves. Unable to work together, the towns competed to attract investment, industry and jobs. Lancaster had been more successful. Faced with the retreat of key industries from its city centre, it was being reconstructed as 'a modern consumption centre preserving the shells of past rounds of economic structure to house new functions' like tourism and higher education (1989: 161). Although they were all influenced by the same large-scale processes of economic change, especially the decline of manufacturing and the rise of new service industries, these different experiences served to underline the importance of 'local uniqueness' in shaping a response. According to Cooke, one of the more generally observable effects was that values of sociability, community, egalitarianism and social justice could be identified 'objectively' with the declining industrial communities of northern Britain, whereas more prosperous southern localities tended to be pervaded instead by questions of competition, monetary value, unit costs and performance indicators (1989: 25). In broad terms, then, patterns of economic and social restructuring were putting communities under pressure, and possibly even undermining the general hold of communal values. Yet to a considerable extent it was from their locations within particular communities, and sets of communal relations, that people were able to fight back. In doing so, they acted in ways that hinged on their own understandings of community, and local belonging, and on their ability to form alliances and cooperate with those around them.

6

THE SOCIAL CONSTRUCTION OF COMMUNITY

The previous chapter described a progressive movement in the sociological analysis of local social situations, away from the idea of 'community' as a matter of relationships grounded in interaction at the local level, towards the examination of increasingly remote and determining sets of processes and structures. This was aimed at meeting the objection that old-style studies of community, by treating communities as if they were free-standing entities, failed to deal adequately with the constraints put upon them by their wider context. The answer was to situate them instead within broader frameworks of social and economic relations, like those of capitalism, class, and power. At certain points in this development, as during the heyday of structuralist Marxism, the resulting accounts were inclined to become excessively impersonal and mechanistic, leaving little scope for much of significance or interest to happen at local level. Harvey (1989a: 148) hints at this, when he suggests that for the idea of community as an autonomous entity we should substitute the notion of a 'set of processes which produce a geographical product'. The processes in question are those of capitalist accumulation, regarded as extraordinarily powerful forces which local social formations find it difficult to withstand. On the whole, Harvey consigns local actors to a merely defensive role, in ill fated struggles to protect home, territory and community against continual disruption (1989b: 238). Otherwise it is clear that he sees 'communities' as the end-product of a long chain of causal influences.

Similarly, Massey (1984) formulated an influential version of local difference as the outcome of particular combinations of structure, for which her key word was 'articulation'. The way in which the structures came together accounted for local variation. Again this appeared to write action out of the equation, or else to ascribe the power to act effectively to capital alone, which seemed to be able to sweep all before it, manipulating local variations to its own advantage, destroying some communities while it favoured others. Despite her socialist credentials, Massey's major work on *Spatial Divisions of Labour* seemed to play down the possibilities for resistance and opposition which local forces might present. Although different from one another, all local communities seemed relatively powerless; this was especially so for industrial and working class communities, pulled apart by the destructive pressures of economic change. Later contributions to the restructuring approach were keen to identify ways in which local circumstances could make a difference, to produce some 'locality effect'; yet it was hard to avoid the sense that always there was a huge weight of social structure bearing down upon them. Where attempts were made to mitigate this pull towards structural determinism, by incorporating a more active conception of community, recognizing the role of subjectivity, action and political mobilization, they gave rise to considerable theoretical tension; for example, in the work of Castells, for whom local resistance seemed to be understood better as the outcome of structural pressures, rather than the work of active, conscious social agents (Smith 2002).

Amidst all of this, we could ask, what became of the people? Although there are tantalizing glimpses of their views and attitudes in the various locality studies, they are rarely given sustained attention. As Smith notes, we never learn who actually lives, works and dies in Harvey's urban spaces. If the earlier community studies suffered from a surfeit of ethnographic detail, in later research the ethnography of daily life and social conduct seems almost to vanish. Just a few enticing clues are offered. For example, the conception of locality as the site of diverse and competing interests suggests there should be ample scope to explore in detail how these interests are shaped, and how they interact with one another. Likewise the lesson that processes of uneven development mean that social groups will be 'spatially constituted and differentiated, with variable local strengths and importance' (Goodwin 1989: 158) leads us back towards the question of how such groups actually relate to one another within their particular spatial terrains. In general, the restructuring approach highlighted the significance of changing patterns of relationships between geography, place and interests, the variety of local configurations which emerged, and the part they played in generating distinctive forms of local action, such as local economic strategies, or programmes for community regeneration (Duncan and Goodwin 1988; Body and Fudge 1984). It offered much potential for in-depth examination of local case studies. Nevertheless, the main focus of interest remained on understanding how these local matters related to the major structural processes and transformations taking place at the level of economy and society as a whole, so that attention was drawn away continually from the local level. There are many for whom this entire direction and style of analysis was misconceived, who would argue that, despite its attempt to capture 'specificities', it failed to give sufficient weight to what occurred at the local level, or to acknowledge the real significance this had for the average member of society. In particular, they would argue, there was a serious gap between the analysis of the structural composition of communities, and an understanding of what they actually meant to those whose lives were led within them.

SOCIAL CONSTRUCTIONISM AND THE CULTURAL TURN

An alternative direction for analysis was already implicit in the preceding discussion. Once community is understood to be 'essentially contested', or as the focus of struggle, rather than simple uniformity, then attention can be turned to the ways in which it is defined and deployed by social actors themselves, in their everyday lives, and in their political imagination. There is much in recent social theory to encourage a turn of this sort, in particular the ascendancy of various kinds of social constructionist perspective. Social constructionism derives from influential currents of sociological thought such as symbolic interactionism and phenomenology, and the work of theorists like Weber, Simmel and Meade. Constructionist approaches treat human beings as active, more or less conscious, agents engaged in the creation of a shared social reality. This makes it important to understand society from their point of view. Knowing what they are about entails investigating their purposes, and the ways in which they give meaning to their situation and behaviours. In other words, the focus moves from efforts to document objective facts and causal relationships to the exploration of subjective consciousness and perception, or from reality itself to how reality is apprehended. This includes examining the production of the various representations and images through which people make sense of their social worlds, and this makes culture, rather than structure, the dominant topic for investigation (Chaney 1994). When interpreting their social world, and their position within it, people are compelled to engage in various kinds of theorizing, and to create a range of explanatory social categories; constructionism undermines the tendency to regard such categories as part of nature. Instead, its basic presupposition is that there are portions of the real world that attain factual status only by virtue of human agreement, and therefore that exist only because people believe them to exist (Searle 1995). 'Community' can be regarded as such a fact, having no independent existence outside the capacity of human beings to conceptualize it. However, because we know that facts of this type are liable to be subjected to immense amounts of debate and disagreement, it is vitally important to know exactly who has been involved in creating them, and why.

The cultural turn and the rise of social constructionism have made themselves felt right across sociology and human geography, and had an impact accordingly on both urban and rural studies (Zukin 1995; Cloke 1997; Cloke and Little 1997; Featherstone and Lash 1999; Devine *et al.* 2005). Decades of criticism of the rural–urban distinction have not overcome the tendency of these two fields of study to continue to develop to a large extent as separate disciplines. Nevertheless, there has been some common movement towards giving greater prominence to such constructionist themes as the diversity of social practices which give meaning to human activities, in both town and country; the role of various kinds of discourse in shaping the way we view such environments; and the manner in which competing social meanings are negotiated and contested. This has encouraged a re-examination of the importance of community, in the light of these cultural and interactionist preoccupations. Interestingly, the influence of cultural studies as a discipline, particularly in Britain, owes a great deal to the work of two scholars who engaged closely with the idea of community, Hoggart (1957) and Williams (1958). The former achieved prominence through his autobiographical account of a disappearing cultural world, that of the working class community. Subsequent researchers in the cultural field have continued to interest themselves in the idea of community as a cultural phenomenon, and as a basis on which distinct forms of culture may rest.

'Community' as social construct

The idea that communities are socially constructed is not new. In fact, once one leaves behind the supposition that somehow they are natural, given or primordial, it becomes inevitable. If they are not to be treated as taken-for-granted facts within the social landscape, then communities have to be seen as resulting from some form of creative process, through which they are built and maintained. This implies that they have a history, and trajectory of development, and that there will be continuing processes through which their existence is reproduced. We have considered several aspects of the construction process already. The sifting of people into relatively homogeneous social groupings, the articulation of shared interests, and mobilization for collective action can all be seen as steps towards the construction of community. Entire communities, like new towns and urban estates, can be 'contrived' through the deliberate decisions of planners, developers and governmental officials (Suttles 1972; Ward 1993). Since governments have not given up looking for 'natural communities' to which to match the delivery of public services, where they cannot be identified agencies will take steps to bring them into being. In order to carry out their own work successfully, they are virtually forced to engage in constructing communities (Ball and Stobart 1997). Finally, existing communities can sometimes move *en masse*, to take up new physical and social locations, and make a new start, as have many migrant and diasporic populations. For example, consideration is being given at present to the possible relocation of sizeable numbers of orthodox Jewish families from the Charedi community of London's Stamford Hill who have outgrown their established location, to new homes in the Thames Gateway development (*Guardian* newspaper, 9 April 2005).

Although all these physical, material and demographic processes enter into the actual creation of communities, the social constructionist spotlight is turned more on the ways in which communities are brought into being through the interpretive activities of their members, and registered among the concepts which they use in everyday talk and interaction. No matter how sniffy sociologists and other experts may be about the value of the idea, 'community' is a term which is in wide popular circulation, and on the tip of many people's tongue when they come to explaining differences in social values, and styles of living that have meaning for them. Community has a form of social existence because people want to believe in it. This is why recurrent attempts to kill off the concept have failed, and why social scientists who wish to stay in touch with the way in which 'lay' members of their society think about it have been compelled to return to the idea, again and again (Day and Murdoch 1993). Researching social relationships in part of Bristol described as a practical 'laboratory of community', a youth worker comments that 'the question "What is community?" has been running around for years, continually exhausting itself, but never dying' (Brent 1997: 68). It was evident that theories of community arose spontaneously in the course of everyday conversation, and influenced people's perceptions and action. In many other situations, it is equally apparent that ideas about and practical expressions of community constitute an essential part of the routine fabric of daily life, and cannot be disregarded merely because intellectuals and academics find them puzzling or unconvincing. Reflecting the ambivalence which so many feel towards the idea, Revill (1993) concedes that 'for good or ill' community plays a key role in how people think about themselves, their personal and social identities, and their subjectivity. It has value as an analytical concept, because it focuses attention on how individuals, groups, and places become tied together through the sense of belonging.

Back to ethnography

Investigating the meanings attached to community among particular social groups involves the use of qualitative methods of participant observation and cultural analysis, rather than amassing statistical information about social and economic structures. As a result there has been a revival of interest in certain forms of ethnographic community study, which has generated a body of new insights that have transformed the way in which researchers perceive community. Unlike earlier examples, these investigations do not aim to provide a complete account of particular ways of life, or exhaustively describe a set of integrated social structures; their purpose instead is to elucidate some of the key interpretive processes through which people sustain their sense of community as a social reality. A leading example is the work of Anthony Cohen, a social anthropologist resolutely opposed to the 'deterministic' assumption that communities are conditioned by economic or political forces. His references to the 'tightly structured intricacy of local life' and the 'tiny spans of close social relationships to which people attribute their fundamental social belonging' (1982: 9) draw us back to the intimacy of the small community and its face-to-face relationships.

Whereas the structuralist gaze has been turned outwards, to discern the external pressures thought to mould contemporary communities, and undermine their integrity, Cohen's attention is directed inwards, to get closer to what he regards as the fundamental human social experiences at the heart of community, and the way in which they take on meaning for those concerned. We could say that his watchword is 'respect for particularity', and the avoidance of unwarranted generalization. Compared with relationships on a larger scale, like those of the nation, region or class, Cohen asserts that the local community holds a greater social reality for people, who know one another better there than they would in a larger, more varied, setting, and share that knowledge with others in a more public way. Hence broader national or 'racial' identities are like empty receptacles, waiting to be filled with particular local experiences (1982: 13). The assertion, though extremely questionable, implies that if we want to know what people are really like, we must meet them on their home territory. The idea that these intimate relationships decide who we are is reiterated by the American sociologist Robert Putnam when he comments that 'for most of us, our deepest sense of belonging is to our most intimate social networks, especially family and friends. Beyond perimeter lie work, church, neighbourhood, civic life and . . . other "weak" ties' (Putnam 2000: 274). From this viewpoint, we should expect any fully social individual to be embedded in such an identity-conferring network of strong ties and close relationships; the further away one moves from these, the weaker the bonds become, and the less socially significant. For both Putnam and Cohen, community consists of these primary bonds, and the sense of belonging that goes with them, and at this level, we could plausibly suggest, all communities are distinctive; to those caught up in them, certainly, they will appear unique, and non-substitutable.

According to Cohen, communities are constituted by processes occurring close to the experiences of everyday life, and they have a largely symbolic existence. His essay on the symbolic construction of community (1985) has been amongst the most influential contributions of recent years. In it, he seeks to sidestep the definitional quagmire into which so many discussions of community have fallen, by switching attention from the attempt to provide objective measurements and descriptions of community, to a consideration of actors' meanings. From his perspective, it is not structures and institutions that define a community, but the feelings and experiences of its members, and the manner in which they express them. Most centrally, they do this by drawing boundaries, between themselves and others, stipulating who 'belongs', and who falls outside the limits of 'their' community. Often these boundaries will be extremely subtle, and possibly quite invisible to anyone who is not part of, or very close to, the community itself. They will be marked by the presence or absence of particular attributes, traits or values. Cohen notes how, when necessary, such differences can be 'elaborated and embellished to maintain the authentic distinctiveness of the community' (1985: 37). Small differences can be accorded great importance. To take an example, in a border territory like Ireland's South Armagh, people who are indistinguishable from one another in most respects may work extremely hard to magnify whatever differences do exist, to turn them into the 'master symbols' by which their community is defined. In this instance, it would be religious affiliation that is seized upon as the essential characteristic, so that being 'Catholic' or 'Protestant' comes to define the identities even of those who neither believe nor practice. This is a process which goes on largely in the minds of the participants, because:

> The symbolic nature of the opposition means that people can 'think themselves into difference'. The boundaries consist essentially in the contrivance of distinctive meanings within the community's social discourse. They provide people with a referent for their personal identities. Having done so, they are then expressed and reinforced through the presentation of those identities in social life.
>
> (Cohen 1985: 117)

Thus Cohen draws our attention to the highly active construction of community, and to the endlessly creative ways in which this can be achieved.

Cohen roots his argument in an attempt to refute prevailing orthodoxies about the 'decline' of community. He agrees that the pressures of modern living, including industrialization, urbanization and the mass media, tend to erode the actual geo-social boundaries around communities. Indeed, contrary to the position taken by the restructuring school, he proclaims that locality is 'anathema to the logic of modern political economy' (1982: 7), which operates to eradicate differences between places and cultures. Yet he denies the conclusion many have taken from this, that society must grow ever more uniform and homogenized. Instead he argues that local differences remain fundamental, since what on the surface appear to be similar behavioural patterns or social forms often conceal a multitude of different meanings. This can be appreciated only if one gets inside communities, to examine their distinctive local cultures and frames of reference. Rapport (1993: 39) makes a similar point, when he warns against the temptation to generalize too freely about the nature of villages, communities, the 'rural', and so on, given that 'the seeming sameness of our categories of description . . . disguise(s) a possible diversity of actual social relations'. The suggestion is that superficial observation will miss what is special about communities, whereas for those who inhabit them, this continues to be of prime importance; what they have in common with 'everyone else' in their wider society matters less than what makes them different and unique. The persistence of community rests then with people's ability to continue to assert and demonstrate their differences, despite pressures to eliminate them.

Cohen's argument is backed with a wealth of anthropological examples drawn from across the world, but mostly from small, rural, contexts. They show how a great array of social groups define themselves by the significance they attach to certain symbols, often projected through particular rituals and ceremonies, participation in which signifies a person's communal membership. For instance, Cohen mentions the Notting Hill Carnival (a British/West Indian gathering) and the Northern Irish marching season. The ties which bind communities together in these examples are not straightforward 'social facts', which can be pinned to some definite, concrete form, but complex social practices, through which individuals are able to identify themselves with the symbols, show that they understand them, and thereby exclude others who lack the same awareness. In both the above instances, the symbolic markers of community would include certain styles of music, dress and bodily deportment. What the symbols actually mean may vary from person to person, or situation to situation, but normally these differences are glossed over, to maintain the appearance of agreement and unity, smoothing out internal variations, whilst highlighting external differences. In the ideal state, they are meaningful to everyone who belongs, and *only* to them. Consequently, statements about community represent a means of identifying with some, and distancing from others. In later work, Cohen has generalized this as a feature of all group life:

> groups have to struggle against their own contradictions, which lie precisely in the fact that they are composed of individuals, self-conscious individuals, whose differences from each other have to be resolved and reconciled to a degree which allows the group to be viable and to cohere.
>
> (Cohen 1994: 11)

Hence, a community is a particular kind of group, consisting of all those who affiliate themselves to, and make use of, a distinctive framework of symbols. Through doing so, they set limits to their variation, and generate a form of collective being. Cohen's examples include groups defined through symbols of kinship, religion, ethnicity and place.

Aspects of Cohen's contribution could be read as reasserting some of the tenets of conventional community research, taking us back into the world of the marginal and esoteric. Throughout his discussion, he uses urban studies as a convenient stalking horse, to make the case for considering again the significance of certain features associated with traditional communities, like the 'total' connection between organization and behaviour, and the complex intertwining of different elements of local life. His critique of the 'myths' of urban sociology, and the Chicago School in particular, to whom he apportions blame for insisting upon structural explanations for alleged rural–urban differences, and variations in associated personality types, makes no mention of the work of Gans, Suttles and others who have tried to ensure that attention is paid to the formation of urban meanings and representations. Almost all the examples collected into Cohen's edited volumes on 'belonging' and the importance of symbolic boundaries (Cohen 1982; 1986) deal with relatively remote or peripheral localities, whose members legitimately feel they have been left out of the mainstream of social development. This adds to the impression that rurality has a special significance for the emergence of fully formed community situations, in which 'people's knowledge of each other is very much more complete than in the heterogeneous urban environment' (1982: 10). Cohen's work is cited widely; perhaps because he does not consider fully any of the relevant urban examples, its impact has been greatest, apart from his fellow social anthropologists, among sociologists and geographers interested in rural matters. However, since he states that the assertion of community in urban-industrial conditions is not an anachronism, but a normal feature of people's sense of self, and a modality of behaviour that is always available to them (1985: 117), then his style of analysis ought to apply equally well to urban settings. Indeed, he refers to the 'innumerable studies' proving community can exist within the city, thereby underlining just how 'irredeemably incorrect' (1985: 27) is the postulate of the decline of community as a general phenomenon.

Community as an act of imagination

Cohen is not alone in seeking to bring the subjective dimensions of community to the fore. Many years earlier, as part of his endeavour to cut the analysis of local social relations adrift from geography, Pahl (1970a) had noted how people could inhabit a 'village in the mind', leading as bucolic a lifestyle as possible, even within the physical spaces of an urban district – a situation depicted in the classic television series *The Good Life*. Equally, it followed, there were those who lived in rural locations, whilst inhabiting mentally the cosmopolitan universe of the city. In the years that have followed, these kinds of anomalies have become much more common, as the linkages between places and lifestyles have loosened, weakening yet further any prospect of making firm distinctions between the attributes of rural and urban existence. Following Anderson (1983), we could say that such people are identifying themselves with certain kinds of 'imagined communities', comprising those whom they believe to have key values, aspirations, or experiences in common with themselves. This highly influential notion was coined by Anderson in an illuminating discussion of national identities, where the 'community' that is imagined necessarily consists of very large numbers of people, who never could know one another at a personal, or face-to-face, level. Even though it is composed of anonymous individuals, Anderson regards the nation as a form of community because the connections between its members are pictured as affirming a 'deep, horizontal comradeship' (1983: 16).

Like the narrower constructions of community dealt with by Cohen, this type of imagining de-emphasizes any internal divisions and contradictions that may exist; for example, national belonging is usually held to be equally firm for all members, regardless of distinctions of class, gender and generation. Inside the nation, these may be the focus of intense disagreement, and even open struggle; people may be aware that they are caught up in divisive relationships of inequality and exploitation; yet these are hidden from or denied to outsiders, against whom the nation presents a solid front. Anderson views this ability simultaneously to be divided and yet represented as united as a fundamental aspect of community, and uses it to throw light on the way in which national belonging is socially constructed and maintained; nowhere does he subject the idea of community itself to any equivalent critical analysis. Indeed this is a weak spot in his thesis, since he tends to treat community as an unproblematic idea, and this leads him to underestimate the extent to which the members of a nation can differ in the form and intensity of their commitment to it. The 'meaning' of a nation among its members is never uncontentious, but always open to interpretation (Day and Thompson 2004). Precisely the same can be said of communities, and it is left to the work of Cohen, and others who have followed his lead, to expose to scrutiny the degree of variation that exists in the nature and type of 'belonging' that ties members to their communities. Cohen's approach puts processes of differentiation and identification right at the heart of what people mean by 'community'.

SIMILARITY AND DIFFERENCE IN COMMUNITIES

In the imaginations of their members, most communities operate in a similar way to nations, through the construction of close similarities and an underlying, seemingly essential, unity among those who 'belong', and the exclusion of those who fail to meet these criteria. Identifying or imagining who you are like necessarily indicates those who you are unlike. In reality, there are always going to be internal differences as well, between individuals and sub-groups, and at a certain level, members know this; but they join together to perpetuate the illusion that these are of secondary importance, or simply do not matter. In the representation of community, it is what people have in common that counts. Unsuspecting observers will find themselves led into taking this proposition at face value, to arrive at the conclusion that communities are marked by deep, unshakeable consensus. This creates the potential for a spiral of confusion, through which 'ordinary members' of actual communities feel compelled to declare that their group possesses all the requisite features of a proper community, while outsiders, including social scientists, accept this as confirmation of what a real community is. As we have seen, for a long while, sociologists treated communities as solid, unified, entities because this is what they had been told they were, by influential informants. They adopted the 'folk models' insiders had developed, as authentic statements about community, and then fed them back for public consumption through their writings, adding an extra layer of authority to them. It took a shift towards a different theoretical and methodological perspective to penetrate this fog of mutual mystification. The alteration in perspective is expressed well in the following comment:

> Rhetorically, communities may represent themselves to themselves, as well as to others, as homogeneous and monolithic, as a priori, but this is an idiom only, a gesture in the direction of solidarity, boundedness and continuity. The reality is of heterogeneity, process and change; of cultural communities as diverse symbolizations which exist by virtue of individuals' ongoing interpretations and interactions.
>
> (Amit and Rapport 2002: 7–8)

As Cohen points out, the relevance of the symbolic character of community is that, so long as people do not press the symbols too hard for their precise meaning, they enable the reality of difference to be represented as the appearance of similarity (1985: 21). There is enough flexibility in interpretation to allow individuals to understand the symbols differently, without noticing that they are not in agreement – especially when they want to believe that they are thinking alike.

Cohen insists that no assumptions should be made about the homogeneity of individual meanings; even so, his work can leave an impression that there is a single model of community, and an agreed set of symbols and markers, to which all insiders can sign up, with equal conviction. His examples focus on ways in which communities show themselves to be united, to both insiders and outsiders. Orange Parades, the Notting Hill Carnival, and the Whalsay Spree are ostentatious occasions for the display and celebration of particular conceptions of community, bringing people together in a spirit of mutual recognition, to exhibit their primordial loyalty. They are moments of Durkheimian 'collective effervescence'. Yet, as Frankenberg and others have shown, events like these are also frequently the focus for bickering and recrimination, times when the pent-up frustration and resentments of living together can boil over. Like family weddings and funerals, gatherings which take people beyond the confines of their normal social intercourse can stimulate heightened levels of both solidarity and conflict. At best then we could say that they allow a temporary suspension of the normal disagreements and hostilities which form part of everyday communal existence, and it would be wrong to suppose on this basis that these divisions are not just as germane to the ongoing constitution of community. The missing element in Cohen's account is any sense that the symbols of community, and the meanings ascribed to them, are negotiable, or subject to open dispute, although ample research in both rural and urban contexts demonstrates this to be the case. A case in point is Notting Hill Carnival, and the way it has changed over time, to reflect different, and frequently contentious, versions of the community it represents (Jackson 1988; A. Cohen 1982).

Unity and disunity in village life

The idea of the village as a mental construct, rather than an objective reality, has been taken up by Strathern. In her work on the Essex village of Elmdon (1981; 1982) she finds that residents make a threefold distinction between 'real Elmdon people', villagers, and the rest. These distinctions come into play when certain rights are asserted, such as claims to local housing, and occasionally to jobs. The core group of 'real' Elmdon people belong to a small handful of farm-labouring families. Other villagers may share their occupational status, but lack the same life-long and generational ties to the village. 'Outsiders' include middle-class incomers and commuters. Despite public assertions of its unity, and complete distinctiveness from neighbouring villages, the people of Elmdon set about organizing their notions of the social world in ways which reveal that it is not an integrated community, since the various population segments offer different versions of how it is subdivided. Furthermore, while everyone seems to accept that these different levels of local 'belonging' exist, the boundaries between them are movable. Strathern suggests that when probed they hold surprisingly little substance, and may not even exert much influence over interaction. Yet to sustain them, people set aside some rudimentary facts, such as the existence of close social ties, including intermarriage, between villages. Thus considerable effort is devoted to maintaining a model of village life and organization that is highly selective, and does not reflect an established reality.

Strathern speculates that this system of representations may go back to some earlier pattern of local social stratification, when conceivably it had some validity, and that today it operates as a veiled way of talking about social class, and about relationships with the world beyond the village. The people of Elmdon use their concepts of 'village' and 'community' to distinguish among themselves, to place people, and to evaluate their status, according to the demands of the situation. Sometimes they conceptualize the village as a closed unit, at others they think more in terms of open networks of social relations; this permits them a great deal of flexibility, including the ability to modify their definition of who is, or is not, a 'villager'. In this context, the essence of 'belonging' lies in the ability to set boundaries between mobile and fixed aspects of the community, or what appears to be given and what can be chosen. The core consists of relatively permanent inhabitants; others are mobile, and mobility implies changes in both geography and social status. On the basis of her research, Strathern suggests that anyone expecting to discover a complete 'real village' will be disappointed, but they may well encounter 'considerable commitment to the idea that every village has its vanishing core of "real villagers" (1982: 274) – vanishing, inevitably, because in a mobile society the more closely the core is equated to those whose ties to the village are fixed forever, the smaller this core is destined to become over time. Her description reminds us of Frankenberg's (1957) account of 'Pentre People', Stacey's contrast between traditionalists and non-traditionalists, and a host of other similar classifications, each of which makes specific sense at the level of a given community, but suggests also some general relationships between 'insiders' and 'outsiders', such as the assignment of privileged entitlements to 'core' members, like the ability to speak for, or lay claim to, the community as a whole. This provides people with a motive to gain entry to the core group, if possible, since this will permit them to share these privileges; but it also makes it highly likely that definitions of membership will be subjected to considerable argument.

When Michael Bell studied the Hampshire village of 'Childerley' (1994), his analysis came to centre on the question of how individuals were able to claim and gain access to the most valued local social grouping. They did so by making use of the rural–urban contrast. No matter how dubious its sociological validity, this has been shown to continue to figure strongly in the thought of many ordinary British people (O. Jones 1995; Halfacree 1995), and Bell discovered that it was a fundamental component of the conceptual frameworks used by Childerley's residents. In their minds, rurality was associated with closeness to nature, genuineness rather than artificiality, and the presence of community. Compared to the town, they believed, there was more community feeling in the countryside, where the pattern of life resembled more closely the way things were in the past. A rural village is a place where you can belong. This cluster of ideas led them to anticipate the existence of a distinctive rural lifestyle, and pattern of social relationships (1994: 91). In a village which is within two hours commuting distance of London, this is what had attracted many who had chosen to settle there. Quite obviously, the extensive critical literature on the 'myth' of the rural idyll had not shaken its hold on these individuals. They inhabited a village in the mind which provided them with more than a vague sense of sentimental attachment and rootedness; it came together with a fairly well developed template for social existence, a model of the social relationships and conduct 'proper' to the countryside. The problem for them was that in many ways the real village failed to live up to this ideal. In their view, it did so largely because among the people surrounding them there were those who did not fit the model, but intruded into it in disturbing ways. Among the incomers especially, many failed to conform to the image of the authentic villager.

The incursion of such people and their 'alien' values and attitudes has been a leading theme in writing about the English countryside for many years (Blythe 1969; Pahl 1965; Newby 1979; Murdoch and Marsden

1994) and has been taken up more recently as a prominent issue in Wales, Scotland and Ireland (Cloke *et al.* 1997; Jedrej and Nuttall 1996; Brody 1974). Processes of rural restructuring and counterurbanization have meant the movement of significant proportions of new people into country districts throughout Britain (and increasingly across much of Western Europe as well). Echoing Pahl, more than thirty years before, Bell notes how this means that rural areas now witness some of the most striking encounters between representatives of different social class and status groups, who cannot avoid one another in rural settlements as easily as they might in more urban settings. As the essays in Boyle and Halfacree (1998) so amply demonstrate, the countryside is populated by an increasingly diverse range of social types, who are categorized and classified by a great variety of nicknames and labels. In Childerley, a key social distinction was made between 'city' and 'country' people, who were held to differ in their origins, backgrounds, tastes and aspirations. Country people had a 'natural' belonging to the rural village, whereas city types behaved inappropriately, wanting to 'tidy up' the landscape, or complaining about the lack of urban services and amenities. This contrast did not correlate straightforwardly with more objective differences of occupation, income or previous geographical location; there were 'city people' with no real experience of living in urban areas, while some genuine locals would rather have been part of the urban scene. Remarkably few Childerley residents could claim to have been born locally, or to have any other direct affiliation to the village; but on a variety of grounds, including type of work, birthplace, or interest in certain activities like riding and hunting, some could be marked out as 'country folk', and therefore 'belong' in a sense that others could not. Bell describes numerous symbolic markers, utilized to 'tell' who was rural, and who was not, including the well known term 'green wellie brigade', used to designate 'townies', which shows how even the apparently simple choice of a certain type of footwear could signify that a person's attachment to rural living lacked authenticity.

Since their identities were not fixed on them by any undeniable set of facts, the majority of people in Childerley found scope to demonstrate their 'elective affinity' to particular ways of life. At the same time, villagers often rejected one another's claims to be genuine members of the local community. Definitions of identity became resources to be used in a complicated game of acceptance and rejection, and tested against a range of criteria. For instance, Bell notes that 'communalism' was a prominent aspect of rurality. People were expected to show readiness to participate in village life, by joining its various voluntary organizations. However, there was no unanimity of opinion about this; members of the local working class were not active members of local bodies, but instead regarded them as vehicles through which others, the wealthy and middle class, tried to dominate the village (see also Day and Murdoch 1993; Pahl 1970a). For their part, those who were more formally active criticized other residents for their apathy and lack of interest in village affairs. These attitudes corresponded to wider variations between more formalized, codified lifestyles led by some, and the relaxed norms adopted by others – again, symbolized by whether visitors were expected to used the front door (formal) or back door (informal). As with Strathern, we see from Bell's account how the life of a village community in contemporary rural England is intersected by cleavages of class and lifestyle, which are reproduced conceptually by participants in ways which allow them space to innovate, while managing the boundaries between different social factions. Bell argues that as well as its implied reference to community, the idiom of rural–urban contrast gave Childerley people the means through which they could address complicated issues of class and class distinction, which they were both embarrassed and obsessed by.

In the above examples, variation and division are integral to the nature of community existence. The strength of community does not consist in universal agreement, but in the way in which different social meanings are played off against one another as people position themselves in village life. They do so by aligning themselves imaginatively with those who they feel share and appreciate their meanings, while separating from those who contradict or challenge them. Jedrej and Nuttall (1996: 100) tell us that 'the indigenous view reveals diversity rather than homogeneity'. To outsiders, all locals may seem the same; but to the insider, they are all different. Yet this perception must be balanced against another of their observations, that anyone who claims to lead a community will be compelled to speak in terms of its natural boundaries and inner harmony. This in turn is hard to reconcile with their next claim, that community as a phenomenon is constituted by the gaze and activities of outsiders. Clearly, the answer is that the two perspectives feed off each other, in a kind of counterpoint, while the interplay between insider and outsider viewpoints creates the opportunities for people to exercise a degree of choice, in deciding which to emphasize, similarity or difference (Cloke *et al.* 1998). Consequently, definitions may change to fit the occasion: at times, the community is reduced to an inner core, those perhaps who may have to be deferred to over key judgements and decisions; at others it expands to become generously inclusive, perhaps when support is being rallied against outside threats, or appeals are being made for contributions towards local projects. Jedrej and Nuttall note the bewildering paradox, whereby community 'continually comes into existence so that it can continually decline' (1996: 93); just as likely, it continually disappears, only to be born again as the need arises. The language of incomers and locals is associated with a whole vocabulary of terms, which sets 'rootedness' and 'connection' against 'invasion' and 'colonization'. Research in the field repeatedly illustrates how this way of talking and thinking simplifies distinctions, and stamps rigidity onto relationships that are fluid, and constantly changing (Allan and Mooney 1998).

The process of breaking community down into its constituent meanings is taken further still by Rapport, in his analysis of the Cumbrian valley settlements of 'Wanet' (1993). Noting how many anthropologists still perpetuate a tradition of writing about communities as if they were uniform moral universes, exhibiting deep-rooted behavioural traditions, Rapport contends that Wanet must be seen instead as 'an assemblage of individual lives which influence, overlap and abut against one another in a number of ways' (1993: 43). His commitment to methodological individualism leads him to refuse to countenance that beyond these individuals there is any 'entity' or even social aggregate which corresponds to an emergent collective reality of community. Instead he is interested in capturing how individuals take part in a construction of social experience which is 'endlessly creative, manifoldly fragmented and inherently contrastive' (1993: x). He contends that they do so by participating in an ongoing series of essentially voluntary exchanges (Amit and Rapport 2002: 140). This leads him to undertake an intensive examination of micro-social regularities – habitual pieces of interaction between individuals – which he claims carry varied meanings for participants on different occasions. Community in Wanet consists of the way in which people make personal sense of their relationships, in patterns of repetitive interaction involving the same limited cast of individual characters, and in relations between themselves and various others who can be categorized as belonging to certain external or 'foreign' social types. Since individuals bring their own interpretive abilities to bear on these processes, there is no agreed version of Wanet; a number of 'communities' are under construction, and being lived in, at the same time.

The intimacy of Rapport's analysis is matched by the extremely detailed portraits he gives of individuals and their conversational exchanges. In this, he joins an established tradition of writing about community from the perspective of selected individual characters (for example, Blythe 1969; Seabrook 1971; Parker 1985), which has gained strength as new emphasis has been placed on the connections between community and individual identity (Revill 1993: 129). However, for Rapport, even an individual does not represent a unitary point of view, a particular angle from which the community can be seen; rather, each person is capable of sustaining several distinct ways of looking at the world. These are used to construct varied and flexible responses to situations, so that familiar elements of thought may appear in new and unexpected combinations. In the case of Wanet, these 'world-views' contain recognizable fragments of the rural idyll, the closed community, trust and respect for local people, as well as rationalizations for behaving badly towards those who do not belong. Individuals employ these in their own idiosyncratic and separate ways. However, their views are coordinated to some extent by the fact that they must take note of similar circumstances, such as the increasingly permanent presence among them of large numbers of outsiders ('offcomers' in local parlance). Rapport accepts that in attending so closely to the multiplicity of individual meanings and motivations, he risks underestimating some of the commonalities in the situation, the shared language and familiar contexts that form taken-for-granted background features of a shared existence (1993: 157). Within each individual's social landscape, a place has been prepared for fellow residents, who expect to understand one another; whereas outsiders almost always represent a threat and a challenge. To be local is to employ appropriate local idioms and to interact in locally accepted ways, but even these practices are under continual pressure to adapt to the changes brought about by repeated, unavoidable, encounters with others, who follow different ways and use different idioms. Wanet cannot be seen as a self-contained social world, any more than Elmdon or Childerley, and the sensitivity shown by Rapport to the intricacies of local social relationships is informed by his own progression, from outsider towards partial acceptance as an insider.

Like Cohen, Rapport believes that British society is exceptionally fragmented and pluralistic, and that its individual members journey during their lifetimes between a seemingly infinite number of bounded groups, which somehow manage to preserve an appearance of being closed and introspective, despite the continual turnover of members. This is achieved in part because there is a 'fetish' for maximizing group distinctions, which means that much of life is spent 'exploring and maintaining discriminatory practices and evaluations and wending ways through social landscapes choc-a-bloc with the diversions of division' (1993: 75). The contribution of social anthropology in recent years has been noteworthy for showing how 'community' remains a prime site at which these mobile individuals attempt to manage complex forms of social closure, inclusion and exclusion, to maintain a sense of continuity in the face of change. As Revill (1993: 120) puts it, understanding community as a product of members' meanings directs our interest towards questions such as how it is possible to generate a sense of stability and coherence from a contested terrain in which 'versions of place and notions of identity are supported by different groups and individuals with varying powers to articulate their positions'.

Among rural researchers, the emphasis has swung towards the examination of relationships of conflict and change, and a recognition of the diverse standpoints from which ideas of community can be expressed. Cloke *et al.* (1997: 148) refer to the 'differentialized experiences of belonging, placedness and cultural affinity in rural lifestyles in particular places', which conveys the feeling of a countryside that is inhabited by people who are very much more varied than is often supposed. Likewise Murdoch and Marsden (1994; see also Bradley and Lowe 1984) remind us of the 'specificity of local processes' and the resulting social distinctiveness of different rural localities. Their research carried out within the narrow confines of Aylesbury Vale in Buckinghamshire, an area under tremendous pressure from population growth and housing development, reveals how the direction being taken by different villages, and the kinds of community they are coming to represent, reflects the particular combinations of social groups they contain, and their varying attitudes and aspirations. There is no single perspective associated with newcomers, nor do all established residents react to change in the same ways; actors utilize a range of conceptions of 'rurality', including ideas about the nature of a village and its social character; and their viewpoints incorporate highly localized elements to do with what they know about local history, and social relationships. Because these many points of view meet and coexist within relatively small settlements, they influence one another, and become woven together in elaborate contests about identity, authenticity, and plans for the future. Despite exceptional levels of social and spatial mobility in their study area, Murdoch and Marsden conclude that feelings of attachment to villages and their immediate environments have grown stronger, rather than declining, as might be expected.

Alongside such studies of the rich variety of mainstream social groups who now claim a place in rural society, greater attention is also being given to the excluded and marginalized groups who constitute the rural 'other' (Cloke and Little 1997), including ethnic and racial minorities, travellers, and those with different sexualities, who have been left out of most studies of rural community. Any lingering assumption that village communities are automatically warm and tolerant places has been tempered by the realization that acceptance into them is conditional upon the possession of certain attributes only; readiness to admit some is premised upon the exclusion of others. Understandings of community will be very different among those who succeed in being included than from the viewpoint of those who are left out. In a situation where membership is debated, and struggled over, it has to be acknowledged that there is no uniquely privileged vantage point from which the full story about rural community can be told; instead there is a range of perspectives, each partial and incomplete.

Stereotypes and stigma in urban contexts

While the content may be specific, there is nothing uniquely rural about these processes of symbolic classification and interpretive reasoning. Suttles (1972) reminds us that from the beginning of urban sociology, there was support for a view that the city was a 'state of mind', and a body of customs and traditions (Park *et al.* 1925), as much as a physical reality. Suttles continues this line of reasoning, by seeing the creation of community identities, distinguishing between different populations, as a main way in which people respond to an urban environment. Cognitive maps and images perform an important function in defining their boundaries, creating simplified geographical and social contours, according to the alleged characteristics of different neighbourhoods and groups. Although they exist only 'in tenuous opposition to one another' and earn their reputation by relative rather than absolute differences (1972: 246), neighbourhood identities assume a very definite social reality. An example he discusses is the attitude prevailing among the well educated inhabitants of Chicago's Hyde Park that they differ from their even wealthier, and possibly socially superior, near neighbours by being less snobbish, more cosmopolitan and more socially caring. On the West Side, by contrast, where there are few other differences of note, greater significance was attached to ethnic origins. In each case, there was an element of fabrication, or clarification, of otherwise blurred distinctions; demarcation lines were drawn more sharply than any objective factors would justify. The outcome is 'a set of social categories for differentiating between those people with whom one can or cannot safely associate and for defining the concrete groupings within which certain levels of social contact and cohesion obtain' (1972: 22).

Studies of urban community are riddled with similar processes of discrimination and separation, in which social groups and neighbourhoods are given special names, assigned relative standing, and expected to comply with distinct patterns of behaviour. Zukin (1995) identifies the language of exclusion and entitlement, and social definitions of visibility and concealment, as dimensions of the 'symbolic economy' that has always been inherent within city living. This is exemplified by a close historical study of an exceptionally rough street in north London, noting how everyday social relationships split it to such an extent that travelling from one end to the other could expose a person to danger of physical attack. Yet while it was *lived* largely as two communities, it was *thought* as one, especially in relation to the outside world (White 1986: 79). Children were particularly active in enforcing this sense of collective identity, and made outsiders who ventured into the area unwelcome. Residents took an apparently perverse pride in the street's bad reputation. Roberts (1971) provides similar evidence for his 'classic' Salford slum. Identical themes appear in Damer's (1989) study of a small housing scheme in Glasgow, generally known as 'Wine Alley'. He describes how popular imagery had it that the inhabitants were 'problem people' – prostitutes, criminals, addicts and drunks – whereas evidence showed this applied only to a small minority. By associating such people with this one small area, the rest of the surrounding neighbourhood of Govan was able to borrow an extra degree of respectability. Damer found that the 'problem' label had stuck to the scheme more or less from its inception, and owed something to the feeling that housing had been allocated to the 'wrong' sort of people, incomers from beyond the immediate vicinity. Within months of their arrival, they had been stigmatized, in the most disparaging terms, as violent, immoral, and mentally incompetent. Again, an element in their response was to endorse and try to subvert some of these negative images, for example by celebrating the exploits of local 'hard men'; but of course, in the eyes of outside observers, this merely confirmed that the original labels were deserved. A variety of external agencies, including the media and local government officials, were complicit in ensuring that the district kept its poor reputation for more than fifty years.

These processes do not apply only to the extreme situations of problem areas and sink estates; rather, they represent general features of community formation. Scott (2005) shows how throughout the interwar period and beyond, the development of suburban estates in Britain produced a fine gradation of such 'rough' and 'respectable' communities, whose residents came to believe they upheld radically different social standards, styles of living, and personal and domestic hygiene. Willmott and Young (1960) were not alone in observing how movement to one of these new estates could necessitate a change of lifestyle, towards greater privacy, material display, and well kept gardens, as people learned to conform to new expectations (Durant 1939; Goldthorpe et al. 1969). Of course, considerations of class and status were central to the formation of these patterns, but there was also a more immediate reflection of the symbolic importance attached to the various signs of being the correct sort of person to live alongside, the 'good' neighbour. According to Scott:

> Unacceptable traits included plainness in speech, strong accents, the free use of tabooed words, children who appeared poorly cared for . . . a forthright approach to personal relations, poor standards of housework . . . and a lack of neighbourly reticence.
>
> (Scott 2005: 29)

Individuals who did not accord with these expectations could be offered instruction, pressurized to conform, or pushed out of the area. Scott notes how, in the language of the times, there was strong support for the view that 'decent people should not mix with slum people'. Over time, distinctions crystallized among people who had begun alike, leading communities to grow more homogeneous. This supports Suttles' contention (1972: 171) that the emergence of territorial identities is especially prone to highlight divisions between groups which claim unchallenged domination over their members; before long they start to emphasize antagonistic interests and indulge in a rhetoric of struggle and exclusion.

Damer proposes a Marxist explanation for these divisions. There are real underlying economic and social cleavages between classes and class fractions, corresponding to their involvement in different sets of productive relations, and allocation between a variety of skills. These will be reflected in the composition of communities. But there is also a heavy influence from 'bourgeois ideology', which brings the familiar contrast between rough and respectable working class ways of life into being, and this ideology is so powerful that it penetrates even the consciousness of the working class itself (1989: 152). By enforcing their 'own' definitions of respectability, he suggests, the working class carries out the socially divisive work of its enemies, the ruling class and the state. In this way, while enlightening us about how images and reputations, of people and of areas, are constructed and reproduced at the local level, Damer attributes them to processes that occur well beyond the community itself, within the wider framework of class and state power. Members of the working class who stand to gain from these distinctions are seen as gripped by a kind of false consciousness. The danger in this approach is that it treats those concerned as largely passive victims of external forces, including ideological pressures. While it is true that members of communities draw on a variety of external sources, including the media and popular culture, when forming their images and impressions of different categories of social actors, the thrust of the constructionist argument is that they are also actively engaged in imposing these categories on those with whom they interact, and in modifying and adapting them to suit their local circumstances.

A more local explanation is provided in a classic study by Elias and Scotson (1965). This also involves the observation of processes through which a particular population segment comes to be stigmatized, as socially inferior, unclean, and disposed to crime and delinquency. Again, this reputation was not merited on any objective measure. Its origins were shown to lie with the movement of assorted newcomers, including war-time evacuees, into a small industrial settlement near Leicester. The people already living there immediately closed ranks against the incomers, who were not at all dissimilar socially from themselves, and took steps to exclude them from positions of local influence. The distinction between 'established' and 'outsider' group-ings became synonymous with respectability and roughness, a trick that was accomplished through selective perception, whereby impres-sions of the established group were modelled on the behaviour (real or supposed) of the 'minority of the best', and outsiders were condemned according to the reputation of the 'minority of the worst'. People were receptive to information about the two groups only when it confirmed these preconceptions. Elias terms this a social 'configuration', with its own logic, setting up a dialectic between the groups that imposed itself upon their individual members. Group pressure ensured that among the established residents not a single example could be found of anyone pre-pared to break ranks with the proprieties of the group, or to associate with the outsiders; while less understandably members of the stigma-tized group also seemed to become reconciled to, and believe in, their inferior position.

Elias argues that the power of the 'established' rested with the cohe-siveness they had built up over the years, and their ability to claim to act as guardians of their locality, and its presumed virtues. They froze out the newcomers, who were never able to cooperate well enough to discipline 'their' minority, so responded instead by withdrawing, or by moving away. Far from being a unique local situation, he suggests there are important underlying regularities which make this a microcosm of some basic social processes, through which relatively powerful social groups succeed in imposing their value judgements on others, and even manoeuvre them into behaving accordingly: 'give a group a bad name, and it is likely to live up to it'. Witnessing these processes at work in the restricted context of a small community made them easier to grasp than they would have been in a larger setting. In a later comment (1994: xxviii), Elias says that, once set in motion, the two factions played out the drama like puppets on a string. The study has been hailed for being so far ahead of its time that it could not be assimilated into the sociological mainstream (Albrow 1997: 42). It was prescient in treating mobility as a major influence on the shaping of community, and it provided an exemplary analysis of the erection of symbolic barriers between interacting groups.

The kinds of stereotyping seen in these examples invariably place the 'other', the villains and evil-doers, somewhere else – at the other end of the street, the opposite side of the estate – or else identify them as some other distant group within the community. As Harvey (1993: 23) notes, denigrating the places inhabited by others is a way of asserting the power and viability of one's own location. Distancing can be both spatial and social. Brent explains how the outer housing estate of Southmead in Bristol

> is split off as a disreputable community from outside, by those who construct themselves as safe and respectable. But this splitting continues inside. There are streets thought of as reputable, and streets powerfully imagined as low, within Southmead. And what is most striking ... is how widely young people have the weight of disreputableness loaded onto them.
>
> (Brent 1997: 78)

Damer notes how, when people described behaviour on Wine Alley, invariably the 'junkies' were located as far away as possible. He suggests there is a similarity with the occurrence in some societies of witchcraft accusations, usually levelled at those who are not close neighbours (1989: 143). Neighbours are known, and from time to time their help may be needed; those further away are an unknown quantity, and can be made to fit the label more easily. More generally, direct and personal knowledge can confound stereotypes, so they are applied best to those with whom one does not actually associate. Differences of age, ethnicity, class and 'race' provide ready-made lines of differentiation, which can be elaborated into clichéd expectations of behaviour and moral worth. What is more striking is the ability of people to conjure these differences out of virtually nothing, as a way of defining the limits around their social groupings. The imaginative power of community is such that it can draw people together by attributing wholly fictitious characteristics and intentions to members of outside groups.

THE LIMITS OF CONSTRUCTIONISM

Cohen (1985: 98) offers us a choice between seeing the constituent social relations of community as repositories of meaning for its members, or as a set of mechanical linkages. For him, community exists in the minds of its members, and must not be confused with geographic or sociographic 'fact'; it is subjectively interpretable, but not objectively observable. However, the choice is loaded by his use of the word 'mechanical', to imply that it is deterministic to pay heed to the real social relationships between individuals. Social relationships can be real without being mechanical, and approaching community as if it is entirely symbolic or 'imagined' risks losing sight of the objective grounding of meanings in actual social relations. For example, in Rapport's account of the interactions between two Wanet families, it is impossible to disentangle symbols and meanings from the everyday materiality of their encounters; they think about each other in ways thoroughly permeated by their experiences of farming practices, business activities, questions of privacy raised by noise, smells and views from their neighbours, small social reciprocities and ongoing feuds. As a counterweight to positivist and structuralist efforts to give the notion of community some objective validity, the stress Cohen and others have put upon its symbolic or rhetorical nature is immensely valuable. But such representations do not remain only in the heads of those who uphold them, because they put them into practice in all sorts of ways. Suttles (1972) argues that they are associated especially with social rules about movement, association and avoidance, connected to ideas of risk, safety, trust and danger. Because they serve such purposes, although partly invented, they cannot be dismissed as 'gratuitous fictions'. He suggests that the key question to pose about such conceptions is not whether they are true, but do they work? More to the point, to what effect do they work? What do they achieve?

Meanings may be constructed symbolically, but they have real consequences in terms of social practice and behaviour, for instance in expressing preferences about those with whom individuals may wish to belong, or associate, and stating expectations about how they will behave. As Cloke and Little infer (1997: 7), in the rural context, it would be inadequate to ascribe definitions of different social types simply to the activity of the imagination, without making connections to processes of discrimination, marginalization and exclusion. In situations of group interaction, conceptualizations of community do not concern only those who are within the group; often they are imposed upon members of subordinate or excluded groups, and enforced by a variety of social sanctions, including denial of access to valued local resources and facilities. At its crudest, farmers and villagers who do not want 'new age travellers' taking up residence locally may put huge boulders on potential parking places. In urban contexts as well, the setting of boundaries between groups, whilst marked by symbolic means, has real and lasting effects. The images people form of particular neighbourhoods, or types of community, impact on their decisions about relocation, their expectations about standards of provision of local amenities and services, and their hopes for the availability of social care and support. The impact can be particularly dramatic when such ideas get into the minds of authoritative agencies, like the police or local government officials. In all these ways, the construction of community is an attempt to create and mobilize particular kinds of social relations, and this cannot be achieved by imagination alone. To succeed in their objectives, as Amit and Rapport (2002: 24) comment, those concerned must overcome innumerable difficulties of 'structure, logistics, persuasion, ideology and opportunity'.

7

THE GLOBAL, LOCAL AND COMMUNAL

ENTER POSTMODERNITY

For well over a century, the decline of community, and the loss that this represents to society, has provided one of the more consistent themes of social commentary and public discourse. From the moment that sociologists began to scrutinize the nature of community, some were eager to predict its imminent disappearance. Yet claims for the rediscovery of community, and arguments about its strengths and defensibility, have been almost as commonplace, and the current generation of sociologists is no different in displaying chronically divided opinions. Powerful arguments are adduced to explain why we should accept that we are witnessing the last stages of community's long decay, whereas others invoke precisely the same circumstances as grounds for celebrating its revitalization, or anticipating its rebirth in new and socially more beneficial forms. From all points of view, there is agreement that the boundaries of community, real and perceived, are being stretched and transformed beyond recognition by the major social processes which influence people's lives. These include the various changes described as 'postmodernity' and 'globalization'. Theorists who analyse these large-scale developments usually seek to explain how they impact upon the various social worlds (local, or otherwise bounded) which people inhabit, and invariably this entails developing some thesis about community and its future.

During the last two or three decades, a clamour of voices has proclaimed that the world is changing in previously unknown ways, with
profound implications for social organization. Setting aside for the
moment the often fierce disputes which rage about the exact nature and
causes of this transformation, it is possible to indicate some of its key
features. That the existing social order has undergone major disruption
and fragmentation is widely accepted. Some regard this as a complete
break with established social principles, while others argue that it
merely extends and crystallizes tendencies which have been operating
for a long time. There is a general belief that change has been rapid and
intense enough to throw into question most of the main outlines of social
structure which previously were taken for granted: frameworks of class,
gender, 'race' and ethnicity have ceased to provide the solid building
blocks from which societies can be assembled. As they fall apart, all
kinds of boundaries and distinctions begin to dissolve. The removal of
barriers, and increasing diversity, encourages the coexistence and interpenetration of many different social worlds (Harvey 1989b: 41), and
this is associated with an expanding variety of social perspectives and
meanings. The most popular terms for describing the current state of
affairs include fracturing, division, difference, plurality and heterogeneity. From the point of view of community, three main aspects of these
changes would appear to be particularly relevant: the dissolution of
place; vastly increased mobility; and the destabilization of identities.
Separately and together, many would argue that these developments
undercut the potential for the maintenance of communal relations.

The changing significance of place

The bulk of the preceding discussion has been concerned with the relationship between ideas and practices of community, and particular
places or territories, a preoccupation shared until comparatively recently
by most of the sociological writing about community. Indeed, there are
many who would support still, implicitly if not explicitly, Warren's
(1963) contention that the central focus of interest for community theory, research and action lies with exploring 'the rich web of social interaction based on common locality'. Communities are often described as
place-based, or place-centred. Even those who might want to query the
restriction of community to situations of geographical closure are left

considering the possibility of 'spatially grounded emergent communal-
ity, of the interactions in place of people as being the basis for an emergent collective identity' (Byrne 2001: 72). The link has been so close
that it has been easy for researchers to slip from dealing with community as primarily a social or cultural phenomenon, to identifying it with
geography alone – to regard community as something that is inherently
spatial, or even to equate it with specific kinds of place. We have seen
how this happens in popular imagery, where community is treated as
synonymous with the rural village, or a particular kind of urban street
or neighbourhood. However, it has also been apparent throughout that
these spatial connotations are far from exhausting the possibilities of
community; neither is a shared geography any guarantee that the other
expected features of community will arise. After many years of study, no
inherent connection has been established between place, and the formation of the distinctive sets of social relationships, forms of sentiment, or
conceptions of common identity that are regarded as typical of community (Fischer *et al.* 1977; Wellman 1979).

On the contrary, there is a formidable literature which problematizes
the relationship between space and social formations (Gregory and Urry
1985; Massey 1994; Harvey 2000). Apart from a few rare, unregenerate
geographical determinists, most now would accept that there is a contingent relationship between place and patterns of social life. As theorists from Wirth and Redfield onwards have sought to establish, the
closeness of social ties and the narrowness and similarity of attitudes
found in many traditional communities owed more to their lack of population numbers, homogeneity of social types, and the insulating effects
of distance and remoteness, than to the nature of the place itself.
Although geographical considerations were among the conditioning factors contributing to shaping different kinds of community, they always
worked together with such key social determinants as cultural resources,
systems of social stratification, and types of predominant economic
activity. So while common locality may enable certain things to happen
socially, it does not compel them. This was confirmed by the failure of
attempts to replicate the characteristics attributed to traditional communities in artificially constructed locations.

Furthermore, we have seen that there is a loosening up of those connections between place and community which did appear to hold. For
example, in the case of the contemporary village, where in any case these

bonds may have existed as much in people's imaginations as in real terms, recent research has shown that people who have moved in precisely in order to become part of community life are living side-by-side with others whose major personal social connections, and principal spheres of activity, lie elsewhere. Different groups use the village in different ways, according to their social class, backgrounds, interests and lifestyles. This leads one set of researchers to conclude that, in terms of the presence of a preponderance of people whose lives actually revolve around the locality itself, the village as a 'totally centred' community is dead. It lives only within the nostalgic ethos of a retrospective rural regret (Gorton *et al.* 1998; Harper 1989). This development contributes to what Murdoch *et al.* (2003: 70) describe as the replacement of the stable structures that once seemed coterminous with rural life with a more fluid pattern of social relationships. They cite Wittel (2001: 51), who states, in a classic restatement of the conventional wisdom, that community entails 'stability, coherence, embeddedness and belonging. It involves strong and lasting ties, proximity and a common history or narrative of the collective'. Place is smuggled into this definition, in the guise of proximity; the implication is that members of a community necessarily inhabit a limited common territory. Such features are said to be pre-given: they precede the individual, and negate the possibility of choice. On these grounds, Wittel argues that a fundamental change has occurred, through the expansion of mobility, and the ability of people to transcend the territorial limits of the local. Freed from traditional restrictions, they can now take part in the active construction of their social bonds. According to his definition, this must mean the abandonment of community.

Murdoch *et al.* apply this to rural circumstances, to suggest the formation of new types of social contacts, within 'community networks' that draw together people who share interests. In this context, it is possible to see the symbolic constructions discussed in the previous chapter being deployed as part of the conscious strategies through which groups attempt to impose their definitions of community onto others. Once they have located themselves in the countryside, 'counterurbanisers' will strive to reinforce those 'rural' aspects which fit their preconceptions (Murdoch *et al.* 2003: 71). This may take the form of resisting 'urban' street-lighting, frequenting farm shops rather than supermarkets, or helping organize village fetes or drama groups.

Murdoch *et al.* report that in one Buckinghamshire village no fewer than thirty new groups and societies had been established, fostering an air of vibrant community life. Ironically, many years previously Pahl (1970a) warned that in seeking to recreate community in their own image, incoming groups, like mobile middle-class commuters, risked destroying whatever vestiges of community still remained. However, like Wittel's argument, this judgement relied on measuring change against a fixed view of what constituted a true rural community. More accurately, one could say that the newcomers hope to become part of, or to appropriate, community, and in doing so inevitably they introduce changes. Throughout the record of writing about rural communities, such people have been held to be responsible for promoting formal organizations, and rendering leadership roles explicit, where formerly a spirit of egalitarianism and informality prevailed, thus encouraging movement along the continuum from *Gemeinschaft* towards *Gesellschaft* (Rees 1950; Pahl 1965). As modern, 'reflexive' individuals, they probably know what they are doing; borrowing ideas about community from a stockpile of cultural resources and socially acquired impressions, they do their best to turn them into realities. This includes the conception of community as a place that is active, and participatory, where people join organizations and do things together.

Urry (1995; see also Lash and Urry 1994) contextualizes this as part of an aesthetic impulse, to bring social life more in line with dominant representations, upheld by actors who exercise considerable skill in the interpretation and evaluation of social practices. As knowledgeable subjects, they reflect upon their conditions of social existence. Urry states that this presupposes extensive mobility, and the ability to make judgements about different places and societies, past and present. It also assumes that those involved have the capacity to bring about the changes they desire. Newby (1979: 167) identified how newcomers brought with them strong views about the desirable social and aesthetic qualities of the village, which he saw as conforming to an 'urban' perspective: villages should be picturesque, ancient and unchanging. Hence they objected strenuously to modern agricultural practices which were not in keeping with these preferences. Through their efforts, country villages, like desirable urban districts, undergo 'gentrification' which turns them into attractive, well-maintained, and commercially valuable sites for the enactment of various 'tasteful' and socially prestigious behaviours. This may preclude the development or continuation of other activities which are deemed to interfere with the preferred outcome; for instance, small industrial enterprises which create noise or mess are unlikely to be viewed favourably, even if they are economically important to some fellow residents. Established features of local life which have no place in the new aesthetic may be eliminated – notorious rural examples include protests about noise from animals, and complaints about mud dropped by farm machinery. In urban situations, there are parallel concerns with having the right kinds of local restaurants, shops and clubs, and observing appropriate patterns of neighbourly civility. The importance attached to these aspirational conceptions of community living helps explain why interest in local matters can be intense among those who appear to have no actual 'roots' in the place. As Urry points out, places become things to be consumed, able to provide people with certain satisfactions, closely connected to their sense of personal identity. Instead of determining how people live, as used to be supposed, places serve as arenas for the realization of particular lifestyles, and are constructed socially to deliver what is required of them. Rather than making people what they are, places can be made, or re-made, to serve particular purposes, and great effort is devoted to advertising and marketing what different places can offer, incorporating the outcomes of these local processes of place-construction and reconstruction.

The disembedding of community

The preceding lines of argument receive much support from contemporary social theorists. Beck (1992) is bold enough to proclaim the demise of traditional forms of community beyond the family. As ascriptive ties of class, race, ethnicity and gender are loosened, he suggests, the limitations and disciplines associated with established neighbourhoods and settlements grow weaker, and people gain greater freedom to make their own choices. There is also more mixing of people from different backgrounds and cultures. This gives individuals the opportunity to develop their own social ties, and build their own social networks, bringing about 'new historical possibilities for self-formation'. Individual choice and reflexivity mean that henceforth social ties will have to be 'established, maintained and constantly renewed by individuals' (1992: 97). Among the possibilities which arise is the rediscovery of neighbourhoods and communal living arrangements, but this time round individuals will participate more actively and consciously in their creation than they could in the past. These features are integral to the formation of a more individualized, 'detraditionalized' form of society, in which people are compelled to make themselves the centre of their own planning and conduct of life. They must select between options, including choosing whether to identify themselves with certain groups or subcultures.

Amidst the search for new kinds of personal and social identity, Beck sees scope for the production of new forms of community. Individualization need not always imply dispersion and fragmentation: in fact, there are significant pressures towards standardization, and the emergence of socio-cultural commonalities which bind individuals together; these include social movements and citizens' groups, whose effectiveness, now that people are liberated from the constraints of place, may not depend upon physical proximity. Wittel (2001) argues that this encourages the replacement of an 'old and out-of-fashion' model of community with relationships that are far more open-ended. He envisages communities as closed social systems, not unlike formal organizations, with clearly defined boundaries. Their disappearance exposes people to contacts which are short-term, but often intense. Maintaining an effective personal network requires a different style of sociality. Wittel illustrates this by examining how individuals 'network' deliberately with one another, in the new media industries, through electronic communications, and at parties and social events. Wellman (2001) argues similarly that community is to be found now in certain kinds of network arrangements, and not among solidary groups.

Behind this account of some immediate forms of social change lies a much deeper narrative, which Wittel reveals when he writes about how communities have been emptied of their meaning by the impact of modernization. Now he suggests a further phase of social disintegration is taking place, as major structures collapse, leaving society 'flattened' and thinned out. As a result of these processes, people are '"lifted out" of their contexts and reinserted in largely disembedded social relations, which they must at the same time continually construct' (Wittel 2001: 65). The reference to disembedding is taken from Giddens (1990), who uses it to indicate the process whereby social activity becomes detached from localized contexts, to be reorganized across larger stretches of space and time. He regards this as a key feature of late modernity, where increased levels of mobility and new forms of communication have undermined the standing of the local community, as a place where relationships of trust and mutual support could be relied upon. Denied knowledge of individuals as fellow members of a community, greater reliance must be placed upon abstract systems of information and expertise. Giddens provides us with the image of relationships being stretched indefinitely, linking places and populations that formerly were unconnected. Harvey (1989b) talks instead of the compression of time and space, as the world seems to 'collapse inwards' upon us. Both have in mind how boundaries are transgressed, or removed, so that elements which 'belong' in one place can turn up in another, in the way that high street shops in advanced economies are stuffed with 'ethnic' goods extracted from other cultures, or supermarkets perpetually display 'exotic' fruits and vegetables, out of season and out of place. Prominent among the displaced elements are people who supposedly belong elsewhere.

The theme of mobility and its repercussions has been taken up by Lash and Urry (1987; 1994), who argue first that contemporary capitalism has become 'disorganized', and disorganizes everything else, so that nothing is fixed, or certain; second, that this plays its part in creating a world that is 'amazingly mobile', and structured into a complex pattern of flows and movements, consisting mainly of the transfer of signs and symbols from one place to another. Ideas, objects and people circulate on an international scale, covering greater distances, at a faster pace than ever before. Modern communication technologies enable direct and immediate contact with people on the other side of the world. Increasingly this means that images, information and commodities are available anywhere and anytime, from any part of the world (Albrow 1997: 44). The escalation of mobility to a qualitatively new level means that we live in a society, or form of social order, that is on the move, built for discontinuity rather than stability. The increased pace and intensity of movement make it harder to distinguish between places, or to remain deeply attached to any of them. Hypermobility, and the penetrability of time–space boundaries, leads to collapse of the framework of relatively solid structures within which social life was once organized. This includes dissolution of the hierarchy of social classes, generational and gender classifications, and bounded geographical units. Society is characterized as becoming 'fluid' (Urry 2000) or 'liquid' (Bauman 2000). According to Harvey, these changes induce a 'sensation of disruption and incoherence in the framing of social life' (1989b: 193) which leaves people searching for meaning and reassurance. These are among the critical features attributed to the condition of postmodernity.

Since communities have been regarded as relatively well established, continuous and stable structures, it is to be expected that the consequences for them will be dire. They represent the 'old' social order, and are unlikely to be able to withstand the pressures of transition to the new. The disappearance of distinctive communities would form part of the 'hollowing out' of society, as the growing dominance of abstract and generalized media of communication and exchange empties existing relationships of their particularity, and meaning. As an example, Giddens (1990) mentions the separation of place from space: places lose their individual meaning and become 'increasingly phantasmagoric' as they are permeated and shaped by distant social influences. Meanwhile people move through space, indifferent to the places they occupy. Various authorities have pointed to the sensation of 'placelessness' as a feature typical of modern life (Relph 1976; Meyrowitz 1985; Kunstler 1993). These changes are said to have radical consequences for personal and collective identity, undermining the foundations on which people once rested their sense of continuity and security. For most, the local community formed an important component of identity, shoring up security, in that it provided a relatively constant social and material environment within which people and things could be relied upon. Its stability underpinned relationships of trust and reciprocity. The disruption of community is a major contributory factor to the state of 'ontological insecurity' Giddens describes. On the other hand, it could be said that the removal of constraints sets individuals free to act as agents of their own destiny, enabling them to contemplate new forms of social organization and activity; as structures melt down, agency takes power (Lash and Urry 1994: 4–5).

The thrust of these arguments would seem to indicate that the whole world is hurtling towards a state of uniformity, in which everybody consumes the same things, thinks the same thoughts, and is at the mercy of the powers of global corporations and big governments. As increasing amounts of movement occur across national and local borders, variations are levelled out, societies become increasingly homogeneous, and differences between societies erode. This is how some interpret the effects of globalization (Ohmae 1991; 1996; Fukuyama 1999). Such a conclusion would be reminiscent of the way certain evolutionary sociologists have argued, from the origins of the discipline. Indeed, although these arguments come loud with proclamations of their originality, they reproduce many of the themes contained in the long record of assertions about the decline of community. As we have seen, even the classic literature was forced to grapple with expectations that rural-urban distinctions and variations between class and lifestyle communities would be submerged eventually by the impact of homogenized 'mass' society. As early as 1893, Durkheim was arguing that the price to be paid for the growing unification of society, through such means as increased travel and more efficient communications, was a loss of collective consciousness, and a weakening of the power of local public opinion. Popularizing such sociological ideas, Packard (1972) described the United States as a 'nation of strangers' where people no longer felt connected to one another, or to places, owing to the breakdown of community living. Nisbet (1953) said this left personal relations morally empty and psychologically baffling. Berger *et al.* (1973) attributed various distressing consequences, including alienation and mental illness, to modern people's sense of homelessness. Similar sentiments can be traced back almost indefinitely through social history (see Fischer *et al.* 1977; Williams 1975). Consequently there must be reservations as to how new and decisive these influences are, or whether it is a case of presenting some rather tired wine in freshly labelled bottles.

RECONSTITUTING THE LOCAL

Among those who pursue this line of thought about more contemporary processes of change there is some agreement that what they are describing is not a unilinear pathway, destined completely to eliminate key social distinctions. This is because there are countervailing forces at work, including the power of individual agency. The capacity to resist universalizing and globalizing forces hinges considerably on the ability of individuals to inject new meaning into their social universes, to reconstruct local differences, and to find ways of reconstituting community. This justifies adopting an attitude of scepticism towards the alleged inevitability of some of the proposed theoretical linkages. When

Fischer and colleagues examined similar claims back in the 1970s, they found that the removal of the constraints tying people to places did not necessarily weaken their sense of local belonging; often indeed they showed signs of stronger commitment, because it was chosen rather than forced. Being able to make choices compensated for the loss of an imposed sense of attachment. For Fischer therefore, 'rootlessness is far less of a problem in modern life than is powerlessness to decide where to plant one's roots' (1977: 186). Also, 'attachment' to place proved to have a number of distinct dimensions, which were not always tightly correlated; they included organizational membership, institutional ties, sociability and affective feelings. This meant people could feel attached to a neighbourhood, or engage in some of its activities, without necessarily liking it, or needing to people it with their social intimates. Fischer concluded that there was no convincing evidence for an overall long-term decline in attachment to place, or in communal sentiments.

Instead, there was potential for greater selectivity in personal connections, as individuals developed their social networks by exercising choice, within a framework of changing constraints. They could respond by strengthening their local ties, or they might prune back their relationships, to maintain fewer, but conceivably deeper, contacts with others at a distance. As well as the maintenance, or even reinforcing, of locality-based relationships, this gave scope for the formation of 'non-place communities'. When compared to the multi-faceted, circumscribed relationships associated with more traditional communities, it was unavoidable that considerable debate would be stimulated as to whether these alternative arrangements represented an 'authentic' form of communal living. There are those, such as Wellman (2001), who entertain little doubt on this score. Defining community in terms of networks of interpersonal ties that provide sociability, support, information, a sense of belonging and social identity, Wellman comments that these properties are not limited to village or neighbourhood networks; rather, there is a proliferation of new types of community networks, some of which are quite independent of place.

Nor should we assume that global forces are necessarily fatal to place-based relationships. Giddens notes how sometimes social bonds can be re-embedded, tied back to local conditions of time and place; for instance, the maintenance of trust among individuals who otherwise are strangers, rather than already known and familiar, may require that on occasion they meet face-to-face, to allow them the chance to test and validate their integrity. In a depersonalized world of movements, direct contact with others may acquire an added value. The example Wittel gives of speed dating, though promiscuous and frenetic, at least has the advantage over meetings conducted impersonally via electronic chat rooms that participants can see and assess one another's demeanour. There are numerous situations in which a visible presence and direct personal interaction are required to access unwritten codes of belonging and acceptance: for instance, young people's knowledge of how to act, dress and speak when 'hanging out' on the street (O'Byrne 1993).

As with the argument put forward by theorists of economic and social restructuring, that rather than removing local differences entirely it made use of, and at times even magnified, them, so globalization may work to preserve and promote certain variations. It may encourage, rather than destroy, differentiation. Robertson (1995) coined the term 'glocalization' to catch the extent to which awareness of global developments could go hand-in-hand with a new sensitivity to local difference, while Lash and Urry refer to 'globalized localization', the apparently contradictory development in which the global system requires the concentration of certain activities at specific places – such as near to global cities, or in mutually supportive clusters. Differentiation and variety are a vital part of the globalization process; for example, tourism, as a major global industry, relies on the sense that people are visiting places that are different and novel (Urry 1995); but at the same time, they may expect to find there things that are familiar, and with which they feel comfortable, such as global chains like McDonalds, Starbucks or Hilton Hotels. There are powerful forces making for the standardization of everyday life, but there are also benefits from maintaining something exceptional. Establishing one's niche in the global environment may be the key to economic and social survival. In the world of books, most large towns will have their brand-name bookstores, but in Wales the town of Hay-on-Wye has achieved international prominence and distinctive character as an entire locality dedicated to books and bookshops, with an accompanying literary festival. Thus it is premature to write off the importance of place altogether, or to suppose that communities can float entirely free from the spatial disposition of limits and opportunities.

The ambiguous place of community

These uncertainties with regard to future developments surrounding community and place are demonstrably significant for some leading theorizations of contemporary change. Contrary to the expectation that globalization must eradicate differences, Featherstone (1993: 175) posits an alternative scenario, that it sensitizes us to a 'differentiated world in which particularities become more evident'. Through increased contact, we learn about many kinds of 'others', whose identities differ from our own. Some of these indeed move closer to us, either physically, or through the media of communication, and by their differences challenge our own sense that what we do, or believe, is 'natural' or normal. Featherstone suggests that one likely reaction is fear, and a 'disturbing sense of engulfment and immersion' (1993: 174), which could encourage a retreat towards the felt securities of ethnicity, fundamentalism and tradition. We know that contact with differences can encourage stereotyping, stigmatization and the building of communal walls. On the other hand, it can foster the kind of tolerant 'postmodern' sensibility which welcomes, values and even celebrates difference and otherness, and tries to build upon them in positive ways. There are those who revel in the sensation of being part of a social setting that is diverse, cosmopolitan, multicultural. The forces of globalization may work to undermine the foundations of communal life; yet in response we may see the strengthening of local alliances and identities (Fisher and Kling 1993; Hall 1993). Bauman (1992: 134) associates postmodernity and self-conscious agency with a 'lust' for community.

Other prominent commentators identify a similar range of possibilities. In his monumental study of the rise of the 'network society' (1997), Manuel Castells accepts that the pressures of globalization and new communicative technologies threaten to overwhelm shared social identities. Left unchecked, these processes would tend to dissolve society as a meaningful social system, to produce a world consisting only of individuals, markets and networks. Unless ways can be found to rework them into new organizational and cultural forms, he believes the primary bonds of community, family and ethnicity will lose all significance. However, rather than a passive acceptance of these tendencies, Castells observes that there has been an extraordinary upsurge in efforts to formulate and express new collective identities, including strong reassertions of the importance of community. Picking up the threads of his earlier research, he contends that this occurs primarily through the mobilization of urban social movements; hence the paradox of increasingly local political activism, in a world structured by global processes. As people struggle to exert an influence over their living conditions, cultural identifications, and political involvements, their resistance to the forces of individualization and social atomization leads them to cluster into movements and organizations that, allowed time, can generate feelings of belonging, and ultimately of communal identity. In fact, for Castells, the construction of communities has become the most important type of identity-building activity in contemporary societies, and often this means attempts to reinstate something like the traditional patterns of social organization. Hence, '[w]hen networks dissolve time and space, people anchor themselves in places and recall their historic memory' (Castells 1997: 66).

Castells repeatedly emphasizes that this kind of identity is generally defensive, involving a step back towards various forms of essentialism, that rely heavily on claims about the inherent bonds bequeathed to people by biology, geography or history. This might be seen as an atavistic gesture towards past determinisms. It has an even darker side, in the demands made for immediate collective self-gratification, for example, by gangs pursuing turf wars, a condition Castells refers to as 'hyper-individualism'. This suggests that many of the communities being produced today in response to globalization and its pressures are engaged in greedy attempts to turn back the clock, and re-establish privileges to which they believe they are entitled. This feeds into contemporary concerns with the rise of various forms of fundamentalism that invoke obligations towards particular communities, and elevate their claims to a position of primordial importance (see, for example, Barber 2003). Castells sees a danger that societies will fragment into a 'constellation of tribes, sometimes euphemistically renamed communities' (1997: 9). But there is a more positive prognosis, in the development of forms of 'project identity', which are forward-looking, and socially transformative; the new social movements are prominent in promoting such identities. The tensions between the two possibilities are represented well in the environmental movement, where literally thousands of small-scale protective groupings, pursuing immediate local interests, share some common ground with other larger, more outward-looking movements, able to take a global view of collective needs and interests, and mobilized for joint action beyond narrow territorial limits. Lash and Urry (1994: 6) also look to the ecological and other social movements of the late twentieth century for evidence of 'new' communities.

David Harvey expresses similarly ambiguous feelings about the role and value of community, an omnipresent concept in his writings on urban change and experience (1989a; 1989b; 1993). He describes how, throughout the entire modern era, stress has been laid on the erosion of geographical barriers, brought about by the spread of universal influences of various kinds. Harvey attaches particular significance in this regard to the power of money, and relationships of capitalist production and exploitation. Yet at the same time, new social meanings have been explored and developed, nurturing the emergence of alternative kinds of local identification. Rather than operating as polar opposites, therefore, particularism and universalism often run side-by-side. The more recent period has seen an intensification of time-space compression, but with similar effects. Despite the pressures making for assimilation and integration, a heightened stress has been put on the specialness of different places, which increasingly compete with one another, and therefore must signal their unique qualities to would-be consumers and investors. This sets a premium on the conscious construction of difference in relation to place. In the same way, the search for reassurance and meaning in the face of constant change and ephemerality leads people to hunt for new forms of community and stability. One symptom of these processes is an explosion of writing about place and localism (Harvey 1993).

For Harvey, the local provides always a possible material basis for the formation of political consciousness and action. In his view, it has relevance especially for the less powerful groups in society, who hope to exert some control over events in their immediate vicinity; consequently places still have the potential to act as reservoirs for collective action, and for the formation of oppositional movements, among those who are 'relatively empowered to organize in place, but disempowered when it comes to organizing over space' (1989b: 303). Of course, this hints at the possibility that not all sections of society are affected equally by the direction of contemporary change.

Harvey doubts, however, whether many of the contemporary forms of constructed, and often highly artificial, communities are sufficiently 'authentic' to guarantee the security and deep sense of belonging once associated with place (1993: 17). Unlike the banal marketing slogans and contrived descriptions that often attach themselves to such manufactured places, the meanings identified with genuine communities tend to be profound, and often inexpressible; to understand them, they must be experienced as they are by those who belong. This is why their loss is so threatening to social 'being' and identity. Nevertheless, despite their increasing shallowness, Harvey accepts that place-based identities continue to provide some of the most pervasive bases for social and political mobilization, taking both progressive and reactionary forms; and they are especially powerful when conflated with other important social differences, like those of class, religion, or ethnicity.

While he recognizes the importance of local mobilization for poor and marginalized groupings, including sexual and ethnic minorities, Harvey leaves little doubt that he is perturbed by the propensity for community formation to take the reactionary route towards exclusionary territorial behaviour and parochialism. The negative connotations of community, as it is articulated by conservative and repressive thinking, tend to outweigh its more positive attributes. As with Castells, Harvey's intellectual roots in Marxism ensure that he finds commitment to 'community' a poor substitute for engagement with political movements that are capable of bringing about genuine large-scale social transformation. Identities based upon place and community are inevitably fragmented, and therefore cannot bear the burden of historical change (1989b: 303); they also depend upon some construction of the past, and the 'motivational power of tradition', which is difficult to sustain in any convincing way in a world of flux and mobility. Instead, tradition and the memory of place itself become something that more and more is manufactured and artificial (see Dicks 2000; Hewison 1987). Despite these shortcomings, Harvey concedes that the drive for security in a world of risk and uncertainty will ensure that there can be no end to the readiness to turn towards community, and even towards the strengthening of certain localistic commitments.

Globalism versus community

According to Byrne (2001: 70) the idea of community has always implied spatial stability and a high degree of spatial closure. This is in keeping with Harvey's image of community as a set of relatively autonomous social relations, contained within roughly given territorial boundaries, able to present its members with a knowable world, of time-honoured routines of life (1989b: 240). Tellingly, however, Harvey has in mind the condition of European feudalism, subsequent to which he would argue the pressure to open up such spaces to global influences has been relentless. The notion of community as a geographically delimited social system has come in for much criticism because it appears to deny the possibility of mobility. It gives the impression of a static population, with minimal contact with the outside world. No wonder Byrne regards community as the complete antithesis to the kind of globalized world which many believe we now inhabit. Featherstone makes the same point about the notion of a local culture, which he says is perceived usually as a particularity which is the opposite of the global (1993: 174). Because such notions seem to have so little bearing on current reality, critics have queued to join Stacey (1969) in rejecting them. A prime example is Martin Albrow, a leading theorist of globalization, who challenges the one-to-one relationship that has been assumed to exist between communities, cultures and territories.

Together with colleagues, Albrow has been involved in a study of the London borough of Wandsworth, to assess the impact of globalization upon local social relations (Eade 1997). They conclude that globalization renders conventional description in terms of neighbourhood and community redundant. According to Albrow, this is reflected in the discomfort ordinary people show when faced with such terms. Indeed, absorbing the effects of globalization is said to demand a wholesale retooling of social, and sociological, concepts, especially their abstraction from any territorial point of reference. Harvey makes a similar point (1989b: 218) when he alleges that a whole string of terms, including city and country, region, locality, neighbourhood and community, have become 'infected' with a nostalgia for the past through which they conjure up place-bound images which fail to match contemporary realities. These conceptual issues reflect the uncertainties surrounding social and cultural theories as core terms start to 'lose themselves in a world of free-floating signification' (Keith and Pile 1993: 6). In a tacit rebuttal of Cohen's work (1985) on the importance of community, Albrow asserts that there is no reason to treat local influences as primordial, or more 'real', because local solidarities can be produced by global processes. The shift towards seeing communities as 'imagined' enables one to understand better the part played by relationships at a distance in determining how the local is perceived. The extent to which imagined connections serve as guiding principles for actual lived social relations shows that '[c]ommunity is in the process of being disembedded . . . to the extent that we can identify its reconstitution on a non-local, non-spatially bounded basis' (1997: 25).

Albrow equivocates somewhat as to whether this means that community is finished as a term, or set to take on a new lease of life more suited to global circumstances. Reviewing existing literature, he notes how it tends to exclude from consideration the movement of people between communities, and their involvement in relationships extending beyond the boundaries of their locality, especially through trade and commerce. Connections with the outside world are systematically ignored. Thus in classic studies of rural community, the social structures delineated seem ill equipped to cope with the existence of mobile individuals, including visitors and tourists; while descriptions of urban communities, like Hoggart's (1957) account of working class Leeds, depict a rhythm of life 'undisturbed by events or outsiders' (Albrow 1997: 41). More recent studies stand accused likewise of failing to make the necessary connections with developing patterns of external relationships, and specifically with processes of globalization. Despite his praise for their ground-breaking work, even Elias and Scotson (1965) are criticized for centring their analysis of shared understandings and interdependencies on a common geographical site, thus anchoring community too firmly to locality. Albrow believes they let slip a golden chance to break this connection, which would have opened the way for others to think about 'locality without community and cultures without locality' (1997: 42). Their readiness to accept social and geographical mobility as normal phenomena should have enabled them to reconceptualize community, as a contingent, even ephemeral, configuration.

In defence of Elias and Scotson, it could be said that nothing about their analysis suggests that the pattern of social relationships they observed was a *necessary* outcome of local conditions. Also, the fact that Elias regards the discriminatory processes at work as generalizable societally, to forms of racial and ethnic relations, means that neither is there a necessary connection to place as such. The formation of the established/outsider pattern described requires some type of regularized social contact between unequally powerful social groupings. Arguably, therefore, place matters for their argument only because, on this particular occasion, it ensured the routine connection between groups which stimulated them to form collective images and stereotypes. Similarly, in many other studies of community place is no more than the staging-ground for the operation of social processes. Albrow is on stronger grounds in highlighting the importance of movement for Elias and Scotson's study, since the process they describe was driven by the attempt to assimilate new, 'foreign' elements into an existing state of affairs. In much of the available material on how conceptions of community are constructed, it is the presence of mobile individuals, or contacts with outsider groups whose influence crosses some boundary-line, that encourages people to routinize and typify the distinctions between insiders and outsiders (Jenkins 1996). Indeed, Bauman (2001a) contends that it is only when they perceive that there is something outside and beyond it that people reflect upon and speak about community; in 'real' communities, when there is no external threat or internal division, there would be no explicit community consciousness.

Apart from rendering true community inert, as part of an unreflective natural order, this claim ignores the fact that few if any of the communities actually studied by sociologists have come anywhere near fitting this description, of a completely closed social world. Even the most remote and ancient of them has existed in a situation where there was contact and exchange with the wider society, and the world beyond. As Wellman (2001) points out, there is plenty of historical evidence for connectivity across large distances, for instance by bands of travellers, soldiers, huntsmen, merchants and prostitutes, who by their roaming linked communities together. Rapport (1993) observes how all the supposedly 'closed' rural communities studied by anthropologists have maintained some trading connections with far distant places; contrary to appearances, they were not self-contained, subsistence economies. He also notes how it has been argued successively that community would be destroyed forever by the bicycle, the car, and the telephone, yet these challenges have been absorbed. The adaptability of small communities to mobility and change is confirmed by Byrne's (2001) account of how nineteenth-century relatives who emigrated from a remote rural home in County Sligo managed to stay in touch with one another, and with their community of origin, from their new locations in England, Australia and North America. Other parts of rural Ireland have benefited extensively from the remittances of expatriate workers, and the enthusiasm and expenditure of tourists (Brody 1974). In the same way, over many years, the small and seemingly isolated Welsh country communities studied by Rees and others supplied the coalfields of industrial Wales with much of their muscle power, and gained from the money and goods that they sent back (Davies and Rees 1960; Day 1998).

As with images of social harmony and order, an exaggerated impression of the enclosed nature of traditional communities forms part of the mythology that generates such a potent sense of subsequent transformation and decline. It serves Albrow's purpose to project this impression, to highlight the differences made by globalism. From his observations in contemporary Wandsworth, Albrow concludes that there is no way of aggregating the individual orientations of its residents into a composite image of community. The diverse nature of the inhabitants, many of whom probably are passing through the area as short-term residents, means that they exist within their own distinctive networks of social relations, spread across widely varying spatial horizons and spans of time. Each occupies a private bubble or 'sociosphere' (1997: 51) from which they can view the locality, and judge whether or not it provides them with some version of community. Some relate only to their nearest neighbours, while others maintain regular connections with friends and relatives in distant lands and cultures. Many appear quite indifferent to place, whereas others find Wandsworth an acceptable location from which to position themselves in relation to world events. As their paths cross, so they form impressions of how others live – for instance, that there are closer social ties among Asians than among whites. Through practices of accommodation and avoidance, they contrive to coexist without impinging too much upon one another; like airplanes on different flight paths, their social worlds are stratified, to avoid collisions. Therefore it is impossible to equate the area with a homogeneous local culture, or characteristic style of life. Albrow offers this as a vision of a new form of existence, the globalized locality.

Albrow's analysis is close to arguments Massey has advanced about the variable geometry of contemporary localities (1993; 1994). To begin with, she mounts a robust defence of the value of local studies. She notes how some commentators object to a focus on local matters, because they feel it diverts attention from questions of more fundamental importance. Her response is that, if properly approached, a concern with the local or 'micro' level can be just as enlightening as more macro analyses; it also needs to be equally informed by theory, so it is mistaken to dismiss it as merely descriptive empiricism (Smith 1987). These arguments have been applied in a similar fashion to a preoccupation with community. Like community, the term 'local' attracts disapproval because it is associated with exclusivity, particularism, even with selfishness. Massey points out that among these critics is Harvey, with his challenge to the 'fetishisms' of locality, place or grouping (1989b: 117). Harvey's scepticism is addressed to postmodernist excesses which encourage uncritical celebration of anything that is different. He contends that this leads to an acceptance of reified statements about place and social divisions. Massey shares his distaste for 'essentialist' definitions which try to fix a single meaning and identity onto places, and develops instead an alternative conception, of places as meeting points for intersecting networks of social relations. As might be expected from her earlier account of spatial divisions of labour, she regards these networks as having been constructed over time, laid down across one another, to interact, decay, and be renewed (1994: 120). Because they coincide in space, they generate outcomes which otherwise might not have happened. Because they interact, conflict is highly probable. Because they extend beyond the locality, it is not possible to determine strict geographical boundaries, or understand locality without examining its external connections. Such considerations rule out the possibility of attaching a definitive meaning to a place: meanings are always multiple, held by different social groups, and subjected to negotiation and debate (see also Wright 1985; O'Byrne 1993). Depending on whose point of view you take, and which set of social relations or processes you choose to emphasize, the meaning of a place will change, as will the nature of the local community.

The significance of the external relationships is that '(t)he global is in the local in the very process of formation' (Massey 1994: 120). In her own neighbourhood of Kilburn, for example, there are very strong connections with Ireland, but also with the Middle and Far East; in an 'English' space, Irish Catholics mingle with Hindus and Muslims. Kilburn is a place with great and distinctive 'character', but it signifies different things to people according to where they are located within 'particular constellations of social relations, meeting and weaving together' (1994: 154). As Massey indicates, the diversity of perspectives they bring to their area ensures that no automatic connection can be made between Kilburn and nostalgia or timelessness. Surveying localities like this leads Albrow to ask where 'community' is to be found; the answer, he decides, is possibly nowhere. He represents this as a new situation, demanding a new vocabulary and body of theory. Yet, while the ability to communicate across spatial differences has increased immeasurably, and there is greater immediacy of contact at a distance, it is questionable whether life in Wandsworth is really so very different from the inner city and cosmopolitan situations explored previously by writers like Gans, Suttles, and Rex and Moore. Nor does the fact that it is located within a global city make it so very unlike the contexts of ethnic and racial mixing to be found in more 'provincial' places like Bradford, Leeds or Oldham. Either globalization is everywhere, or it is a less dramatic break with the past than Albrow suggests.

Furthermore, Albrow recognizes, like Massey, that processes of disembedding and time-space compression possess very different consequences for different social groups. He mentions the 'single yuppie' and 'the unemployed lad next door', while Massey brings it home with the image of the person who waits by a bus stop, returning from shopping at the local store, while overhead a plane carries a neighbour on a business or holiday trip to a foreign country. With some assurance, we can predict that the person travelling by bus is likely to be older, poorer, female, and more place-bound. While it is true that people are participating now in a widening range of diverse global processes, in the majority of cases they still have their feet firmly on the ground, anchored into place. In his study of working class Londoners, O'Byrne (1993) met young people who hardly ever left the limits of their estate, and who showed no knowledge of other parts of London, or its emblematic landmarks. It might seem that globalism had passed them by, except that beyond doubt their music and clothing would be deeply inscribed by external influences. O'Byrne reminds us that all working class cultures, and all communities, have been shaped by an interplay between local and non-local forces. Relationships between insiders and outsiders have always been at their core. Greater awareness of global developments and relationships did not prevent those he interviewed from expressing fierce local loyalties. Their sense of community, and what it represented, remained strong, and they were well aware of the many pressures working against it. The maintenance of community life in the area represented a fragile social achievement, the construction of 'a tentative social order in a world of flows' (1993: 74); even so, most of those questioned retained a definite sense of place and belonging. Amidst the pressures of globalizing forces, 'community' still figured for many as an indispensable tool with which to try to make sense of how society worked, and where they belonged within it.

THE COMMUNITARIAN IMPULSE

Warnings about the perils of community abound in the literature on postmodernity. Castells (1997: 66) discerns a readiness to flee towards undifferentiated cultural communes, as actors attempt to protect themselves from the challenges of pluralism and flexibility, by shrinking their world back to more manageable proportions. Harvey (1989b: 351) fears an inevitable slide into parochialism, myopia and sectarianism. In these accounts, community stands for a narrow, controlled, homogeneous social formation; its instincts are authoritarian and repressive. Others emphasize instead the importance of social bonds, relationships of intimacy and trust, and social networks of association, and focus on the social damage done when they are lacking. For them, community represents a virtuous ideal of human warmth and solidarity. The rival pulls of these possibilities set up a tension in many discussions. Lash and Urry (1994) comment that new instances of community are as likely to be communitarian social movements, or race-baiting neotribes. Harvey (2000) scrutinizes recent attempts to revitalize urban design and architecture and finds a curious blend of forward-looking utopianism and nostalgia for the way things used to be. Urban planners invoke 'community' as the solution to an overly materialistic and socially fragmented existence, but in practice reinforce tendencies towards spatial separation and exclusion. These alternatives are rehearsed in abstruse discourse around the meaning of 'communitarianism', but they also play out in more immediate political debates about the role communities should play in the regulation of behaviour and social controls, and promotion of active citizenship. The lead in these controversies has been taken by American social theorists, continuing a line of discussion that goes back to the era of progressivism, and its defence of the values of small town America.

Communitarianism came to prominence during the 1980s, when it was debated among a group of leading political philosophers (see Tam

1998; Frazer 1999). Its most prominent sociological exponent is Amitai Etzioni, who has been instrumental in popularizing the term in a series of books (1995; 1997; 1998), and through his position as the lynchpin in a political grouping spreading the message in its journal, *The Responsive Community*. Etzioni traces the term 'communitarianism' back to the mid-nineteenth century, and acknowledges the influence of a long line of sociological thinkers, including Tonnies, Durkheim, Nisbet, and in more recent times Bellah *et al.* (1991) and Selznick (1992). His own concern with normative order goes back to influential work he undertook in the 1960s on the nature of control in formal organizations (Etzioni 1964). If we take his conception as the best known application of the approach, communitarianism purports to represent the middle ground between the individualism of the market and the collectivism of the state. Etzioni claims to be uninterested in resurrecting the conservative tradition of regret for the loss of community as the custodian of established order and social discipline; nevertheless there are extremely strong moral overtones to his arguments. The core thesis has to do with striking a correct balance between rights and responsibilities. In Etzioni's view, Western societies, especially America, have gone too far in the direction of favouring unlimited individual 'rights' and expectations, so that ever increasing demands can be made upon society, which are not matched by an equivalent readiness to carry out social duties and obligations; people are more interested in what they can get than what they should give. This is because the extent to which individual morality needs to be rooted in effective communities, with shared values and rules, has been forgotten. In Britain, influenced by the work of Giddens (1994b), New Labour governments have flirted with a politics of the 'third way', incorporating elements of the communitarian agenda.

Etzioni's style is deliberately folksy, and his claims are backed mainly by anecdotes and tales of personal experience; but always there is an underpinning reference to sociological theorizing and research. The position he adopts resembles most nearly that taken by Durkheim (1964), when making the case for mediating structures interposed between society and the individual, to regulate needs and curb aspirations. Where Durkheim looked to corporate groups, centred on occupational and professional identities, Etzioni refers us more generally to 'communities'. These he defines as webs of social relationships which bind people together, carry an emotional charge, and support a culture of shared meanings and values. Communities can exert a collective 'moral voice', enabling pressures to be applied to ensure that individuals conform to group expectations. We are assured that this can be accomplished through informal means, of 'gentle chastisement' and moral encouragement, which is less oppressive than the intervention of the state or judicial system. Etzioni acknowledges that in reality communities can behave in ways that are oppressive and abhorrent; however, he regards these as 'errant' examples, deviations from the norm of reasonable cooperation and tolerance which he identifies with the true 'spirit of community' (1995). In modern circumstances, he believes, there is no real prospect of a return to closed, monopolistic relationships which dominate the individual. Since most people exist within a multiplicity of social groupings, such as those based upon residence, work, faith and leisure, as well as class and ethnicity, normally they can opt between a number of plausible and competing communities. Following Janowitz (1967), these could be termed communities of 'limited liability'. This ensures that the demands of any one group will be tempered by commitments to another. For Etzioni, the main enemy now is not authoritarian collectivism, but 'radical individualism' and libertarianism, which deny the necessity for social control and collective responsibility. Communitarianism is said to take a more balanced view of the relationship between personal autonomy and respect for others.

According to Etzioni, strengthening community to counteract excessive individualism will provide an answer to some major societal problems, of crime, disorder and incivility. Many of the examples he gives seem trivial – neighbourly interventions about mowing lawns, supervising children's behaviour, observing speed limits; but there are also more worrying suggestions to do with naming and shaming miscreants, tagging offenders, and keeping out those deemed to be unsuitable neighbours. Etzioni's exposition of his underlying theme, the need to regain an 'authentic' commitment to core social values, harks back to an outdated sociological functionalism and belief in social consensus. This is borne out by his depiction of communities as nesting inside one another, building up from the local towards the national and ultimately international scale. The image of a good society seems closely modelled on the 1950s, allegedly a time of low anti-social behaviour, when core values were widely shared and strongly endorsed (1997: 60). By contrast, society today is said to suffer from 'a severe case of deficient we-ness and the values only communities can properly uphold' (1995: 26). However, if we accept that it is problematic to treat local societies as undifferentiated and inherently unified, then such a description becomes still more implausible when taken to the level of society as a whole; and in pluralistic, multicultural contexts, it appears completely meaningless.

The conservative twist to the argument is amplified when praise for community is accompanied by advocacy for better parenting skills, more conventional family structures, a stronger work ethic, and the role of the community in supervising and disciplining deviant conduct. Etzioni tells us that morality fails where social fabric is frayed, because 'people move around a lot and lose most social moorings' (1995: 33). In a throwback to assumptions more characteristic of pre-industrial times, he adds that every community should be expected to do 'the best it can to take care of its own' (1995: 146). Many commentators take such prescriptions to be a recipe for return to old-fashioned social practices, based on obsolete values. Along with the restoration of community, they expect to see the reinstatement of old lines of gender and generational 'authority', and an assertion of the rights of the majority over minorities of all types. Etzioni and his supporters deny this, insisting that they take full cognizance of contemporary diversity, and devolved forms of power. They refer to a system of checks and balances which will hold the ring between irresponsible individualism and social compulsion. However, events in real life have shown vividly how putting power into the hands of a community, especially one that is free to define itself, can go hideously wrong; recent examples include vigilante actions against alleged malefactors, such as when communities gang up to drive out suspect drug-dealers or paedophiles, or, in one notorious example, a paediatrician. As Elias (1994) has insisted, communal processes of labelling and stereotyping at local level may be the starting point for much nastier forms of ethnic partition and social division.

The idea of community is obviously central to the communitarian standpoint, and yet its supporters have been roundly criticized for the vagueness with which they use the term (Frazer 1999; Little 2002). Etzioni's contribution systematically blurs the boundaries between what has been established factually about real communities, and the attributes associated theoretically with community as an ideal, thus confusing communities as entities with 'community' as a quality. His model of nested communities allows him to merge together many different sets of social relationships, including those of society as a whole, the nation-state, neighbourhoods, ethnic and professional groups. Tam (1998) throws the net even wider to include extended families, schools and business enterprises – in fact, virtually any group within which people interact. Others also extend the idea of community to encompass shared sporting interests, reading groups, parent–teacher associations, and so on (Little 2002: 11). This eclecticism makes it very much easier to appeal to 'the community' as the solution to all kinds of social difficulties, in the hope that some form of collective intervention will materialize to sort things out. Politicians in particular are attracted by such nebulous uses of the term, but they are of little value in assisting with the clear analysis of problems, especially when, as Frazer (1999: 73) points out, there are often perfectly acceptable, and more precise, alternative terms already in use for such groupings.

As formulated by Tam (1998), the aim of the communitarian movement is to achieve the spread of inclusive communities. These would provide their members with equal powers to participate in processes of collective deliberation and decision making. Tam is explicit that this does not indicate any desire to restore traditional patterns, especially as these were often marked by hierarchical domination and elitism. Looking forward, he wants to see a 'harmonious integration of diverse interests' (1998: 220), enabling communities to uphold the values of wisdom, love, justice and fulfilment. Sociologically, Tam derives from Durkheim's depiction of organic solidarity and 'moral individualism' the view that *bona fide* community would provide room for individual development within a framework of cooperation, supported by social bonds of care and respect. Like Etzioni, he has many proposals to make about how groups should conduct themselves, and suggestions as to what a communitarian society would look like; but there is an almost total absence of any analysis of how existing structures of power and inequality are to be dismantled, or recognition that doing so is likely to meet with fierce resistance from those who currently benefit from them. This strain of utopianism is well in line with the communitarian thinking of earlier religious and political movements which upheld community as the ultimate destination, and achievement, of humanity. When implemented, such ideals have invariably been broken on the contradictions between openness to all, and insistence on compliance with the conditions and characteristics of membership (Kumar 1987).

These tensions continue to bedevil communitarianism, as can be seen from its relationship to feminism and other radical movements. To begin with, feminists felt certain affinities with communitarianism, including the value it attaches to relationships of personal trust, reciprocity and solidarity; its desire to reconstruct society in fundamental ways; and the emphasis it placed on the relevance of taking action within everyday local and mundane contexts (Frazer and Lacey 1993; Frazer 1999). For both feminists and communitarians, the personal is political. However, initial support gave way to disillusionment. Careful conceptual analysis leads Frazer to conclude that the term 'community' is too problematic to provide the basis for a convincing model of political relationships. As an idea, it is too vague and open-ended, and shot through with value judgements and emotional appeals (1999: 60).

In particular it fails because it seems unable to handle the reality of how individuals move between different communities in the course of their daily lives and life courses. Iris Marion Young (1990) attacks it more vigorously, alleging that community necessarily forms part of a conservative and oppressive discourse. Like many of those who have engaged in the debate, her wrath is directed against the *ideal* of community, as embodied in communitarianism, and is not informed by any examination of empirical researches. In her view, it is self-evident that community 'denies and represses social differences' (1990: 227); its pursuit is incompatible therefore with the distancing of time and place that must exist between people who engage in real social relationships. While they may have things in common, they are never identical with one another, and should not be treated as the same. Hence total community is an unrealizeable goal, but one which has dangerous consequences for those who value it. Their desire for social wholeness encourages its advocates to adopt 'mystical' ambitions, which submerge individuality into group-identity. Others also believe that communitarianism threatens to obliterate individual autonomy, by dissolving the self into imposed social roles (Phillips 1993).

Against this, Young wants to foster the richness and creativity of city life, and public contexts where people can meet as strangers, secure in their differences, whilst achieving some level of mutual recognition and everyday cooperation. Her ideal is one of 'differentiation without exclusion'. In making this case, Young stands for all those who have asserted the values of cosmopolitan, urbane existence against the restrictions of an enclosed social world. Whilst allowing that urban differences will guarantee misunderstanding, rejection, withdrawal, and conflict between individuals, Young contends that it is the 'myth' of community which translates these into group segregation, harassment, violence and social injustice. It does so by imposing homogeneity onto variety. Rather than a solution to urban problems, then, it is responsible for many of them. Young is a leading advocate of the 'politics of difference', the need to give due recognition to the multiplicity of ways in which people are differentiated and identified. It is her view that assertions of the unity of community tend to ride roughshod over such differences. In the case of the women's movement specifically, treating women as a 'community' could not cope with the variations of class, race, sexuality and ability which existed between them. As a result, some women were either excluded, or made to feel invisible. Although less strident in her rejection of the term, Frazer agrees (1999: 167) that 'the idea of community, with its emphasis on sharing, inevitably conduces to an emphasis on shared cultural identity and pronounced boundaries'. Therefore it is a divisive, rather than integrative, construct.

Social capital versus social repression?

The influential political scientist Robert Putnam shares Etzioni's view that recent decades in America have witnessed a decline in community involvement, or 'civic engagement', from a peak in the early 1960s. He acknowledges that his concern with developments in the stock of 'social capital' is a close conceptual cousin of the long-standing debate about community decline. The two forms of social capital he distinguishes, 'bridging' and 'bonding' capital, represent respectively ways of strengthening ties within the group (exclusiveness), or between the group and the outside world (inclusion). Hence they reflect the same underlying dynamic, or dilemma, as has surfaced continually with respect to community: must internal coherence and strength be won only at the cost of creating barriers and accentuating division? Throughout his key text, Putnam (2000) reiterates a core finding from the community studies tradition – the close connection between the structural foundations of community, and the values and attitudes displayed by its members. Repeatedly he informs us that civic virtue is at its most powerful when embedded in dense networks of reciprocal social relations; networks of community engagement foster 'sturdy norms' of reciprocity, and 'an effective norm of generalized reciprocity is bolstered by dense networks of social exchange' (2000: 19–20; 136). The decline of involvement, as measured by a host of statistics on group membership and participation, has serious consequences then, because it undermines people's readiness to trust and cooperate with one another. Much of the change in question has taken place at local level, with falling membership and activity in voluntary associations, churches, and community groups. Overall, Putnam concludes, 'thin, single-stranded, surf-by interactions are replacing dense, multi-stranded, well-exercised bonds' (2000: 184). This disintegration of social bonds matters, because evidence suggests that social capital (or strong communities) can help make people healthier, happier, more informed, and better able to solve collective problems: 'community connectedness' produces positive results. Judging by polling data, the majority of Americans seem to be aware that with the loss of community ties 'something bad is happening'.

Social capital is a tricky concept to pin down (Field 2003). It signifies very many things in Putnam's discussion, including moral cohesion, altruism, feelings of obligation, trust, and cooperation. At times it appears synonymous with community, at others it is interpreted more as an aspect, or product, of communal relations. Although it has a dark side, in the ability of groups to use their social capital to advance their own interests at the expense of others, mostly it is viewed extremely positively. Unlike Young (1990), Putnam believes there is no necessary trade-off between the strengths of community and the virtues of tolerance, equality and democratic involvement; indeed, he produces evidence to suggest that these are among the benefits which accrue from high levels of social capital. However, he does note that 'social divisiveness is the central normative issue raised by communitarianism' (2000: 361). He ends with an appeal for an era of 'civic inventiveness' to restore American community, which resembles Etzioni's programme for communitarian intervention.

The protagonists in these debates operate from fundamentally different value positions, and with different understandings of the relationship between individuals and society. Rather than 'shared particularity', Young values 'unassimilated otherness'. She endorses the politics of difference, against those of sameness. The communitarians are more concerned with raising the level of social control, to restore lost collective virtues. This is in response to, and reaction against, the postmodern, globalizing influences Young appears to welcome. On the one hand, stress is laid on creativity, freedom, tolerance and diversity, whereas the other position is primarily about control, discipline and regulation. Nevertheless there are some common themes. From the radical stand-point, Harvey (2000) raises the issue of how the embeddedness and organized power of the 'militant particularisms' associated with com-munity can be reconciled with a more universal understanding capable of producing necessary social change. This is grappled with by Putnam in very different language, when he considers what sort of balance can be struck between bonding and bridging capital, the latter requiring an ability to transcend our own social identities, so as to connect with peo-ple unlike ourselves. He values the local heterogeneity which forces us to deal with diversity, rather than the avoidance that comes from sur-rounding ourselves with others who are just the same. A form of resolu-tion is offered by Brent (1997), who reminds us that these issues of similarity and difference, inclusion and exclusion, are unavoidable fea-tures of social existence; all group formation entails making distinctions between those who belong and those who do not (compare Payne 2000). Community therefore is inherently a site of difference and division. No sooner are its boundaries drawn up than they are put into question by the emergence of some new distinction. Contrary to the view expressed by Young, that community necessarily elevates unity to a supreme virtue, Brent's practical experience of working with community projects leads him to conclude that community formation is intrinsically about creating difference; it is diversity, not unity, that constitutes the space of modern communities.

8

NEW DIRECTIONS FOR COMMUNITY

There is wide acceptance that we live now in a complex society of highly diverse groupings and affiliations, and that this renders notions of primary allegiance to a single, undifferentiated, primordial community irrelevant. As Little (2002: 155) puts it, it is because each of us is a member of different communities and associations that society is made up of individuals who have separate identities. Our social identities are not given, but constructed out of the intersection of a variety of memberships and commitments. This is a view asserted most clearly among radicals and postmodernists, who derive from it their readiness to respect social diversity, and the claim to recognition and rightful existence of many different communities. Young (1990: 236) comments that 'in our society most people have multiple group affiliations, and thus group differences cut across every social group'. The urban milieu she espouses consists of a vast array of networks, associations and small 'communities', which she believes can coexist and intermingle without being forced into a common identity. Frazer (1999: 151) notes that when questioned about their sense of belonging, people readily express multiple loyalties and identifications. As a result, in geographic terms, they construct highly individualized maps of social relations in different areas, with varying degrees of clarity, and make distinctions between their own subjective perceptions, and the public images and representations of space with which they are familiar. The validity of these claims is conceded by more conservative social theorists. Thus Etzioni depicts society as comprising many 'overlapping and interlaced communities' (1997: 205), while Putnam's concern for rebuilding levels of social capital leads him to advocate participation in and engagement with an expanding range of bodies and groups, from sports teams and choirs to grassroots social movements. Furthermore, all agree that these groupings take a number of different forms, and that many have no obvious spatial reference.

Where debate rages is around the limits to this proliferation, and the extent to which it is compatible with genuine community. Frazer and Lacey (1993: 200–1) refer to a range of 'communities' organized on a variety of lines; these include workplaces, families, and consciousness-raising groups. They also tell us that both sociology and ordinary common sense point to the existence of multiple 'communities within communities', defined by particular practices, crafts, traditions, discourses and languages. It is no surprise, then, that they are driven to ask what prevents the individual subject, faced by such incredible diversity, from collapsing into total incoherence. They suggest that the desire to avoid this is what drags many back towards some conception of a homogeneous, unifying community. Etzioni would be a prime example. He is hostile to what he terms 'unbounded pluralism' and 'unqualified diversity', and fears that if pursued to the limit they will result in the division of society into warring tribes. Somewhat amusingly, he accuses his radical critics, the advocates of the politics of difference, of encouraging such exclusiveness, by fixating on single aspects of identity, such as colour, gender or ethnicity. For their part, they would see Etzioni's call for a 'supracommunity' to bind all the varying allegiances together, and enforce an overarching shared morality, as encouraging the coercive suppression of differences which ought to be allowed to flourish. These arguments have major implications both for our understanding of the nature of communities in the twenty-first century and for any designs there might be to intervene practically within them.

REFORMULATING COMMUNITY FOR MODERN TIMES

A pluralistic conception of society as composed of many different kinds of groupings implies that a variety of different elements will enter into a person's social identity. They do so in combinations which, if not unique, are shared with only a limited number of others. Thus any given individual may be categorized in various ways, according to their race, ethnicity, nationality, gender, sexuality, class, education, place of residence, and so on. Unless any of these dimensions is so powerful that it dominates the rest, there is scope for manoeuvre between the various affiliations; individuals can be thought of in several different ways, or can exercise some choice as to how they wish to identify themselves. What they do about this may vary between situations (Jenkins 1996; Bauman 2001b), since different identities will appear appropriate to different circumstances. It could be argued that there is nothing very new about this, since individuals have always undertaken a number of different social roles at the same time, necessarily exhibiting separate facets of their identity in different contexts. However, there is an assumption that traditionally these roles were organized in such a way as to maintain overall coherence: for example, a man typically might be expected to combine the roles of husband, father, breadwinner and workmate. Communities played an important part in reinforcing this coherence, by constituting audiences before which most or all of these roles had to be performed. Now society is believed to be far more differentiated and diverse; different spheres of social life have grown apart, and much greater effort is needed to make them cohere (Crook *et al.* 1992). For instance, under current arrangements within the family unit, owing to divorce and cohabitation, 'father' is no longer assumed to be synonymous with 'husband', or even 'partner'.

Postmodernist theorists contend that the major forces which once shaped identity have lost strength, and many celebrate this as a liberation. It makes it possible to escape the social constraints which formerly prescribed membership of particular communities, and opens up new possibilities for choice and innovation. They welcome this because it enables the expression of new and more complex identities, in new forms of community. A renewed sense of community is promised, whereby individuals will be free to customize their social contacts, by selecting among a wide range of options (S. G. Jones 1995). For Bauman (1992: 36), insistence on plurality is the seminal feature of the postmodern world-view, shifting attention from earlier ideas of coordination and integration towards the recognition of many coexisting communal settings. On the other hand, others depict the postmodern individual as increasingly lost, stripped of dependable social coordinates, desperately searching for new ways of experiencing meaningful relationships with others. Consequently, according to Lash and Urry (1994) the invention of new substitute communities has become almost chronic. During a time of unprecedented individualization, there is a paradoxical upsurge of interest in the idea of community. In the light of this, Frazer and Lacey (1993) ask for a revised conception of community, capable of embracing diversity and fragmentation. There are a number of prominent candidates, which deviate to a greater or lesser extent from the traditional conception.

As a reminder of what this involves, Little (2002: 156) cites a version of Etzioni's definition of community, as involving 'criss-crossing affective bonds', a moral culture, and a shared history and identity, and states that it represents 'a fairly innocuous view'. However, Etzioni's aim is to establish a basic distinction between community, and other forms of human association, such as interest groups. When he writes elsewhere of community as a 'web of relationships', able to address a broad band of human needs, he clearly intends something more substantive by it than membership of a bowling club, or even a consciousness-raising group. Others take a similar line, when they identify communities in terms of a range of activities and interests, capable of implicating the whole person (Selznick 1992) or as social formations which engage individuals at the level of their identity (Frazer 1999: 143). Communities of this type confer meaning upon their members, and hold a central position in their social existence. Little seriously underestimates what he is demanding when he says that 'all' that is required for community is a shared identity, not based on self-interest, and a code of morality, recognized by its members; this is far from the 'limited' definition he implies, and certainly a long way removed from many current usages. The gap between such traditionalist definitions and O'Byrne's possibly more realistic vision of contemporary community as the construction of 'a tentative social order in a world of flows' (1993: 74) is enormous. At the same time, critics are concerned that alternative conceptualizations can dilute the meaning of community to vanishing point.

The key point about the 'new communities' is that they are not determined by destiny or 'fate', but chosen, largely according to taste and interests. True, certain interest-based communities have always existed, alongside communities of place, and origin. Examples would be the formation of specialist religious communities, such as monasteries, and various kinds of utopian or 'alternative' collectives, like communes

(Abrams and McCulloch 1976). These are intentional communities which tend to involve a highly exclusive, 'elitist' type of membership, and to exist in a state of separation from the world. Less rigorous communities, still entailing a degree of choice and voluntary commitment, have been formed around particular occupations, political ideologies and belief systems. Now, however, choice has been elevated to a guiding principle of community formation. More and more, people take their identities and social meanings from groupings which they have elected to join, thereby implicitly reserving the right to leave again if circumstances change. Voluntary involvement with communities fits a society which attaches high importance to notions of individual accomplishment and self-fulfilment. Individuals who engage in the kinds of reflexive identity-building projects described by writers like Beck and Giddens will chafe at the restrictions imposed upon them by the limitations of birth, geography and upbringing. Their preference will be for relationships that have been achieved, rather than ascribed, and they will evaluate the options more self-consciously, in terms of the rewards they can bestow. The question that arises is whether this provides a sufficient basis upon which to construct a shared form of life. Shields (1992: 109) asks this, when he queries if community can exist in the absence of the old 'universals' such as class structure, which once provided predictable criteria for separating insiders from outsiders. Without such guidelines, individual identities would appear less rooted, and more vulnerable to manipulation and exploitation. Conversely, it could be argued that people will be more attached to definitions of themselves and others when they have had a hand in creating them.

From communities to networks?

Network is a term which has moved closer towards the centre of social analysis as established patterns of social structure have appeared to dissolve. Lash and Urry (1994) suggest that without it the new world of flows could not be comprehended, while Castells (1997) argues that we inhabit a society of networks, in which direct and fixed relationships have been replaced by more open and mediated sets of connections. Network was already a well established term within the field of community analysis, where it has been used to explain patterns of migration and settlement (Mitchell 1969), to account for how contrasting behavioural norms were enforced by the social circles that surrounded families (Bott 1957), and to provide a general framework for the comparison of types of community (Frankenberg 1966). Murdoch *et al.* (2003) reiterate a point made by Fischer *et al.* (1977), that network analysis provides a way of reconciling the examination of social structures with an awareness of individuals as active participants in the construction of their own social worlds. Blokland and Savage (2001; see also Wellman and Leighton 1979) note how substituting an exploration of networks for investigations of community might avoid the seemingly endless debate as to whether or not community has been lost, saved or liberated. A focus on networks takes away the holistic connotations of 'community', making it a question instead of the quality and pattern of interpersonal relations.

A network can be defined in terms of the set of linkages in which the individual is embedded, and their interconnections. Networks centre on the individual in a way that communities do not; they radiate outwards from actors, tracing the connections of their various social relationships. Since there may be a number of distinct fields of relationships, an individual can belong to more than one social network. The conventional view taken of communal networks has been that they are reinforced by the coincidence of the personal networks of their members, superimposed across several fields, to create a dense, relatively enclosed set of relationships. Even in the absence of formal organization, this will promote a high degree of cohesion. At the extreme, a community could be thought of as a single all-encompassing network, making escape the only option for those whom it fails (Wellman 2001: 232). However, since it is in the nature of networks to remain open-ended, usually there will be some connections which leak out beyond the confines of a community's boundaries. Moreover, the network will look subtly different from the perspective of each individual member, allowing different perceptions of the whole. In general, networks are designed to be more flexible, adaptable, and to require less wholehearted commitment, than a fully integrated community. As a tool of analysis therefore, they seem better suited to exploring complex, overlapping and interlinked relationships among mobile individuals.

Networks do more than link people together; they provide the basis for social cohesion and cooperation. Fischer *et al.* (1977: 199) comment that as well as providing support to individuals they also place demands on them, and influence their attitudes and values. In other words, they foster some form of collective being. This varies according to the character of the network. More concerted social support can be expected from denser social networks, for example. The literature on social capital has produced many similar observations; its conclusions point to the significance of network properties like homogeneity, stability, and closure, in promoting or sustaining social capital. There are numerous references in *Bowling Alone* to the importance of dense networks of social interaction, and regular interaction among a diverse set of people (for instance, Putnam 2000: 21–2). Networks are distinguished according to whether they are single-stranded and episodic, or involve interactions that are intensive, repeated and multistranded. These differences are deemed relevant because they explain the levels of trust and reciprocity that result. Rich, stable and dense networks are held to be conducive to good health, well-being, strong economic performance and civility; communities that are 'well networked' tend to thrive (Field 2003). The closer a network approximates to the traditional measures of community, the stronger it is in social capital. The main proviso is that to do really well networks must stretch out to connect with other networks or groupings that can deliver additional resources not available from amongst members themselves. As well as bonding, they need to 'bridge'.

Wellman (2001) states that the personalized social network has become a dominant form of contemporary social organization. Technological developments have helped transfer community away from place, into households, and increasingly to persons. Mobile phones and internet connections enable people to engage in person-to-person community. This ensures that a rising proportion of interaction is based on achieved social characteristics, such as lifestyle or voluntary interests. Social ties are fragmented, with different individuals supplying different needs. Consequently there has been a loss of the 'palpably present and visible local community' which supported strong identities and belonging; communities now are 'far-flung, loosely-bounded, sparsely-knit and fragmentary' (2001: 227). Wellman provides much supporting evidence for his view; but when relationships become so disconnected, fragmented and individualized, it is a mystery why he persists in calling them 'community'. The networks he describes provide none of the reinforcement and solidity needed to ensure the maintenance of social norms and controls. In fact, among the implications of living in networks, he notes a decrease in control, and in commitment to specific social milieux. Most of the interaction occurs between small fragments of the overall network, in communications between pairs of individuals, or among couples, and given the manner in which it is constituted, only the individual at its centre is likely to have much sense of its totality. Networks of this sort may develop their own ways of doing things, employ particular turns of phrase, share certain items of information; but they exert none of the symbolic power of more established communities. Although its members may experience feelings of community and enjoyment in being together within it, a network in itself does not constitute a community.

Lifestyles

Lifestyle groupings come closer to meeting the criteria for community laid down above, because they are capable of unifying many social networks within a set of shared cultural codes and preferences, and can be marked as well by other trappings of community, such as an association with particular spaces or locales, distinctive markers of identification, and occasional social gatherings. The word 'lifestyle' suggests that there is considerably more to it than the mere act of consuming; it implies a design for living, possibly even a way of conducting oneself across a lifetime. To adopt a particular lifestyle is to take up a pattern of activity and consumption which indicates to others the sort of person you are, and the lifestyle choices made by individuals can contribute critically towards their self-definition. Those who share a similar lifestyle can be assumed to have comparable attitudes and values, to make similar comparisons between themselves and others, and probably show a propensity to come into contact from time to time. The dynamics of group affiliation produce differentiation and distance between such groupings; approval for a particular lifestyle often denotes disapproval for others. Thus lifestyle groupings can take on a collective identity, and it is not unusual to hear them referred to as 'communities'. As sets of attitudes, values, and manners held in common by numbers of individuals, there are obvious similarities between the idea of lifestyle, and that of 'subculture', which to a great extent it appears to have superseded. A number of distinct 'cultures' or lifestyles have been identified within the contemporary middle classes, for example, such as those centred on exercise and healthy living, and a more 'postmodern' way of living that combines elements of these with emphasis on indulgence in eating and drinking (Savage *et al.* 1992). Others meanwhile have been exploring the possibilities of living in an 'environmentally sound' way. Lifestyles can exist within class formations or, like 'sexual lifestyles', cut across them.

People are likely to have some sense of 'belonging' to a given lifestyle, and through it can identify themselves with others who are like-minded. Lifestyle provides a point of reference against which to stabilize a sense of self, and find the security which might have been supplied previously by membership of a community. Thus it is a moot point whether people can affiliate themselves to more than one lifestyle at a given time. On the other hand, lifestyles are flexible and developing, and subject to continual negotiation among their adherents, and apart from the personal investments required, there is little to prevent anyone swapping one lifestyle for another. Some problems with the term are indicated by its very close connections with the worlds of marketing and consumer research (Crook *et al.* 1992: 60; Solomon and Englis 1997; Shields 1992). Here people are classified into lifestyle categories with the prime or sole intention of selling them things. This lays them open to manipulation by commercial interests, and the media, intent on the commodification of particular ways of living. As well as involving patterns of conduct, it is generally accepted that lifestyles centre on the consumption of particular items and experiences. Their rise to ascendancy can be interpreted then as a victory for consumer capitalism and the social relations of consumption. Harvey (2000: 113) notes accordingly how entire 'lifestyle communities' can be created and dissolved in the interests of commercial return. While it would be mistaken to write off consumers as merely passive victims of commercial exploitation, in the light of the pressures exerted by advertising and the mass media, questions must be raised about the genuineness of many of the choices involved.

Since what people consume is linked so closely to their economic assets, lifestyle differences are intimately connected with developments in social stratification: the emergence of a 'privatized' working class during the 1960s, for example, could be seen as the formation of a new style of life. In market research, lifestyle classifications are regarded as more accurate than broader class categories. Chaney (1996) associates lifestyles in general with the privatization of communal life. Although agreeing that lifestyles afford distinctive ways of being that differentiate people in their everyday lives, he distinguishes them from more stable 'ways of life' grounded in the long-term intimacy of communities; lifestyles are more fluid and ambiguous and do not absorb the whole person in the same way. Elsewhere Chaney (1994) points to the peculiar significance of lifestyle configurations in suburbia. Suburban districts represent those largely neglected 'placeless places', where a large proportion of the contemporary population resides. Suburbs have a reputation for soulless homogeneity and anonymity, but in the context of prevailing uniformity, small differences become important. In contents and decoration, the suburban home is a prime site for the display of lifestyle choices. Although home- and family-centred, these are not solely for private consumption, because they are also on public display, and make statements about who the residents are. Included in this is often the portrayal of particular kinds of community. As Chaney has it (1994: 164), in order to provide experiences that can be consumed, inhabitants collude in creating the appearance of community. It is in suburbia that Etzioni's communitarian disciplines seem most likely to come into their own, and where 'neighbourhood watch' schemes flourish. As well as maintaining good order, such practices have a positive effect on house values. A long line of critics has portrayed suburban life as essentially materialistic, superficial and censorious.

Since participation in particular forms of community is a core component of many lifestyles, it is no surprise that with the advent of consumer culture, 'community' itself becomes a commodity for sale. Living spaces are created and packaged to afford certain kinds of communal experience. Competition over access to lifestyles helps to organize the process through which individuals and households distribute themselves spatially. By occupying particular locations, and following prevailing lifestyle patterns, they indicate who they are. Some analysts go further, to argue that it is the very act of consuming, or shopping, that has become the key expression of community. Just as marketplaces once provided meeting points for traditional communities, now it is in the shopping centre perhaps that community becomes real, where one can observe and evaluate competing lifestyles, and feel closest to those one most resembles (Shields 1992).

Neotribalism

In several places we have encountered references to the possibility of communities developing into 'tribal' formations. The debate surrounding communitarianism is haunted by the prospect of the 'Balkanization' of society into small, self-enclosed, sectional groupings fiercely defending their own particular social and physical territories. A number of writers have highlighted the significance of modern forms of 'tribalism'. Maffesoli (1996) for one argues that it is premature to talk of society being reduced to nothing more than a mass of individuals. Instead he sees people engaged on a furious search for those who feel and think as they do. 'Feeling' is especially important, because a characteristic modern phenomenon is the formation of communities with more than simply shared interests in common; they share a passion, or enthusiasm. It is the cohesive aspect of social sharing that leads Maffesoli to speak of this as tribalism, and to describe the outcome as 'neotribes' united around shared sentiments. These would include friendship networks, peer groups, and 'affinity groupings' of various kinds, such as sports fans, punks, or those with shared sexual tastes. Maffesoli considers that there has been a growth in the significance of small groups and existential networks; people are prepared to dissolve their individuality into such groupings, which provide them with warmth and companionship. His intellectual reference points include Weber's concept of the emotional community (*Gemeinde*), and the sociology of the Chicago School. Eventually this leads him towards the (re)discovery of an 'urban mosaic', comprising 'a succession of territories in which people in a more or less ephemeral way take root, close ranks, search out shelter and security' (1996: 139). Introducing Maffesoli's book, Shields describes such groupings as the central feature and key social fact of our experience of everyday living. During the course of a normal day, he says, we might move between several such groups, drawing from them our sense of 'being together' with others. The examples Shields cites are diverse, embracing groups of workmates, consumer lobbies, service users, and even the American National Rifleman's Association. Elsewhere Shields (1992) applies the idea of neotribes to groups organized around distinctive lifestyles. Putnam (2000: 149) accepts that such groups offer some antidote to social disconnection, by 'redefining community in a more fluid way'. He also notes that they tend to concern themselves with the emotional needs of the individual, providing care, support and intimacy. 'Self-help' groups of various kinds figure prominently among the neotribes.

Neotribes identify themselves by distinctive clothing, common ways of behaving, and displays of theatricality. Their social relationships tend to be intense, but short-lived, and Maffesoli comments that their existence is marked by fluidity, occasional gathering, and dispersal. In some instances, they are completely ephemeral, organized only for the occasion. A good example of a neotribe is the new age travellers described by Hetherington (2000; see also McKay 1996). For a short while, these bands of nomadic young people, pursuing an 'alternative' lifestyle, formed a strong elective community held together by emotional ties. As well as adopting common modes of appearance and conduct, they expressed shared beliefs and values and engaged in a range of interaction and cooperation, including providing economic and social support to one another. Periodically, during festivals, as well as in confrontations with the authorities and members of more mainstream social groups, they experienced intense sensations of belonging together, of the sort that some would qualify as the inner core of community. Frazer (1999: 83) notes that communities can generate feelings of 'communion', that are both euphoric and fleeting. These are times when the individual can feel lost within the group, and connected to others in ways that transcend normal, everyday reality. Travellers themselves placed much emphasis on such experiences, the 'buzz' or 'vibes' they got from being together (Hetherington 2000: 78). Hetherington classifies travellers as part alternative lifestyle, part youth subculture, and part social movement, based around a set of common lifestyle choices. For many other groups inhabiting the countryside, they represented a major challenge, threatening to destabilize the accepted order of things by transgressing all kinds of real and symbolic boundaries. Halfacree (1998) extends Maffesoli's framework to the other rural social groupings against whom they were pitched, like farmers and rural newcomers. Each could be seen as constituting a distinct neotribe, with its own symbolic apparatus, sets of rituals, and ambitions to seize control of space to exclude others, so that the countryside resembles a tribal battleground between competing lifestyles.

The idea of neotribalism seems especially suited to the situation of young people, in that there is both a rapid turnover and evident diversity of youth 'styles' and subcultures. Analysing youth perceptions of the arts and cultural media, Willis (1990) notes that young people are particularly bereft of traditional resources for social meaning, membership and security. There are no 'organic communities' in which they can find a home. What he discerns instead is a mass of 'proto-communities', which form and reform around shared interests, fashions, and desires. This might take place around a one-off event, like a rave or Live Aid concert, without necessarily any direct communication among those involved, just the knowledge of something shared. Willis describes such groupings as shifting, insubstantial, recombining; they are unplanned and unorganized. To this extent, they resemble a loose crowd, or spaced-out queue of people, but with the potential to become a more closed communicative circle. He cites (1990: 143) the example of the Hillsborough disaster, which turned a mass of football supporters into a community of mourners, able to act collectively in ritual displays of grief, and in quasi-political action against hostile media reporting. Emotional intensity, or a sense of communion, bonded them together more firmly as a group. However, it should be noted that the majority of the supporters involved were already embedded firmly in a given place (Liverpool) and class (the working class). Echoing Raban's (1975) account of the 'soft' city, Willis states that following the steep decline in traditional sources of identity and meaning communal walls 'zigzag wildly around the urban mass', making it hard to predict where individuals will choose to affiliate themselves. Lash and Urry (1994) suggest that it is in the parts of society where network connections are weakest that we will meet the neotribes; as well as their example of groups of 'race-haters', we might include here the disaffected bands of urban youth described by Campbell (1993).

The new social movements

In his analysis of the network society, Castells (1997) argues that people resist processes of individualization and social atomization by gathering together into new forms of communal organization. Faced with the dissolution of their established identities, they rediscover themselves through mobilization into social movements. While often these start life as defensive groupings, they can develop into projects for social change. For Castells, the key to their survival and success is a communal logic, which narrows down the scope for individual self-determination by imposing certain shared definitions of identity onto members. Castells warns that this can result in a lack of communication, between movements, and with other agencies, so that much-needed social meaning may be gained at the expense of division or conflict. Other recent theorizations of social movements have laid similar stress on their cultural dimensions, and their significance for the formation and reconstruction of identities (Melucci 1989; Buechler 2000). Lash and Urry's remark that in times of social disorganization and uncertainty people can opt to 'throw themselves into' community seems particularly apt when applied to contemporary movements, since they tend to make exceptionally wide-ranging demands on people's energies and commitments. They do so by requiring a restructuring of interpersonal relationships and the everyday experiences of those who participate, sometimes amounting to the wholesale reworking of individual biographies. In certain respects such movements can be thought of as formal organizations, with a set of rational, instrumental concerns, to do with mobilizing resources and achieving specific aims. In their ambition to effect significant social change, they belong within the sphere of politics. But they are also intensely social in their impact upon everyday life: feminism, anti-racism, movements for sexual liberation, or for animal rights and welfare all imply more than a set of lifestyle 'choices'; they promulgate ethical and behavioural standards which penetrate deep into the realms of everyday activity, eroding the distinction between public and private life, and making connections between the local, the national and the global (Buechler 2000: 154). With this level of anticipated commitment, it is natural that members may come to see the movement as their 'home'.

New social movements adopt their own form of loosely structured, networking organization, but reinforce it with multiple forms of interaction and exchange. In this way they can build up the interactive networks of multilayered communication characteristic of communities. Castells uses the term 'the women's community' to encompass the host of feminist organizations, support networks, clinics, refuges and cultural associations which have sprung up specifically to serve the needs of women. He also describes the formation in San Francisco of the first visibly organized gay community, with its autonomous institutions, bars, clubs and street festivities. This is replicated now in many other major cities, while a more diffuse sense of the existence of a homosexual community is used widely to refer to those who identify themselves as gay or lesbian, or become involved in the cultural, political and sexual issues surrounding such identities (Weeks 1996; Weeks and Holland 1996). Like the women's movement, examination of the gay 'community' shows it to consist of a complicated variety of different organizations and sub-communities, organized around several nucleuses, so that rather than a single phenomenon, 'diverse communities are a reality', because 'sexualities today are lived in a variety of communities of identity, of interest and of politics' (Weeks and Holland 1996: 177). Clearly such communities are socially constructed phenomena. Weeks (1996) refers to the idea of a sexual community as a 'necessary fiction', called into being by the self-identifications and imaginings of its participants, to meet conditions of isolation and oppression, and to cope with particular crises, like that surrounding HIV/AIDS. The 'community' is a loose collection of many elements, including dozens of organizations and local action groups, that exists 'because its members feel it should'. It enables them to develop and express a particular identity, to formulate collective values and ways of behaving, and build links. As it develops a set of 'dense interconnections, networks, relationships and experiments in living' (1996: 77), it grows into something more like a community of lived shared experiences.

Buechler (2000) distinguishes between social movements which are grounded in pre-existing identities, with historical and structural depth, such as those organized around race, gender, ethnicity and faith, and others in which identity has to be built from scratch. The latter would include the anti-globalization and peace movements, vegetarians and 'greens'. Fluidity and flexibility is greater in the second type of movement, but in all cases, movement members have the potential to form a distinct community, in that they share certain characteristics, and corresponding forms of consciousness. True to the ethos of postmodernity, Buechler (2000: 194) indicates that a person can possess multiple collective identities, and so presumably belong to several movements, and that there is a shifting dynamic between these. Like communities, movements persist as the collective accomplishments of their members, maintained through ongoing interaction and negotiation. Movements can merge and fragment in line with the changing salience of different identifications for individual lives; for example, lesbian communities emerged out of the women's movement, while over time the scope of the identity label 'black' has shifted, widening and narrowing to fit changing circumstances.

Virtual community

Maffesoli (1996) includes electronic networks among his neotribal groupings. These might seem to take the characteristics of 'new' community to an extreme, since they involve individuals participating in relationships which exist only somewhere in 'cyberspace', by virtue of the networks and connections of communication technologies. Advocates hail the advent of virtual communities as finally setting individuals free from social, geographical, even biological constraints, enabling them to associate at will with those who are truly like-minded (Rheingold 1993; S. G. Jones 1995; Holmes 1997). According to some, this amply compensates for the loss of other, more tangible, kinds of community, by transferring social solidarity into new channels. Electronic media promise a solution to the problem of mobility, because no matter where the participants are, or how often they move, they can stay in touch. Space is compressed almost to nothing, making it possible for individuals anywhere to establish contact with one another. The possibilities for the invention of new communities are endless. Furthermore, since communication at present is by text alone, most of the usual social identifiers are removed from those involved, and this anonymity is said to facilitate more egalitarian and democratic forms of interaction. Participants can assume identities to suit their purposes, for example by disguising their gender. Nothing could be more open and fluid than communication via the net. Compared to real, physical, communities, some regard those constructed on the internet as 'utopian' collectivities, a realm of uninhibited difference and choice. Others are less convinced. They argue that immersion in virtual reality represents a withdrawal from involvement in the embodied social and political relationships of the 'real' world and its communities. The complexities of human engagement are thinned down to the status of one-dimensional transactions, which call upon only a fraction of the individual's capacities (Doheny-Farina 1996; Willson 1997). In addition, there is little to authenticate these commitments as genuine. The degree of potential disengagement is shown in the extent to which participants can become caught up in various kinds of games and fantasy worlds; here community is not just imagined, it is literally imaginary.

Responding to these negative perceptions, Baym (2000) describes a thoroughly postmodern phenomenon, a 'tribe within a tribe', consisting of fans of television soap-operas who participate in online newsgroup discussions about them, and explains how it comes to be a social world that *feels* like a community. Regular participants develop shared understandings, and habitualized ways of acting, and take a shared pleasure in their communications. Those involved can be said to accumulate a collective memory, with elements of consensus, and agreed ethical standards. For Baym, the newsgroup itself resembles an interpersonally complex social world, while beyond this, there are further exchanges of personal information, offers of mutual support, and in some cases actual meetings and friendships. Baym suggests that, like any other social grouping, the newsgroup is structured into 'community' through the existence of recurrent social practices; it is an ongoing construction of its members. However, when asked, even those taking part expressed reservations as to whether this was 'really' a community, rather than just a group. As a group, it is somewhat strange, since members are usually alone when they participate. According to Baym (2000: 209), being part of an audience, or an online community, is about having a group of friends, with whom one engages in a set of activities, and from those connections there grows a world of feelings and relationships. Yet it would seem that the majority of those involved remain quite passive and solitary, receiving from and giving to their 'community' little beyond the exchange of electronic messages. Holmes (1997) likens this to maintaining a community in existence by floating messages in bottles. There is no guarantee that the messages will be received and understood in an act of collective apprehension, and few consequences follow.

Electronic networks enable people to form effective lobbies, exchange information, fulfil useful educational purposes, and supply comfort and advice. They may constitute important threads within a larger community of involvement, such as a social movement; but on their own, they represent a highly attenuated version of community. Viewed as they tend to be almost exclusively from the standpoint of the individual, the emphasis naturally falls on what it feels like to take part, rather than on what is achieved. Like many other forms of new 'community', online conversations provide occasions for individuals to 'focus upon themselves in the presence of others' (Wuthnow 1994: 170). The price paid for such narcissism is a very weak sense of social obligation and accountability. In his discussion of the 'wired neighbourhood', Doheny-Farina (1996) contrasts the creation of such 'globalized virtual collectivities of alienated and entertained individuals' with the more solid nature of local 'placed' communities. He suggests that in cyberspace the image or 'sense' of a community has been substituted for the real thing; but this can provide no answers to the needs for protection, healing and social support that people normally vest in communities. Virtual gatherings cannot match the complex integration of private and public life, or the critical mass of interdependent interests, found in actual geo-physical communities. In his view, therefore, computers are seen best as adjuncts to communities which already exist, not a replacement for them.

THE LIMITS OF THE NEW COMMUNITIES

Analyses of the kind briefly reviewed above are concerned to highlight the heterogeneity of contemporary society, the plurality of its communal groupings, and the extent to which they take shape through contact with one another, in relationships of accommodation or opposition. This means that their outlines are never fixed, or stable, but always in a state of becoming; for example, people continually join, leave, or move between them, making their boundaries impossible to pin down. Membership is provisional, and with this degree of overlap and mobility, no group can count on the undivided allegiance of its members. The fluidity of the underlying reality is reflected in the way the various categorizations blur into one another: lifestyle groupings become neotribes, neotribes provide the invisible support network for new social movements (Melucci 1989), the language of social movements weaves in and out of descriptions of the new sexual communities (Weeks 1996), and what to begin with looks like a single community soon dissolves into many. It is not only 'nostalgic communitarians' (Holmes 1997: 31) who might point to an ensuing loss of comprehensiveness of interaction. We get a sense of this by contrasting these alternative forms of community with the meaningful personal relationships presupposed in Williams' (1975) conception of the 'knowable community', where people come to know one another 'in the round'. By comparison, the new forms of community appear one-dimensional. They offer a rich menu of choices, but engage only with fragments of the individual. For this reason, those describing them tend to employ qualified terms like 'pseudo-community', 'proto-community', and so on.

Networks are not communities at all, but provide some foundations for their potential formation. Lifestyles, neotribes and virtual communities are all marked by high degrees of voluntarism; they form because individuals choose to identify with, or imagine themselves into, membership. Their existence depends on these acts of self-identification, and therefore lacks solidity and permanence (Bauman 1992: 136). There is a wide gap between Maffesoli's vision of a neotribal society of tiny cells of conviviality, and the possibility of people joining together to act to maintain favoured ways of life, or engage in collective projects to change them. Social movements are more promising; they certainly have the capacity to absorb fully the lives of individuals, and bind them together in relationships of close cooperation. Yet, as Putnam (2000) points out, most members are far less deeply involved than the activist core, while large numbers confine their investment to the occasional mail subscription or donation. For the most part, groupings of this kind lack the density and multiplexity of the relationships traditionally associated with community (Frazer 1999); their members have only partial awareness or knowledge of one another, and at any time they choose may go missing from the group. In addition, the majority of the groupings considered are expressive or aesthetic in tone; they focus on the richness of the experiences they can provide for individuals and, above all, on their emotional needs. The stress is on the feelings inspired by community. Even in the case of the multitude of task-oriented small groups mentioned by Putnam, a high proportion of them are concerned to make the individual feel better. In essence, therefore, for many, community today has come to mean this feeling of being cared for, or 'belonging', and no end of groups claim to be able to provide it.

In fact, virtually any social collectivity can lay claim to some elements of 'the communal', in terms of bonds of shared orientation, markers of appropriate behaviour, or common symbols. These provide the membership badges displayed by youth cultures, religious and political movements, class fractions, consumer groupings and so on, all of which can masquerade as communities. Given the abundance of possibilities, the experience of community promises to be ubiquitous: we can all belong to communities, and as many of them as we like; it is up to us to decide which to identify with. Not only do people conjure up communities from whatever they feel they have in common, but there are many others only too ready to fabricate them, as things that can be bought into. Internet marketeers apply the label 'community' to random collections of website visitors (Wellman 2001: 228). This leads Frazer (1999) to inquire whether there is any property, shared between people, which does not lend itself to a proclamation of community. In the same way that there are said to be 'communities' of business people, or jazz fans, is it conceivable that we could perhaps find people referring to themselves as the 'freckled community'? The answer would seem to depend on whether they thought they could get something out of it. Wellman (2001: 248) contends that today community is a 'game', ruled by considerations of autonomy, opportunity and uncertainty, which implies that community can be whatever people want to make of it. Others, like Bauman (1992) and Sennett (1998) insist that commitments of this type cannot generate lasting social bonds. In Bauman's terms, most contemporary communities are no more than pegs on which to hang identities for the time being. There is nothing to signify the sense of obligation or responsibility towards others that might hold people in a continuing relationship, even when things turn difficult. Membership always carries the implied warning 'until further notice'. Sennett (1998: 30) laments the erosion of long-term qualities of character, such as loyalty, commitment and resolve. In the absence of more tangible social relations, not even the short-lived enthusiasm of being together with others of a similar kind can be sustained. The crowd at a Glastonbury music festival may feel themselves to be in such communion; they may even link hands to pledge their commitment to solving world poverty; but then they disperse, and go home, and cease to think about their collective unity.

Interestingly enough, in all the examples mentioned above, there is evidence of people seeking to go beyond the limits of their existing contacts, to meet actually in the flesh, and develop closer, fuller, relations with one another. It is when they meet at picnics and social gatherings that collaborators in e-communities are able to establish the trust missing from their electronic interactions. Those who belong to youth cultures, or sexual communities, invariably establish particular venues and routines through which they firm up their connections in personal encounters. Lifestyle consumers parade their possessions where others can see and appreciate them. In these ways, a sense of community can be embedded more firmly. Of course, there are exceptions, where such efforts are unnecessary because communities already are well embedded. Conventional community ties tended to draw their strength from certain kinds of pre-existing social bonds, especially family, religion, occupation, ethnicity and class. Despite all the changes that have occurred, these still provide the operational relationships underpinning communities where identities seem most secure, and most resilient in the face of globalization and postmodernity. Unsurprisingly, these are also the communities which attract odium from some for being narrow and exclusive. In recent years, with the waning of other influences, ethnicity in particular has come to the fore as a prime source of communal cohesion, often but not always in conjunction with religion. In a globalized, mobile world, ethnicity has become for many a dominant form of structuring framework, within which to negotiate their sense of belonging and identity. Ethnic ties bind people together at a local and geographically limited level, but can also unite dispersed populations into meaningful communities across large distances.

In the way that villages used to produce close encounters between social classes (Pahl 1965), urban districts now bring different ethnicities into close proximity, both sharpening and challenging their communal boundaries (Cantle 2002; Webster 2003). As well as the formation of local and fundamentalist communities, we see the emergence of new hybrid and diasporic groupings (Eade 1997; Hall 1990). In response to such diversity, existing communities also find themselves driven into adopting a more ethnic clothing, becoming aware of their ethnicity where previously it was unchallenged, and unconscious (Collins 2004). As the conflicts surrounding the development of London's Docklands have shown (Foster 1999), the defence of local community and the rights of the 'established' very easily spill over into racism and xenophobia. Riots in the northern ex-industrial towns of Britain in 2001 also highlighted how far a combination of economic restructuring, selective migration, and symbolic stereotyping and stigmatization had gone to split the population into separate ethnic enclaves (Webster 2003). The promotion of cultural identity and difference had played its part in the development of racism and segregation. Webster notes an unresolved tension between particularistic, potentially exclusive community cohesion, and universalistic, potentially inclusive social cohesion (Webster

2003: 114). In a formulation reminiscent of Etzioni, he concludes that the latter is a question of the moral regulation that gives rise to social solidarity within and between groups. Ironically, policy discourse evokes 'community' as the solution to these communal problems, by trying to shift the limits of community to incorporate all the warring factions, into a so-called 'community of communities' (Runnymede Trust 2000). Yet again, 'community' is put to work, to paper over the cracks in social relations.

WORKING WITH COMMUNITY

As recent calls for greater 'community cohesion' demonstrate (Cantle 2002), despite the many conceptual and empirical difficulties that we have been exploring, there is no sign that the term 'community' is going to go away, either from the everyday discourse of 'ordinary' people, or from the rhetoric of those who seek to govern and manage them. On the contrary, the capacity of 'community' to mean so many different things, sometimes all at once, makes it an invaluable political resource. Many ongoing struggles between social groups are conducted in its name, both at the local level and in the wider society. Claims for goods and resources, including political recognition and esteem, are legitimized by invoking the needs of the community. Exhortations to rally around communal interests have played an important part in mobilizing the new social movements, and as Hoggett (1997: 1) asserts, the idea of community is nowhere more ubiquitous than in contemporary social and public policy. Discussions of problems of immigration, crime, terrorism and anti-social behaviour rarely proceed far without mention of the part played by communities, as either cause or cure. No matter how difficult it is to be clear about its meaning, 'community' has come to possess a definite social reality because it is inscribed so deeply in a thick web of activities and practices such as community programmes, community groups of various kinds, projects like community arts or community health and welfare, and the physical fabric of community centres. These practices and facilities all involve people doing things with, or to, communities. This in turn produces an extensive apparatus of community workers, facilitators, activists and experts, who together constitute quite a significant industry, with a substantial turnover of financial assets. Apart from the practitioners themselves, there are those who reflect and comment upon their practice, and provide them with relevant training and education. Even when taking opposing sides, they have a mutual interest in maintaining the social visibility of community, which makes them the 'community community', and they employ a vocabulary littered with terms such as community activism, community development, participation and community-based action. Yet by now we know that, although it seems to offer something for everyone, community is an exceedingly fragile hook from which to hang so much.

Community as a tool for intervention

The popularity of community as a tool of political and social intervention has risen and fallen along with shifts in government thinking, and in prevailing social and economic circumstances (see Mayo 2000; Clarke *et al.* 2002). Well before the formation of a communitarian 'movement' in the 1990s there were many who looked to communities as sources of action or forms of mobilization, to work with or to counteract currents of social change. Action at the level of community is viewed as a way of working on those social relationships deemed closest to individuals, and their most intimate social groupings, and therefore likely to be particularly effective in bringing about changes with a lasting impact. Involving a wider community can provide reinforcement and support for those who are undertaking new ventures; for example, the designation of certain localities as 'educational priority areas' in the late 1960s was intended to generate the local backing needed to help parents and pupils adopt new attitudes towards achievement in school. Since then, similar ideas have lain behind numerous interventions in the fields of community health, policing, crime prevention and social care. Weeks (1996) argues that campaigns for safer sex as a response to the AIDS epidemic became successful when they won the support of a community of activists and voluntary organizations, inspired by a philosophy of collective self-help. Practical efforts of this sort have been influenced by, and in turn exerted an influence upon, emerging theoretical perspectives on community. Indeed, some of the most direct applications of sociological ideas and methods have occurred in the broad area of 'community work', and this has meant that disagreements about the nature and meaning of community have been translated fairly immediately into differences of practice and approach.

Forms of community activism can be traced back a long way, but have obtained an increasing clear definition as they have become more formal and professionalized (Lees and Mayo 1984; Clarke *et al.* 2002; Twelvetrees 1998). Even so, there continue to be significant inconsistencies and contradictions in practice, which reflect the influence of divergent perspectives and commitments. For example, methods of 'community development' were refined in the context of colonial relationships in developing countries, where they were seen as a means of helping local people to adjust to new economic and cultural expectations and to adopt more 'modern' forms of behaviour. These included self-reliance, individualism and readiness to value economic growth. There were always some who challenged such approaches, as ways of pacifying potential opposition, and incorporating it within a dominant Western ideology. Development would be encouraged, providing it followed certain predetermined directions. When the approach was transferred back home, to the West, the same debates arose. Definitions of community development, like those cited by Clarke *et al.* (2002: 30–3), incorporate references to such worthy aims as enabling communities to grow; strengthening and bringing about change in communities; encouraging communities to tackle problems for themselves; and securing the active involvement of people in the issues which affect their lives. Communities are treated as agents, able to assume responsibility, define objectives, and act to meet them. There is a strong theme of collectivism, in that action with communities entails working together, reinforcing shared ties, encouraging solidarity and self-help. The emphasis on cooperation and collaboration could be seen as a valuable counterweight to rampant individualism; it reminds people that they belong together and need to show consideration for one another. However, concealed within words like 'growth', 'strength' and even 'development' itself is an implicit model of the 'good' community. A community which can stand on its own feet, with a clear sense of purpose, and which can mobilize its own resources to achieve useful ends, is considered to be a more developed, healthier community than one that cannot. Skilled community practitioners of various types exist to help communities grow along this path. But they are rarely neutral when it comes to evaluating what sorts of goals and values communities choose to pursue. It is not possible so easily to separate the form of community from its content. As with the former colonial powers, the temptation to encourage or insist upon particular outcomes is extremely strong. Much of the literature on community development deals with this simply by assuming that, when approached correctly, communities are naturally progressive, liberal and inclusive; or else that practitioners will provide their services only where these positive values can be ensured. When they make the 'wrong' choices, communities find themselves condemned for being too self-centred, too exclusive, or reactionary.

Since development is often offered as part of a package, within funded programmes, these substantive outcomes are built in as part of the deal. Communities are developed *in order* to be more economically effective, to play a larger role in decision-making, or to exercise greater control over social misbehaviour. An insidious pressure is applied to comply with definitions that someone else has laid down, even if this risks missing the point about the nature of the community in question. A classic example is the 1970s Community Development Project (CDP), which followed the lead set by the United States' 'War on Poverty' in targeting action on a number of places in Britain identified as exhibiting persistent deprivation. The assumption was that this was attributable to 'malfunctions' in family and community. A dozen teams of researchers and development workers were sent in to investigate the causes, including the possibility that the areas concerned suffered from a local 'culture' of poverty. Instead, the majority of teams concluded that the sources of the problems lay elsewhere, in the wider social structure of class inequality, so that action taken at local level would have only very marginal impact. Blame was being placed on the victims for matters beyond their control. This was not a message government wanted to hear, and support for the project was withdrawn. Although the CDP represented a failure in official terms, it proved to be a seed-bed for urban sociologists, and an influential source for what became the restructuring analysis (for discussions, see Cockburn 1977: 123; Frazer 1999: 153). Key elements of the approach have become standard practice in subsequent state interventions, such as the 1980s Urban Programme, and schemes under City Challenge and the Single Regeneration Budget in the 1990s. These include dispatching outsiders into communities to assess their needs; shifting responsibility for action towards their members; and devising innovative forms of local policy. Cockburn (1977) labelled this approach the 'community package' and interpreted it as an attempt by central government to manage conflict, and to gain more knowledge of, and better control over, local conditions.

This form of community action is 'top-down'. It tries to ensure that the target communities learn to conform to external expectations. If successful, communities can be coopted as instruments of social policy or regulation. For this reason, it has been applied primarily to communities defined as 'poor', marginal or deprived, including those in rural areas; after all, what need is there to apply such techniques to situations where social relationships are already considered well-organized and resourced, and meeting accepted social objectives? A view is encouraged thereby that intervention is required only where communities are in some way lacking, or pathological, and in need of normalization. Quite often, to be designated as a needy community in these terms implies that there is not (yet) really a 'proper' community there at all. A recent example of this approach is the programme launched in 2000 in Wales, Communities First. This identified 142 Welsh communities as needing support, mostly defined as multiply deprived local authority wards or sub-ward areas. Ten are non-spatial 'communities of interest'. Each community will be eligible for comparatively long-term public funding, to create and follow through a local action plan for community regeneration. The programme has received a cautious welcome from experts, who describe it as 'a centrally planned programme to be driven by professionals who will coordinate the best way to spend government resources' (Clarke *et al.* 2002: 86). This suggests that the communities themselves will not be in control of the programme, but could be controlled by it.

Radical community action

On the whole, community workers do not become involved with such programmes because they want to carry out the wishes of government, even though ultimately government may pay their salaries. They are far more likely to be motivated by a desire to do something helpful for communities and their members. Very often this will be seen as involving going against the wishes of the authorities. Community development practice is influenced therefore by an alternative tradition of radical community action, which tries to ensure that the weak are given a voice, and assisted to overcome the barriers inhibiting their full and equal participation in society. In North America there is a tradition of community activism, which sees it as the role of the professional organizer, or agitator, to help build community, using common interest as a motivating factor in creating broad-based coalitions of groups (Clarke *et al.* 2002: 41). In Britain, militant social workers and community activists have engaged in confrontational direct action designed to force government and local authorities to respond to the needs of particular groups and localities. Notions of 'empowerment' and advocacy encourage the pursuit of campaigning methods designed to raise consciousness and increase the ability of marginalized groups to engage in protest. Such an approach is obviously more compatible with a conflict model of community relations than with the managerialist thrust of official programmes for community development (Cockburn 1977; Lees and Mayo 1984). The activist takes the side of the community, or community group, against the state, big business and, if need be, the wider society. Community-based protest tactics have been employed by a wide range of special interest groups, including people with disabilities, language activists and environmentalists. Here too there is a selective tendency for activists to offer their support only to certain approved causes, linked to movements like anti-racism, feminism and civil rights (Mayo 2000). Community action of this kind easily aligns itself with the politics of difference and identity.

We saw earlier how communities are the site for the spontaneous formation of many kinds of action groups, so that there is often fierce competition between groups for resources and support. The fact that there are many different competing conceptions of community accentuates this, by ensuring that groups cut across one another. For this reason, there is a stream of critical thinking which doubts whether 'community' represents a viable basis for significant political mobilization. Cockburn (1977: 159) claims that the idea of community action 'rings with implausibility' because it refers in the main to very fragmented responses to local 'service' issues. It is directed towards the problems people encounter as consumers, which tend to be short-term, highly specific, and divisive. It is also populist, in suggesting that such forms of action are open to all groups and interests, regardless of class barriers. Saunders (1979) agrees that community action usually involves a narrow social base, pursuing limited objectives. More often than not, its concern is with blocking some initiative, rather than doing anything more positive. Furthermore, the notion of community encourages a consensus view, that with goodwill on all sides, cooperative solutions can be found; this makes such activity accommodative and facilitative, rather than genuinely oppositional. The outcome is a mass of what Bell and Newby (1976: 204) described as 'briefly spluttering local action groups'. These objections are levelled principally at territorially based groupings, but could apply just as well to the work of many of the groups which battle on the grounds of shared interests. Measured against the standard of achieving significant social transformation, most community action appears to revolve around small issues and minor gains. Frazer (1999: 160) notes how much of the literature consists of stories of victories and defeats, highlighting the trials and tribulations of community organizing (for examples, see Hoggett 1997; Clarke *et al.* 2002). Saunders (1979: 130) observed that successes could be chalked up, without posing any fundamental threat to dominant economic and political interests. Critiques of this kind rest on a prior commitment to theories of basic social division, along lines of class, race or gender, in the light of which action at community level comes across as inherently pluralistic and disjointed. Activists often try to solve this by creating alliances and coalitions to broaden action and link up with wider movements.

Clearly, both radicals and officialdom can engage in community building activity for instrumental reasons: community becomes a vehicle for the achievement of their ulterior purposes, and since they meet in the spaces created by the various community projects and programmes, community development practice is bound to be riddled with tensions between adherents of 'top-down' and 'bottom-up' approaches. As the studies reported in Hoggett (1997) show, reconciling the wishes of communities with the aims of public policies can be an immensely frustrating business, and accusations of tokenism, unreasonableness, manipulation and lack of representation fly in all directions. Many schemes for community involvement end in failure, or very limited achievement, leaving behind a residue of discontent. The problem of disappointed expectations is familiar to those who work with communities and community groups, as is the difficulty of sustaining organization and action for sufficient periods of time. Community action often seems best suited to short bursts of enthusiasm (Frazer 1999), whereas policy objectives are more long-term. On the other hand, changes in policy direction and funding initiatives make it difficult for community groups to think far ahead, when their resource base is uncertain. Rapid turnover of personnel and frequent organizational changes are commonplace. There is then a major disjunction between the ill-defined, fluid and contested nature of 'community' and the relatively well organized, codified sphere of government. To a considerable extent, an answer has been sought through the professionalization of community work and community development methods.

Involving the communities: mobilization or incorporation?

There was a time when working with communities was a relatively marginal activity, associated more with church-based, welfare and philanthropic bodies than with government. Systems of representative democracy, local government, and government agencies were supposed to deal with policy issues, without the direct entanglement of communities. Now, however, community involvement has been mainstreamed, as a routine aspect of policy implementation, and few initiatives emanate from government without some anticipation that communities will be implicated in their delivery. If communities themselves are not mentioned, 'active citizens', located in their various communities, will be (Hill 1994). It has become standard practice to insist that bodies like local development corporations, housing trusts, National Health Trusts and local authorities obtain regular feedback from, or consult with, 'their' communities. In their turn, groups and organizations which apply for funding under government programmes, or from one of the independent organizations providing support for action at community level, will be expected to provide detailed information about themselves and the communities they represent, and explain how they intend to match the various performance criteria and targets by which success is measured. Monitoring and evaluation have become key components of project work. These activities require particular skills and expertise, which are not always available within the community. Either new ways of working must be learned, or assistance will be sought from among the various consultants, facilitators, and intermediaries who specialize in these tasks. Roles that used to be undertaken as voluntary commitments have become full-time occupations, and as the demand for advice and support has grown, a distinct literature has developed to provide communities with the necessary toolkit (for examples, see Francis and Henderson 1992; Hawtin *et al.* 1994). This enables communities, and other appropriate bodies, to carry out tasks such as local needs assessments, community audits and village appraisals. They can construct community profiles, and analyse the structure of social relationships within and around the community. In effect, the community study method has been reinvented, as something communities do to themselves, in order to gain access to necessary resources. Basic social scientific techniques of quantitative and qualitative research have been adapted so that they can be understood and used by community members.

These developments lend themselves to both positive and negative interpretations. As a statement of aspirations, there is little to quarrel with in Francis and Henderson's definition of the purpose of community work (1992: 17) as 'helping people to work together in their community, to grow in confidence and competence, in order to tackle their priorities and needs'. It puts community members firmly at the centre, and allows them to determine aims and objectives. Ideas of participation and self-determination figure strongly in contemporary accounts of community development processes. Techniques have been developed, ranging from surveys to interactive planning exercises, to enable the views of all sections of a community to be taken into account (Day *et al.* 1998). Statements of the approved procedures for effective community work advocate obtaining the active involvement of the community, with the inclusion of all its elements, and the importance of capacity-building measures to strengthen any areas of weakness. In these ways, community development can be seen as aiming to raise levels of social capital. As well as empowering the community and its members, this is regarded as ensuring better results, because the community takes ownership of the process, and its outcomes. In particular, this is said to increase the sustainability of the results. Yet there are limitations to what can be achieved. First, many exercises of the kind are half-hearted and superficial, and done with the intention of arriving at predetermined results. Experience of this type of activity breeds a great deal of cynicism. Second, the frameworks within which community development methods are applied often force communities to adjust themselves to fit a particular template; for example, to set up certain types of recommended committee and leadership structures, ostensibly to ensure there is 'clarity' in decision making. Agencies feel more comfortable relating to organizations than they do to amorphous community relationships. Third, there are worries that when these methods are employed, they disclose lingering assumptions about the intrinsic possibilities for harmony and agreement. This is despite the recognition in the relevant texts that communities are complex, may not be able to resolve all their differences, and can engage in reprehensible behaviour like racism. Faced with these realities, community workers sometimes find themselves being urged to adopt the role of counsellors, expected to lead a divided community towards cooperation and conflict resolution.

There is much to admire in the values avowed by most workers and activists who engage in the community development process. In general, they aim to foster principles of fair treatment, compassion, reciprocity and consideration, and to strengthen the networks of cooperation required to achieve collective ends. In doing so, they promise to bring actually existing communities closer to the normative ideal. They also direct their efforts mainly towards the more vulnerable members of society, or those who feel themselves to be most oppressed. Nevertheless, throughout the development of community work practice, anxieties have been expressed that rather than promoting the real interests of communities it could result in their incorporation into structures of power and control determined by others, whether this be the state, the social relations of capitalism, or the 'moral majority'. How can one be sure that the interests served are genuinely those of the people on the ground? What happens when the expressed wishes of a community conflict with the purposes of the powerful? Very often, in practice, an attempt will be made to redefine the community, or modify its formal structures, to secure a more satisfactory outcome. The powerful show a sometimes surprising ability to absorb pressures from below. Cockburn (1977: 118) observes that no sooner was community activism and protest put into practice than it was welcomed as a sign of healthy democratic disagreement, and integrated as part and parcel of political pluralism; conflict was diverted into competition between groups, and some groups, especially those willing to be more moderate and cooperative, found favour over others. The steady professionalization of community work has also encouraged an impression that it is now a service, provided by well educated middle-class experts for poor working class and ethnic minority people in areas of economic and social decline, and therefore liable to become rather patronizing and controlling. Uncertainties as to who benefits from community activism have persisted throughout a series of changes in both theoretical perspectives and social conditions (Taylor 1995), and emerge at the present time in warnings that efforts to develop communities may become dissipated amongst ever increasing numbers of rival 'identity' groups, making them susceptible to competitiveness and manipulation.

The most searching critical commentary on these developments has been produced by Rose (1996), who claims that community has moved right to the heart of public administration, and also of individual existence. In line with postmodernist arguments, he suggests that a new form of awareness has emerged, in which society is deconstructed into many different kinds of communities, leaving individuals to be identified according to the particular networks of affiliation within which they are located. People are seen as owing primary responsibility to these personal networks of communal ties, rather than to any sense of society as a whole. Government increasingly works by finding ways of regulating and orchestrating these relationships. Government through community involves devising strategies which transform communities into instruments of regulation or reform (Rose 1996: 334). This allows key tasks to be devolved away from the centre, relieving the state of some of its burden. Thus techniques of participation, empowerment, and involvement in decision making shift responsibility towards the individual and the community. Communities are called upon to play a more active part in ensuring their own safety and security, by hiring private protection or making sure they exclude the criminals. Greater responsibility for health and welfare is allocated to self-help groups and community campaigns. Economic policies seek to encourage local enterprise and initiative. Where they do not exist to fulfil these functions, communities may have to be created. Groups and organizations that are prepared to assume responsibility, and be accountable, on behalf of the community are sought out, or stimulated into existence. Although this can be presented as demonstrating greater sensitivity towards the needs of communities, it suits the interests of government to cultivate such mechanisms of self-regulation. Amongst other devices, Rose indicates that attachment to particular 'lifestyle communities' can be mobilized to establish firmer control over behaviour and consumption practices. Sociology plays a part in this, by gathering information about, interpreting and explaining the nature of different communities.

For Rose, the practice and expertise of community work, including the preparation of audits, reports and assessments, performs a vital role in rendering community calculable, as a means of government. In line with his arguments, the website of the UK government's Active Community Unit defines its vision as one of 'strong, active and empowered communities – increasingly capable of doing things for themselves, defining the problems they face and then tackling them together'. A number of current initiatives turn the spotlight onto community. As noted above, the urban disturbances of 2001 led to the commissioning of studies into the problem of 'community cohesion', which made connections with parallel debates about social inclusion and exclusion, social capital and participation. The problem was seen to lie in the degree of separation between different communities, which bred fear and intolerance. It was noted that there was an unfair tendency to problematize communities of ethnic minority and black people, while overlooking groups of white people living in equally or more deprived circumstances (Cantle 2002). Efforts to combat this should be devoted to bringing the communities together, and promoting shared values. Local community cohesion plans should be prepared. In other words, problems should be managed at community level. The tendency is still to attribute major social difficulties to problem people, and problem areas. There is little to reassure critics like Byrne (1999), who perceive such approaches as excluding communities from strategic power, and failing to connect with the realities of social division and inequality. Lest it should be thought that these concerns are exclusively urban, recent rural policies have also highlighted a range of new concerns and concepts, such as the value of 'countryside capital', new interests in community capacity-building, forms of social enterprise, and questions of local empowerment and exclusion (for example, Countryside Agency 2003). Indicators of community 'vibrancy' have been developed which position different local communities as 'vibrant', 'active', 'barely active' and 'sleeping'. Although rural communities continue to win praise for providing desirable social environments, 'really existing' communities are expected to *prove* that they deserve this reputation. If not, then they must work to remedy the problem, for instance by ensuring that a broad cross-section of the community becomes engaged in planning and decision making processes. In such ways, the vision of a community in which everyone is involved, pulling together for the common good, continues to exercise a deep influence on the minds of policy makers and their advisors, and to determine how different social groups are treated.

IN CONCLUSION: THE FUTURE OF 'COMMUNITY'

There is a very considerable distance between the kinds of geographical, and usually deprived, communities that are mainly targeted by governmental policies, and the freewheeling, imaginative groupings of internet enthusiasts and lifestyle celebrants who see themselves as representing the future of community. That the same word can be used to encompass both gives some sense of the versatility that has enabled the idea of community to display such resilience in the face of innumerable critiques. Time and again, no sooner is it pronounced to be dead than it springs back to life again, usually in some slightly modified form. Rose's argument that community now has become a central tool of contemporary governance implies that we will see policy moving increasingly away from its place-bound, administrative, conventional definitions, to chase the emergent definitions of the new communities. We see this already in the favourable positioning offered to communities of faith and ethnicity, who are assured that their differences will be recognized and respected, so long as they fit within the framework of the larger, national or societal community. Over time, they also will be subjected to the attentions and measurements of the community workers, to ensure they are in good health. Meanwhile, there are many who continue to look for sources of security and stability in recreating where necessary what they suppose to be the traditional communities of the past – whether these are prettified versions of rurality, or in some cases conceivably ethnically purified urban districts. There seems little point in sociologists lamenting the confusions and obscurities which surround the notion of community, when it is being put to work so intensively and determinedly by the members of society. Neither does it seem relevant to seek to legislate which of the meanings is more correct. Much of the interest lies rather in seeing how they are used to accomplish such different purposes.

At every level, it does appear community is contested, and contestable. There is disagreement about its essential meaning, and endless argument about what it signifies in terms of entitlements and responsibilities, and for whom. The clash between different interpretations fuels much that is dynamic in modern social life. Those who welcome ethnic diversity as a valuable addition to a pluralistic society, for example, find themselves confounded when others interpret ethnic community as enjoining them to reinstate older, restrictive codes of conduct and values. It turns out that liberals and fundamentalists alike can justify their positions in terms of the values of 'community', so that they must battle for hearts and minds to achieve their aims. In such circumstances, there is nothing intrinsically warm and cosy about community, as is often suggested, because it can be a rallying call to conflict. Even at the mundane level of the practice of community work and community development, there is as much argument as consensus, because those involved bring different aspirations and expectations to their understanding of community. Farrar (2001: 343) has proposed that community is understood best as an imaginative tool used by people as they go about their business of constructing an idea of a better society. This implies that community is always about change, and that such change is a positive expression of dreams of a better life. Unfortunately ideas of community can be taken up just as readily to resist change, and enact what some would regard as nightmarish possibilities. There is no escaping the social ambivalence involved in deciding who belongs, and who does not, and this ensures that the social features associated with community will not go away, but will continue to erupt in new, often unexpected forms. Consequently, ideas of community are likely to continue to be embedded at the centre of social theory. By following the career of the concept as it has twisted and turned with changes of sociological perspective and social reality, we do learn two key lessons. First, that community is among the more active construction sites in society, with lots of different people hard at work. Second, that the reality of community as discovered by empirical research is a great deal messier than the abstract and idealized versions used by theorists, whether these theorists are in academia, or located closer to the fields and streets of actual communities.

BIBLIOGRAPHY

Abercrombie, N., Hill, S. and Turner, B. S. (1984) *The Penguin Dictionary of Sociology*, Harmondsworth: Penguin.

Abrams, P. and McCulloch, A. (1976) *Communes, Sociology and Society*, Cambridge: Cambridge University Press.

Albrow, M. (1997) 'Travelling Beyond Local Cultures: Socioscapes in a Global City', in J. Eade (ed.) *Living the Global City: Globalization as Local Process*, London: Routledge.

Albrow, M., Eade, J., Durrschmidt, J. and Washbourne, N. (1997) 'The Impact of Globalization on Sociological Concepts: Community, Culture and Milieu', in J. Eade (ed.) *Living the Global City: Globalization as Local Process*, London: Routledge.

Allan, J. and Mooney, E. (1998) 'Migration into Rural Communities: Questioning the Language of Counterurbanisation', in P. Boyle and K. Halfacree (eds) *Migration into Rural Areas: Theories and Issues*, Chichester: Wiley.

Allen, V. (1981) *The Militancy of British Miners*, Shipley: The Moor Press.

Althusser, L. (1969) *For Marx*, London: Allen Lane.

Amit, V. and Rapport, N. (2002) *The Trouble with Community: Anthropological Reflections on Movement, Identity and Collectivity*, London: Pluto Press.

Anderson, B. (1983) *Imagined Communities*, London: Verso.

Anderson, N. (1923) *The Hobo*, Chicago, IL: University of Chicago Press.

Anderson, P. (1965) 'Origins of the Present Crisis', in P. Anderson and R. Blackburn, *Towards Socialism*, London: Fontana.

Arensberg, C. M. (1939) *The Irish Countryman: An Anthropological Study*, New York: Macmillan.

Arensberg, C. M. and Kimball, S. T. (1940) *Family and Community in Ireland*, London: Peter Smith.

Badcock, B. (1984) *Unfairly Structured Cities*, Oxford: Blackwell.

Bagguley, P., Mark-Lawson, J., Shapiro, D., Urry, J., Walby, S. and Warde, A. (1990) *Restructuring: Place, Class and Gender*, London: Sage.

Ball, R. and Stobart, J. (1997) 'Getting a Fix on Community Identity: The Catalyst of the Local Government Review', in P. Hoggett (ed.) *Contested Communities: Experiences, Struggles, Policies*, Bristol: The Policy Press.

Barber, B. R. (2003) *Jihad vs. McWorld*, London: Corgi Books.

Barr, A. (1996) *Practising Community Development*, London: Community Development Foundation.

Bauman, Z. (1992) *Intimations of Postmodernity*, London: Routledge.

—— (2000) *Liquid Modernity*, Cambridge: Polity Press.

—— (2001a) *Community: Seeking Safety in an Insecure World*, Cambridge: Polity Press.

—— (2001b) *The Individualized Society*, Cambridge: Polity Press.

Baym, N. K. (2000) *Tune in, Log on: Soaps, Fandom and Online Community*, London: Sage.

Beck, U. (1992) *Risk Society: Towards a New Modernity*, London: Sage.

Beck, U., Giddens, A. and Lash, S. (1994) *Reflexive Modernization: Politics, Tradition and Aesthetics in the Modern Social Order*, London: Sage.

Becker, H. (1963) *Outsiders: Studies in the Sociology of Deviance*, Illinois: Free Press.

Bell, C. and Newby, H. (1971) *Community Studies: An Introduction to the Sociology of the Local Community*, London: George Allen and Unwin.

—— (1976) 'Community, Communalism, Class and Community Action: The Sources of New Urban Politics', in D. Herbert and R. Johnston (eds) *Social Areas in Cities*, Chichester: Wiley.

Bell, M. M. (1994) *Childerley: Nature and Morality in a Country Village*, London: University of Chicago Press.

Bellah, R., with Madsen, R., Sullivan, W. A., Swidler, A. and Tipton, S. M. (1991) *The Good Society*, New York: Alfred A. Knopf.

Berger, P., Berger, B. and Kellner, H. (1973) *The Homeless Mind*, New York: Vintage.

Berry, B. J. L. (1965) 'Internal Structure of the City', *Law and Contemporary Problems* 3: 111–19.

—— (1973) *The Human Consequences of Urbanisation*, London: Macmillan.

Beynon, H. (ed.) (1985) *Digging Deeper: Issues in the Miners' Strike*, London: Verso.

Beynon, H. and Austrin, T. (1994) *Masters and Servants: Class and Patronage in the Making of a Labour Organisation*, London: Rivers Oram Press.

Birch, A. H. (1959) *Small Town Politics*, Oxford: Oxford University Press.

Bird, J., Curtis, B., Putnam, T., Robertson, G. and Tickner, L. (eds) (1993) *Mapping the Futures: Local Cultures, Global Change*, London: Routledge.

Blackwell T. and Seabrook, J. (1985) *A World Still To Win: The Reconstruction of the Post-war Working Class*, London: Faber.

Blokland, T. and Savage, M. (2001) 'Networks, Class and Place', *International Journal of Urban and Regional Research* 25, 2: 221–6.

Blythe, R. (1969) *Akenfield*, Harmondsworth: Penguin.

Body, M. and Fudge, C. (1984) *Local Socialism*, Basingstoke: Macmillan.

Boddy, M., Lovering, J. and Bassett, K. (1986) *Sunbelt City?*, Oxford: Oxford University Press.

Boissevain, J. (1975) 'Towards a Social Anthropology of Europe', in J. Boissevain and J. Friedl (eds) *Beyond the Community: Social Process in Europe*, The Hague: Department of Education and Science of the Netherlands.

Booth, C. (1902) *Life and Labour of the People of London*, London: Macmillan.

Bott, E. (1957) *Family and Social Network*, London: Routledge and Kegan Paul.

Boyle, P. and Halfacree, K. (eds) (1998) *Migration into Rural Areas: Theories and Issues*, Chichester: Wiley.

Bradley, H. (1996) *Fractured Identities: Changing Patterns of Inequality*, Cambridge: Polity Press.

Bradley, T. and Lowe, P. (1984) *Locality and Rurality*, Norwich: Geo Books.

Braine, J. (1957) *Room at the Top*, London: Eyre and Spottiswoode.

Brent, J. (1997) 'Community Without Unity', in P. Hoggett (ed.) *Contested Communities: Experiences, Struggles, Policies*, Bristol: The Policy Press.

Brody, H. (1974) *Inishkillane: Change and Decline in the West of Ireland*, Harmondsworth: Pelican.

Brook, E., and Finn, D. (1978) 'Working Class Images of Society and Community Studies', in Centre for Contemporary Cultural Studies, *On Ideology*, London: Hutchinson.

Brown, R. K. and Brannen, P. (1970) 'Social Relations and Social Perspectives Amongst Shipbuilding Workers', *Sociology* 4: 71–84 and 197–211.

Buechler, S. M. (2000) *Social Movements in Advanced Capitalism: The Political Economy and Cultural Construction of Social Activism*, Oxford: Oxford University Press.

Bulmer, M. (ed.) (1975a) *Working Class Images of Society*, London: Routledge and Kegan Paul.

—— (1975b) 'Sociological Models of the Mining Community', *Sociological Review* 23, 61–92.

—— (ed.) (1978) *Mining and Social Change: Durham County in the Twentieth Century*, London: Croom Helm.

—— (1986) *Neighbours: The Work of Philip Abrams*, Cambridge: Cambridge University Press.

Burgess, E. (1925) 'The Growth of the City', in R. E. Park, E. W. Burgess and R. D. McKenzie (eds) *The City*, Chicago, IL: University of Chicago Press.

Byrne, D. (1989) *Beyond the Inner City*, Milton Keynes: Open University Press.

—— (1995a) 'Community and the Dispossessed Working Class', paper presented to the conference on Ideas of Community, University of the West of England.

—— (1995b) 'Deindustrialization and Dispossession', *Sociology* 29: 95–116.

—— (1999) *Social Exclusion*, Buckingham: Open University Press.

—— (2001) *Understanding the Urban*, London: Palgrave.

Calhoun, C. (1982) *The Question of Class Struggle: Social Foundations of Popular Radicalism during the Industrial Revolution*, Oxford: Blackwell.

Campbell, B. (1993) *Goliath: Britain's Dangerous Places*, London: Methuen.

Cannon, I. C. (1967) 'Ideology and Occupational Community: A Study of Compositors', *Sociology* 1: 165–87.

Cantle, T. (2002) *Community Cohesion: A Report of the Independent Review Team*, London: Home Office.

Carter, H. (1972) *The Study of Urban Geography*, London: Edward Arnold.

Castells, M. (1977) *The Urban Question: A Marxist Approach*, London: Edward Arnold.

—— (1978) *City, Class and Power*, London: Macmillan.

—— (1983) *The City and the Grassroots*, London: Edward Arnold.

—— (1997) *The Power of Identity*, Oxford: Blackwell.

Champion, A. (ed.) (1989) *Counterurbanisation: The Changing Pace and Nature of Population Deconcentration*, London: Edward Arnold.

Chaney, D. (1994) *The Cultural Turn: Scene-setting Essays on Contemporary Cultural History*, London: Routledge.

—— (1996) *Lifestyles*, London: Routledge.

Charlesworth, S. J. (2000) *A Phenomenology of Working Class Experience*, Cambridge: Cambridge University Press.

Christenson, T. (1979) *Neighbourhood Survival: The Struggle for Covent Garden's Future*, London: Prism Press.

Clarke, J. (1979) 'Capital and Culture: The Post-war Working Class Revisited', in J. Clarke, C. Critcher and R. Johnson, *Working Class Culture: Studies in History and Theory*, London: Hutchinson.

Clarke, S., Byatt, A. M., Hoban, M. and Powell, D. (2002) *Community Development in South Wales*, Cardiff: University of Wales Press.

Cloke, P. (1997) 'Country Backwater to Virtual Village? Rural Studies and The "Cultural Turn" ', *Journal of Rural Studies* 13, 367–75.

Cloke, P. and Little, J. (eds) (1997) *Contested Countryside Cultures*, London: Routledge.Cloke, P., Goodwin, M. and Milbourne, P. (1997) *Rural Wales: Community and Marginalization*, Cardiff: University of Wales Press.

—— (1998) 'Inside Looking out; Outside Looking in: Different Experiences of Cultural Competence in Rural Lifestyles', in P. Boyle and K. Halfacree (eds) *Migration into Rural Areas: Theories and Issues*, Chichester: Wiley.

Coates, K. and Silburne, R. (1973) *Poverty: The Forgotten Englishmen*, Harmondsworth: Pelican.

Cockburn, C. (1977) *The Local State: Management of Cities and People*, London: Pluto.

—— (1983) *Brothers: Male Dominance and Technological Change*: London: Pluto Press.

Cohen, A. (1982) 'A Polyethnic London Carnival as a Contested Cultural Performance', *Ethnic and Racial Studies* 5: 23–41.

Cohen, A. P. (ed.) (1982) *Belonging: Identity and Social Organisation in British Rural Cultures*, Manchester: Manchester University Press.

—— (1985) *The Symbolic Construction of Community*, London: Tavistock.

—— (ed.) (1986) *Symbolising Boundaries: Identity and Diversity in British Cultures*, Manchester: Manchester University Press.

—— (1994) *Self Consciousness: An Alternative Anthropology of Identity*, London: Routledge.

—— (2002) 'Epilogue', in N. Rapport (ed.) *British Subjects: an Anthropology of Britain*, Oxford: Berg

Cohen, P. (1972) 'Subcultural Conflict and Working Class Community', Working Papers in Cultural Studies, reprinted in P. Cohen (1997) *Rethinking the Youth Question*, Basingstoke: Macmillan.

—— (1997) 'Beyond the Community Romance', *Soundings* 5: 29–51.

Collins, M. (2004) *The Likes of Us: A Biography of the White Working Class*, London: Granta Books.

Collison, P. (1953) *The Cutteslowe Walls: A Study in Social Class*, London: Faber.

Cooke, P. (ed.) (1989) *Localities: The Changing Face of Urban Britain*, London: Unwin Hyman.

Coulter, J., Miller, S. and Walker, M. (1984) *State of Siege: Politics and Policing in the Coalfields*, London: Canary Press.

Countryside Agency (2003) *Rural Economies: Stepping Stones to Healthier Futures*, London: Countryside Agency.

Craib, I. (1997) *Classical Social Theory*, Oxford: Oxford University Press.

Crenson, M. A. (1971) *The Un-politics of Air Pollution: A Study of Non-decisionmaking in the Cities*, Baltimore, MD: Johns Hopkins University Press.

Cressey, P. G. (1932) *The Taxi Hall Dancer*, Chicago, IL: University of Chicago Press.

Critcher, C. (1979) 'Sociology, Cultural Studies, and the Post-war Working Class', in J. Clarke, C. Critcher and R. Johnson, *Working Class Culture: Studies in History and Theory*, London: Hutchinson.

Crompton, R. (1998) *Class and Stratification*, 2nd edn, Cambridge: Polity Press.

Crook, S., Pakulski, J. and Waters, M. (1992) *Postmodernization: Change in Advanced Society*, London: Sage.

Crow, G. (2002) *Social Solidarities: Theories, Identities and Social Change*, Milton Keynes: Open University Press.

Crow, G. and Allen, G. (1994) *Community Life: An Introduction to Local Social Relations*, Hemel Hempstead: Harvester Wheatsheaf.

Crow, G. and Maclean, C. (2000) 'Community', in G. Payne (ed.) *Social Divisions*, Basingstoke: Macmillan.

Dahl, R. A. (1961) *Who Governs? Democracy and Power in an American City*, New Haven, CT: Yale University Press.

Damer, S. (1989) *From Moorepark to 'Wine Alley': The Rise and Fall of a Glasgow Housing Scheme*, Edinburgh: Edinburgh University Press.

Davies, C. A. and Jones, S. (eds) (2003) *Welsh Communities: New Ethnographic Perspectives*, Cardiff: University of Wales Press.

Davies, E. and Rees, A. D. (1960) *Welsh Rural Communities*, Cardiff: University of Wales Press.

Davies, J. G. (1972) *The Evangelistic Bureaucrat*, London: Tavistock.

Day, G. (1998) 'A Community of Communities? Similarity and Difference in Welsh Rural Community Studies', *The Economic and Social Review* 29, 3 July: 233–57.

Day, G. and Fitton, M. (1975) 'Religion and Social Status: *Bucheddau* and Its Implications', *Sociological Review* 23, 4: 867–91.

Day, G. and Murdoch, J. (1993) 'Locality and Community: Coming to Terms with Place', *Sociological Review* 41, 1: 82–111.

Day, G. and Thompson, A. (2004) *Theorizing Nationalism*, London: Palgrave.

Day, G., Morris, E. and Knight, P. (1998) *Where Do We Go From Here? A Review of Community Participation Methods*, Conwy: Wales Council for Voluntary Action.

Dempsey, K. (1990) *Smalltown: A Study of Social Inequality, Cohesion and Belonging*, Melbourne: Oxford University Press.

Dennis, N. (1970) *People and Planning*, London: Faber.

Dennis, N. and Erdos, G. (1992) *Families without Fatherhood*, London: Institute of Economic Affairs.

Dennis, N., Henriques, F. and Slaughter, C. (1969) *Coal Is Our Life: An Analysis of a Yorkshire Mining Community*, London: Tavistock (first published 1956).

Devine, F. (1992) *Affluent Workers Revisited*, Edinburgh: Edinburgh University Press.

Devine, F., Savage, M., Scott, J. and Crompton, R. (eds) (2005) *Rethinking Class: Culture, Identities and Lifestyle*, London: Palgrave.

Dickens, P. (1988) *One Nation? Social Change and the Politics of Locality*, London: Pluto Press.

—— (1990) *Urban Sociology: Society, Locality and Human Nature*, London: Harvester Wheatsheaf.

Dickinson, R. E. (1964) *City and Region: A Geographical Interpretation*, London: Routledge and Kegan Paul.

Dicks, B. (2000) *Heritage, Place and Community*, Cardiff: University of Wales Press.

Doheny-Farina, S. (1996) *The Wired Neighbourhood*, New Haven, CT: Yale University Press.

Duncan, S. (1989) 'What is Locality?', in R. Peet and N. Thrift (eds) *New Models in Geography*, London: Edward Arnold.

Duncan, S. and Goodwin, M. (1988) *The Local State and Uneven Development*, Cambridge: Polity Press.

Dunleavy, P. (1980) *Urban Political Analysis: The Politics of Collective Consumption*, Basingstoke: Macmillan.

Durant, R. (1939) *Watling: A Survey of Social Life on a New Housing Estate*, London: P. S. King.

Durkheim, E. (1964) *The Division of Labour in Society*, Glencoe, MN: Free Press (first published 1893).

Eade, J. (ed.) (1997) *Living the Global City: Globalization as Local Process*, London: Routledge.

Elias, N. (1994) 'Introduction', in N. Elias and J. L. Scotson, *The Established and the Outsiders*, 2nd edn, London: Sage.

Elias, N. and Scotson, J. L. (1965) *The Established and the Outsiders*, London: Frank Cass.

Emmett, I. (1964) *A North Wales Village*, London: Routledge.

—— (1982) 'Place, Community and Bilingualism in Blaenau Ffestiniog', in A. P. Cohen (ed.) *Belonging: Identity and Social Organisation in British Rural Cultures*, Manchester: Manchester University Press.

Engels, F. (1845) 'The Condition of the Working Class in England', reprinted in K. Marx and F. Engels (1956) *On Britain*, Moscow: Progress Publishers.

Ennew, J. (1980) *The Western Islands Today*, Cambridge: Cambridge University Press.

Etzioni, A. (1964) *Modern Organizations*, Englewood Cliffs, NJ: Prentice Hall.

—— (1995) *The Spirit of Community: Rights, Responsibilities and the Communitarian Agenda*, London: HarperCollins.

—— (1997) *The New Golden Rule: Community and Morality in a Democratic Society*, London: Profile Books.

—— (ed.) (1998) *The Essential Communitarian Reader*, Oxford: Rowman and Littlefield.

—— (2004) *From Empire to Community: A New Approach to International Relations*, London: Palgrave.

Evans, G. E. (1956) *Ask the Fellows Who Cut the Hay*, London: Faber.

Farrar, M. (2001) *The Struggle for 'Community' in a British Multi-ethnic Inner City Area: Paradise in the Making*, Lampeter: Edwin Mellor Press.

Featherstone, M. (1993) 'Global and Local Cultures', in J. Bird, B. Curtis, T. Putnam, G. Robertson and L. Tickner (eds) *Mapping the Futures: Local Cultures, Global Change*, London: Routledge.

Featherstone, M. and Lash, S. (eds) (1999) *Spaces of Culture*, London: Sage.

Featherstone, M., Lash, S. and Robertson, R. (eds) (1995) *Global Modernities*, London: Sage.

Fevre, R. (1989) *Wales is Closed: The Quiet Privatisation of British Steel*, Nottingham: Spokesman.

Field, J. (2003) *Social Capital*, London: Routledge.

Fischer, C. S., Jackson, R. M., Stueve, C. A., Gerson, K., Jones, L. M. and Baldassare, M. (1977) *Networks and Places: Social Relations in the Urban Setting*, New York: The Free Press.

Fisher, R. and Kling, J. (eds) (1993) *Mobilising the Community: Local Politics in the Era of the Global City*, London: Sage.

Foster, J. (1999) *Docklands: Cultures in Conflict, Worlds in Collision*, London: UCL Press.

Fox, R. (1978) *The Tory Islanders: A People of the Celtic Fringe*, Cambridge: Cambridge University Press.

Francis, D. and Henderson, P. (1992) *Working with Rural Communities*, Basingstoke: Macmillan.

Frankenberg, R. (1957) *Village on the Border*, London: Cohen and West.

—— (1966) *Communities in Britain: Social Life in Town and Country*, Harmondsworth: Penguin.

—— (1976) 'In the Production of Their Lives: Men (?) . . . Sex and Gender in British Community Studies', in D. Barker and S. Allen (eds), *Sexual Divisions and Society: Process and Change*, London: Tavistock.

Frazer, E. (1999) *The Problems of Communitarian Politics: Unity and Conflict*, Oxford: Oxford University Press.

Frazer, E. and Lacey, N. (1993) *The Politics of Community: A Feminist Critique of the Liberal-Communitarian Debate*, London: Harvester Wheatsheaf.

Fried, A. and Elman, R. (eds) (1974) *Charles Booth's London*, Harmondsworth: Pelican.

Fukuyama, F. (1999) *The Great Disruption: Human Nature and the Reconstitution of Social Order*, London: Profile Books.

Gans, H. (1962) *The Urban Villagers*, Glencoe, MN: Free Press.

—— (1968) 'Urbanism and Suburbanism as Ways of Life', reprinted in R. Pahl (ed.) *Readings in Urban Sociology*, Oxford: Pergamon.

Gibbon, P. (1973) 'Arensberg and Kimball Revisited', *Economy and Society* 4: 479–98.

—— (1988) 'Analysing the British Miners' Strike of 1984–5', *Economy and Society* 17, 2: 139–94.

Giddens, A. (1984) *The Constitution of Society*, Cambridge: Polity Press.

—— (1990) *The Consequences of Modernity*, Cambridge: Polity Press.

—— (1994a) 'Living in a Post-Traditional Society', in U. Beck, A. Giddens and S. Lash, *Reflexive Modernization: Politics, Tradition and Aesthetics in the Modern Social Order*, London: Sage.

—— (1994b) *Beyond Left and Right: The Future of Radical Politics*, Cambridge: Polity Press.

—— (1998) *The Third Way: The Renewal of Social Democracy*, Cambridge: Polity Press.

—— (2000) *The Third Way and Its Critics*, Cambridge: Polity Press.

Gilbert, D. (1992) *Class, Community and Collective Action: Social Change in Two British Coalfields, 1850–1926*, Oxford: Clarendon Press.

Gill, O. (1977) *Luke Street: Housing Policy, Conflict and the Creation of the Delinquent Area*, Basingstoke: Macmillan.

Glass, R. (1953) *The Social Background of a Plan: A Study of Middlesbrough*, London: Routledge.

—— (1955) 'Urban Sociology: A Trend Report', *Current Sociology* IV, 4: 5–76.

—— (1966) *Conflict in Society*, London: Churchill.

Goffman, E. (1961) *Asylums: Essays on the Social Situation of Mental Hospital Patients and Other Inmates*, Harmondsworth: Penguin.

Goldthorpe, J. H., Lockwood, D., Bechhofer, F. and Platt, J. (1969) *The Affluent Worker in the Class Structure*, Cambridge: Cambridge University Press.

Goodman, R. (1972) *After the Planners*, Harmondsworth: Penguin Books.

Goodwin, M. (1989) 'The Politics of Locality', in A. Cochrane and J. Anderson (eds) *Politics in Transition*, London: Sage.

Gorton, M., White, J. and Chaston, I. (1998) 'Counterurbanisation, Fragmentation and the Paradox of the Rural Idyll', in P. Boyle and K. Halfacree (eds) *Migration into Rural Areas: Theories and Issues*, Chichester: Wiley.

Green, D. G. (1996) *Community Without Politics: A Market Approach to Welfare Reform*, London: Institute of Economic Affairs.

Gregory, D. and Urry, J. (eds) (1985) *Social Relations and Spatial Structures*, Basingstoke: Macmillan.

Halfacree, K. (1995) 'Talking About Rurality: Social Representations of the Rural as Expressed by Residents of Six English Parishes', *Journal of Rural Studies* 11: 1–20.

—— (1998) 'Neo-tribes, Migration and the Post-productivist Countryside', in P. Boyle and K. Halfacree (eds) *Migration into Rural Areas: Theories and Issues*, Chichester: Wiley.

Hall, S. (1990) 'Cultural Identity and Diaspora', in J. Rutherford (ed.) *Identity: Community, Culture, Difference*, London: Lawrence and Wishart.

—— (1993) 'Culture, Community, Nation', *Cultural Studies* 7: 349–63.

Hall, S. and Jefferson, T. (1976) *Resistance through Rituals*, London: Hutchinson.

Hall, T. (1981) *King Coal*, Harmondsworth: Penguin.

Hannerz, U. (1969) *Soulside: Inquiries into Ghetto Culture and Community*, New York: Columbia University Press.

—— (1980) *Exploring the City: Inquiries Towards an Urban Anthropology*, New York: Columbia University Press.

Harper, S. (1989) 'The British Rural Community: An Overview of Perspectives', *Journal of Rural Studies* 5: 161–84.

Harris, C. C. (1987) *Redundancy and Recession*, Oxford: Oxford University Press.

—— (ed.) (1990) *Family, Economy and Community*, Cardiff: University of Wales Press.

Harris, R. (1972) *Prejudice and Tolerance in Ulster*, Manchester: Manchester University Press.

Harrison, P. (1983) *Inside the Inner City: Life Under the Cutting Edge*, Harmondsworth: Penguin.

Harvey, D. (1989a) *The Urban Experience*, Oxford: Blackwell.

—— (1989b) *The Condition of Postmodernity*, Oxford: Blackwell.

—— (1993) 'From Space to Place and Back Again: Reflections on the Condition of Postmodernity', in J. Bird, B. Curtis, T. Putnam, G. Robertson and L. Tickner (eds) *Mapping the Futures: Local Cultures, Global Change*, London: Routledge.

—— (2000) *Spaces of Hope*, Edinburgh: Edinburgh University Press.

Hawtin, M., Hughes, G. and Percy-Smith, J. (1994) *Community Profiling: Auditing Social Needs*, Buckingham: Open University Press.

Henriques, F. (1969) 'Introduction' in N. Dennis, F. Henriques and C. Slaughter, *Coal Is Our Life: An Analysis of a Yorkshire Mining Community*, 2nd edn, London: Tavistock.

Hetherington, K. (2000) *New Age Travellers: Vanloads of Uproarious Humanity*, London: Cassell.

Hewison, R. (1987) *The Heritage Industry: Britain in a Climate of Decline*, London: Methuen.

Hill, D. M. (1994) *Citizens and Cities: Urban Policy in the 1990s*, Hemel Hempstead: Harvester Wheatsheaf.

Hill, S. (1976) *The Dockers*, London: Heinemann.

Hobsbawm, E. (1994) *Age of Extremes: The Short Twentieth Century 1914–1991*, London: Michael Joseph.

Hoggart, R. (1957) *The Uses of Literacy: Aspects of Working Class Life*, London: Chatto and Windus.

—— (1988) *A Local Habitation*, London: Chatto and Windus.

Hoggett, P. (ed.) (1997) *Contested Communities: Experiences, Struggles, Policies*, Bristol: The Policy Press.

Hollowell, P. (1968) *The Lorry Driver*, London: Routledge and Kegan Paul.

Holmes, D. (1997) 'Virtual Identity: Communities of Broadcast, Communities of Interactivity', in D. Holmes (ed.) *Virtual Politics: Identity and Community in Cyberspace*, London: Sage.

Holton, R. J. and Turner, B. S. (1989) *Max Weber on Economy and Society*, London: Routledge.

Hunter, F. (1953) *Community Power Structure*, Chapel Hill, NC: Chapel Hill Books.

Jackson, B. (1968) *Working Class Community: Some General Notions Raised by a Series of Studies in Northern England*, London: Routledge and Kegan Paul.

Jackson, B. and Marsden, D. (1962) *Education and the Working Class*, London: Routledge and Kegan Paul.

Jackson, P. (1988) 'Street Life: The Politics of Carnival', *Society and Space* 6: 213–27.

James, E. (2003) 'Research on Your Own Doorstep: Welsh Rural Communities and the Perceived Effects of In-Migration', in C. A. Davies and S. Jones (eds) *Welsh Communities: New Ethnographic Perspectives*, Cardiff: University of Wales Press.

Janowitz, M. (1967) *The Community Press in an Urban Settting: The Social Elements of Urbanism*, Chicago, IL: University of Chicago Press.

Jarvis, H., Pratt, A. C. and Cheng-Chong Wu, P. (2001) *The Secret Life of Cities: The Social Reproduction of Everyday Life*, Harlow: Prentice Hall.

Jedrej, C. and Nuttall, M. (1996) *White Settlers: The Impact of Rural Repopulation in Scotland*, Luxembourg: Harwood Academic Publishers.

Jenkins, R. (1983) *Lads, Citizens, and Ordinary Kids: working-class Youth Lifestyles in Belfast*, London: Routledge and Kegan Paul.

—— (1996) *Social Identity*, London: Routledge.

Jones, O. (1995) 'Lay Discourses of the Rural: Development and Implications for Rural Studies', *Journal of Rural Studies* 11: 35–49.

Jones, S. G. (1995) 'Understanding Community in the Information Age', in S. G. Jones (ed.) *Cybersociety: Computer-mediated Communication and Community*, London: Sage.

Joyce, P. (1980) *Work Society and Politics*, Brighton: Harvester Press.

Keith, M. and Pile, S. (eds) (1993) *Place and the Politics of Identity*, London: Routledge.

Kerr, C. and Siegel, J. (1954) 'The Inter-industry Propensity to Strike: An International Comparison', in A. Kornhauser, R. Dubin and A. M. Ross (eds) *Industrial Conflict*, New York: McGraw Hill.

Kornhauser, W. (1959) *The Politics of Mass Society*, Glencoe, MN: The Free Press.

Kumar, K. (1978) *Prophecy and Progress: The Sociology of Industrial and Post-Industrial Society*, Harmondsworth: Pelican.

—— (1987) *Utopia and Anti-Utopia in Modern Times*, Oxford: Blackwell.

Kunstler, J. (1993) *The Geography of Nowhere*, New York: Simon and Schuster.

Lane, T. and Roberts, K. (1971) *Strike at Pilkingtons*, London: Fontana.

Lash, S. and Urry, J. (1987) *The End of Organised Capitalism*, Cambridge: Polity Press.

—— (1994) *Economies of Signs and Space*, London: Sage.

Lee, D. and Newby, H. (1983) *The Problem of Sociology*, London: Hutchinson.

Lees, R. and Mayo, M. (1984) *Community Action for Change*, London: Routledge and Kegan Paul.

Little, A. (2002) *The Politics of Community: Theory and Practice*, Edinburgh: Edinburgh University Press.

Littlejohn, J. (1963) *Westrigg: The Sociology of a Cheviot Parish*, London: Routledge and Paul.

Lockwood, D. (1966) 'Sources of Variation in Working-Class Images of Society', *Sociological Review* 14, 3: 249–67, reprinted in M. Bulmer (ed.) (1975) *Working-Class Images of Society*, London: Routledge and Kegan Paul.

Long, N. (1977) *An Introduction to the Sociology of Rural Development*, London: Tavistock.

Lowe, S. (1986) *Urban Social Movements: The City after Castells*, Basingstoke: Macmillan.

Lukes, S. (1974) *Power: A Radical View*, Basingstoke: Macmillan.

Lynd, R. and Lynd, H. (1929) *Middletown: A Study of American Culture*, New York: Harcourt Brace.

—— (1937) *Middletown in Transition*, New York: Harcourt Brace.

McCourt, F. (1996) *Angela's Ashes*, London: Flamingo.

Macintyre, S. (1980) *Little Moscows: Communism and Working-Class Militancy in Inter-war Britain*, London: Croom Helm.

MacIver, R. M. and Page, C. H. (1961) *Society: An Introductory Analysis*, London: Macmillan.

McKay, G. (1996) *Senseless Acts of Beauty*, London: Verso.

Mackenzie, R. T. and Silver, A. (1968) *Angels in Marble: Working-Class Conservatives in Urban England*, London: Heinemann.

Maffesoli, M. (1996) *The Time of the Tribes: The Decline of Individualism in Mass Society*, London: Sage.

Malinowski, B. (1944) *A Scientific Theory of Culture and Other Essays*, Chapel Hill, NC: University of North Carolina Press.

Mann, M. (1973) *Workers on the Move*, London: Cambridge University Press.

Maraspini, A. L. (1968) *The Study of an Italian Village*, The Hague: Mouton.

Marris, P. (1967) 'Motives and Methods: Reflections on a Study in Lagos', in H. Miner (ed.) *The City in Modern Africa*, London: Pall Mall Press.

—— (1982) *Community Planning and Conceptions of Change*, London: Routledge and Kegan Paul.

Marx, K. (1973) *Grundrisse: Foundations of the Critique of Political Economy*, Harmondsworth: Penguin.

Massey, D. (1984) *Spatial Divisions of Labour: Social Structures and the Geography of Production*, London: Macmillan.

—— (1993) 'Power-Geometry and a Progressive Sense of Place', in J. Bird, B. Curtis, T. Putnam, G. Robertson and L. Tickner (eds) *Mapping The Futures: Local Cultures, Global Change*, London: Routledge.

—— (1994) *Space, Place and Gender*, Cambridge: Polity Press.

Mayhew, H. (1861) *London Labour and the London Poor*, London: Griffin, Bohn and Co.

Mayo, M. (1994) *Communities and Caring: The Moral Economy of Welfare*, Basingstoke: Macmillan.

—— (2000) *Cultures, Communities, Identities*, London: Palgrave.

Melucci, A. (1989) *Nomads of the Present: Social Movements and Individuals Needs in Contemporary Society*, London: Hutchinson.

Meyrowitz, J. (1985) *No Sense of Place*, Oxford: Oxford University Press.

Mills, C. W. (1956) *The Power Elite*, New York: Oxford University Press.

Mitchell, J. C. (1969) *Social Networks in Urban Situations*, Manchester: Manchester University Press.

Mitford, M. R. (1938) *Our Village*, London: Dent Everyman (first published 1824).

Mogey, J. M. (1956) *Family and Neighbourhood*, Oxford: Oxford University Press.

Moore, R. (1974) *Pitmen, Preachers and Politics*, Cambridge: Cambridge University Press.

Moore, R. M. (1982) *The Social Impact of Oil: The Case of Peterhead*, London: Routledge and Kegan Paul.

Murdoch, J. and Marsden, T. (1994) *Reconstituting Rurality: Class, Community and Power in the Development Process*, London: UCL Press.

Murdoch, J., Lowe, P., Ward, N. and Marsden, T. (2003) *The Differentiated Countryside*, London: Routledge.

Murray, C. (1990) *The Emerging British Underclass*, London: Institute of Economic Affairs.

Newby, H. (1977) *The Deferential Worker*, London: Allen Lane.
—— (1979) *Green and Pleasant Land: Social Change in Rural England*, London: Hutchinson.
—— (1987a) *Country Life: A Social History of Rural England*, London: Sphere Books.
—— (1987b) 'Community and Urban Life', in P. Worsley (ed.) *The New Introducing Sociology*, Harmondsworth: Penguin.
Newby, H., Bell, C., Rose, D. and Saunders, P. (1978) *Property, Paternalism and Power: Class and Control in Rural England*, London: Hutchinson.
Nisbet, R. A. (1953) *The Quest for Community: A Study in the Ethics of Order and Freedom*, New York: Oxford University Press.
—— (1967) *The Sociological Tradition*, London: Heinemann.
Noble, T. (2000) *Social Theory and Social Change*, Basingstoke: Macmillan.
O'Byrne, D. (1993) 'Working class Culture: Local Community and Global Conditions', in J. Eade (ed.) *Living the Global City: Globalization as Local Process*, London: Routledge.
Ohmae, K. (1991) *The Borderless World: Power and Strategy in the Interlinked Economy*, London: Fontana.
—— (1996) *The End of the Nation State: The Rise of Regional Economies*, London: HarperCollins.
Packard, V. (1972) *A Nation of Strangers*, New York: McKay.
Pahl, R. (1965) 'Class and Community in English Commuter Villages', *Sociologia Ruralis* 5: 5–23.
—— (1966) 'The Rural Urban Continuum', *Sociologia Ruralis* 6: 299–329.
—— (1968) (ed.) *Readings in Urban Sociology*, Oxford: Pergamon.
—— (1970a) *Patterns of Urban Life*, London: Longman.
—— (1970b) *Whose City?*, London: Longman.
—— (1975) *Whose City?*, 2nd edn, Harmondsworth: Penguin.
—— (1984) *Divisions of Labour*, Oxford: Blackwell.
—— (1996) 'Friendly Society', in S. Kraemer and J. Roberts (eds) *The Politics of Attachment*, London: Free Association Books.
Pahl, R. and Winkler, J. (1974) 'The Coming Corporatism', *New Society* 10 October: 72–6.
Park, R. (1957) *Human Communities*, New York: Free Press.
Park, R. E., Burgess, E. W. and McKenzie, R. D. (1925) *The City*, Chicago, IL: University of Chicago Press.
Parker, T. (1985) *The People of Providence: Interviews from an Urban Housing Estate*, Harmondsworth: Penguin.
Parkin, F. (1971) *Class Inequality and Political Order*, London: Paladin.
Parry, J. (2003) 'The Changing Meaning of Work: Restructuring in the

Former Coalmining Communities of the South Wales Valleys', *Work, Employment and Society* 17, 2: 227–46.

Parsons, T. (1951) *The Social System*, Glencoe, MN: Free Press.

Payne, G. (ed.) (2000) *Social Divisions*, Basingstoke: Macmillan.

Perkin, H. (1969) *The Origins of Modern English Society 1780-1880*, London: Routledge and Kegan Paul.

Phillips, D. L. (1993) *Looking Backwards: A Critical Appraisal of Communitarian Thought*, Princeton, NJ: Princeton University Press.

Pickvance, C. (1976) *Urban Sociology: Critical Essays*, London: Tavistock.

—— (1999) 'Democratization and the Decline of Social Movements', *Sociology* 33, 2: 353–72.

Platt, J. (1971) *Social Research in Bethnal Green*, London: Macmillan.

Poulantzas, N. (1973) *Political Power and Social Classes*, London: New Left Books.

Pryce, K. (1986) *Endless Pressure*, 2nd edn, Bristol: Bristol Classical Press.

Putnam, R. (2000) *Bowling Alone: The Collapse and Revival of American Community*, New York: Simon and Schuster.

Raban, J. (1975) *Soft City*, London: Fontana.

Rapport, N. (1993) *Diverse World-views in an English Village*, Edinburgh: Edinburgh University Press.

—— (ed.) (2002) *British Subjects: An Anthropology of Britain*, Oxford: Berg.

Redfield, R. (1947) 'The Folk Society', *The American Journal of Sociology* 52, 3: 293–308.

—— (1955) *The Little Community: Peasant Society and Culture*, Chicago, IL: University of Chicago Press.

Rees, A. D. (1950) *Life in a Welsh Countryside*, Cardiff: University of Wales Press (reprinted 1996).

Rees, G. and Thomas, M. (1991) 'From Coalminers to Entrepreneurs? A Case Study in the Sociology of Re-industrialization', in M. Cross and G. Payne (eds) *Work and the Enterprise Culture*, London: Falmer Press.

Relph, E. (1976) *Place and Placelessness*, London: Pion.

Revill, G. (1993) 'Reading Rosehill: Community, Identity and inner city Derby', in M. Keith and S. Pile (eds) *Place and the Politics of Identity*, London: Routledge.

Rex, J. (1988) *The Ghetto and the Underclass: Essays on Race and Social Policy*, Aldershot: Avebury.

Rex, J. and Moore, R. (1967) *Race, Community and Conflict: A Study of Sparkbrook*, Oxford: Oxford University Press for the Institute of Race Relations.

Rex, J. and Tomlinson, S. (1979) *Colonial Immigrants in a British City: A Class Analysis*, London: Routledge and Kegan Paul.

Rheingold, H. (1993) *The Virtual Community: Homesteading on the Electronic Frontier*, Reading, MA: Addison-Wesley.

Riesman, D. (1950) *The Lonely Crowd: A Study of the Changing American Character*, New Haven, CT: University of Yale Press.

Roberts, K.(1978) *The Working Class*, London: Longman.

—— (2001) *Class in Modern Britain*, London: Palgrave.

Roberts, R. (1971) *The Classic Slum: Salford Life in the First Quarter of the Century*, Manchester: Manchester University Press.

Robertson, R. (1995) 'Glocalization: Time–space and Homogeneity–Heterogeneity', in M. Featherstone, S. Lash and R. Robertson (eds) *Global Modernities*, London: Sage.

Robson, B. T. (1969) *Urban Analysis*, Cambridge: Cambridge University Press.

Rose, G. (1968) *The Working-Class*, London: Heinemann.

Rose, N. (1996) 'The Death of the Social? Re-figuring the Territory of Government', *Economy and Society* 25, 3: 327–56.

Rosser, C. and Harris, C. (1965) *The Family and Social Change*, London: Routledge and Kegan Paul.

Runnymede Trust (2000) *The Future of Multi-ethnic Britain*, London: Profile Books.

Sabel, C. (1982) *Work and Politics*, Cambridge: Cambridge University Press.

Salaman, G. (1974) *Community and Occupation: An Exploration of Work/ Leisure Relationships*, Cambridge Papers in Sociology no. 4, Cambridge: Cambridge University Press.

—— (1975) 'Occupations, Community and Consciousness', in M. Bulmer (ed.) *Working-Class Images of Society*, London: Routledge and Kegan Paul.

Samuel, R. (ed.) (1977) *Miners, Quarrymen and Saltworkers*, London: Routledge and Kegan Paul.

Saunders, P. (1979) *Urban Politics: A Sociological Approach*, London: Hutchinson.

—— (1981) *Social Theory and the Urban Question*, London: Hutchinson.

—— (1985) 'Space, the City and Urban Sociology', in D. Gregory and J. Urry (eds) *Social Relations and Spatial Structures*, Basingstoke: Macmillan.

—— (1986) *Social Theory and the Urban Question*, 2nd edn, London: Hutchinson.

—— (1990) *A Nation of Home Owners*, London: Unwin Hyman.

Savage, M and Warde, A. (1993) *Urban Sociology, Capitalism and Modernity*, London: Macmillan.

Savage, M., Bagnall, G. and Longhurst, B. (2005) 'Local Habitus and Working class Culture', in F. Devine, M. Savage, J. Scott and R. Crompton (eds) *Rethinking Class: Culture, Identities and Lifestyle*, London: Palgrave.

Savage, M., Barlow, J., Dickens, P. and Fielding, T. (1992) *Property, Bureaucracy and Culture: Middle-class Formations in Contemporary Britain*, London: Routledge.

Savage, M., Barlow, J., Duncan, S. and Saunders, P. (1987) 'Locality Research: The Sussex Programme on Economic Change and the Locality', *Quarterly Journal of Social Affairs* 3, 1: 27–51.

Scott, J. (2000) 'Class and Stratification', in G. Payne (ed.) *Social Divisions*, Basingstoke: Macmillan.

Scott, P. (2005) 'Visible and Invisible Walls: Suburbanisation and the Social Filtering of Working class Communities in Interwar Britain', unpublished ms., University of Reading, Department of Management.

Seabrook, J. (1971) *City Close-up*, Harmondsworth: Penguin.

—— (1984) *The Idea of Neighbourhood: What Local Politics Should Be About*, London: Pluto Press.

Searle, J. R. (1995) *The Construction of Social Reality*, Harmondsworth: Penguin.

Selznick, P. (1992) *The Moral Commonwealth: Social Theory and the Promise of Community*, Berkeley, CA: University of California Press.

Sennett, R. (1998) *The Corrosion of Character*, New York: Norton and Company.

Sewel, J. (1975) *Colliery Closure and Social Change*, Cardiff: University of Wales Press.

Shields, R. (1992) 'The Individual, Consumption Cultures and the Fate of Community', in R. Shields (ed.) *Lifestyle Shopping: The Subject of Consumption*, London: Routledge.

Short, J. (ed.) (1971) *The Social Fabric of the Metropolis*, Chicago, IL: Chicago University Press.

Short, J. R. (1984) *The Urban Arena: Capital, State and Community in Contemporary Britain*, London: Macmillan.

—— (1996) *The Urban Order*, Oxford: Blackwell.

Sillitoe, A. (1958) *Saturday Night and Sunday Morning*, London: W. H. Allen.

Simmel, G. (1903) 'The Metropolis and Mental Life', reprinted in P. Kasinitz (ed.) *Metropolis: Centre and Symbol of Our Times*, Basingstoke: Macmillan.

Smith, N. (1987) 'Dangers of the Empirical Turn: Some Comments on the CURS Initiative', *Antipode* 19: 59–68.

Smith, P. (2002) 'Power in Place: Retheorizing the Local and the Global', in J. Eade and C. Mele (eds) *Understanding the City: Contemporary and Future Perspectives*, Oxford: Blackwell.

Solomon, M. R. and Englis, B. G. (1997) 'Breaking Out of the Box: Is Lifestyle a Construct or a Construction?', in S. Brown and D. Turley (eds) *Consumer Research: Postcards From the Edge*, London: Routledge.

Stacey, M. (1960) *Tradition and Change: A Study of Banbury*, Oxford: Oxford University Press.

—— (1969) 'The Myth of Community Studies', *British Journal of Sociology* 20, 2: 134–47.

Stacey, M., Batstone, E., Bell, C. and Murcott, A. (1975) *Power, Persistence and Change: A Second Study of Banbury*, London: Routledge and Kegan Paul.

Stein, M. (1964) *The Eclipse of Community*, New York: Harper and Row.

Strangleman, T. (2001) 'Networks, Place and Identities in Post-Industrial Mining Communities', *International Journal of Urban and Regional Research* 25, 1: 253–67.

Strathern, M. (1981) *Kinship at the Core*, Cambridge: Cambridge University Press.

—— (1982) 'The Village as an Idea: Constructs of Village-ness in Elmdon, Essex', in A. P. Cohen (ed.) *Belonging: Identity and Social Organisation in British Rural Cultures*, Manchester: Manchester University Press.

Suttles, G. D. (1968) *The Social Order of the Slum: Ethnicity and Territory in the Inner City*, Chicago, IL: University of Chicago Press.

—— (1972) *The Social Construction of Communities*, Chicago, IL: University of Chicago Press.

Tam, H. (1998) *Communitarianism: A New Agenda for Politics and Citizenship*, Basingstoke: Macmillan.

Taylor, M. (1995) 'Community Work and the State: The Changing Context of UK Practice', in G. Craig and M. Mayo (eds) *Community Empowerment: A Reader in Participation and Development*, London: Zed Books.

Taylor, N. (1973) *The Village in the City*, London: Maurice Temple Smith.

Thompson, F. (2000) *Larkrise to Candleford*, Harmondsworth: Penguin.

Tonnies, F. (1955) *Community and Association*, London: Routledge and Kegan Paul (first published 1887).

Townsend, P. (1957) *The Family Life of Old People*, London: Routledge and Kegan Paul.

Tunstall, J. (1962) *The Fisherman*, London: MacGibbon and Kee.

Twelvetrees, A. (1998) (ed.) *Community Economic Development: Rhetoric or Reality?*, London: Community Development Foundation.

Urry, J. (1995) *Consuming Places*, London: Routledge.

—— (2000) *Sociology Beyond Societies: Mobilities for the Twenty-first Century*, London: Routledge.

Urry, J. and Murgatroyd, C. (1985) *Localities, Class and Gender*, London: Pion.

Vidich, A. and Bensman, J. (1958) *Small Town in Mass Society: Class, Power and Religion in a Rural Community*, Princeton, NJ: Princeton University Press.

Wacquant, L. and Wilson, W. J. (1989) 'The Cost of Racial and Class Exclusion in the Inner City', *Annals of the American Academy of Political and Social Science* 501: 8–25.

Waddington, D., Wykes, M. and Critcher, C. (1991) *Split At the Seams? Community, Conflict and Change After the 1984–5 Coal Dispute*, Milton Keynes: Open University Press.

Ward, C. (1993) *New Town, Home Town: The Lessons of Experience*, London: Calouste Gulbenkian Foundation.

Warde, A. (1985) 'The Homogenization of Space? Trends in the Spatial Division of Labour in 20th Century Britain', in H. Newby, J. Bujra, P. Littlewood, G. Rees and T. Rees (eds) *Restructuring Capital: Recession and Reorganisation in Industrial Society*, London: Macmillan.

Warner, W. Ll. and Lunt, P. (1941) *The Social Life of a Modern Community*, New Haven, CT: Yale University Press.

Warren, R. (1963) *The Community in America*, Chicago, IL: Rand McNally.

Warwick, D. and Littlejohn, G. (1992) *Coal, Capital and Culture: A Sociological Analysis of Mining Communities in West Yorkshire*, London: Routledge.

Wates, N. (1976) *The Battle for Tolmers Square*, London: Routledge and Kegan Paul.

Wates, N. and Knevitt, C. (1987) *Community Architecture: How People Are Creating Their Own Environment*, Harmondsworth: Penguin.

Weber, M. (1947) *The Theory of Social and Economic Organisation*, New York: The Free Press.

—— (1978) *Economy and Society*, eds G. Roth and C. Wittich, Berkeley, CA: University of California Press.

Webster, C. (2003) 'Race, Space and Fear: Imagined Geographies of Racism, Crime, Violence and Disorder in Northern England', *Capital and Class* 80: 95–122.

Weeks, J. (1996) 'The Idea of a Sexual Community', *Soundings* 2: 71–84.

Weeks, J. and Holland, J. (eds) (1996) *Sexual Cultures: Communities, Values and Intimacy*, Basingstoke: Palgrave Macmillan.

Wellman, B. (1979) 'The Community Question', *American Journal of Sociology* 84: 1201–31.

—— (2001) 'Physical Place and Cyberplace: The Rise of Personalized Networking', *International Journal of Urban and Regional Research* 25, 2: 227–53.

Wellman, B. and Leighton, B. (1979) 'Networks, Neighbourhoods and Communities: Approaches to the Community Question', *Urban Affairs Quarterly* 14: 363–90.

Westergaard, J. (1965) 'The Withering Away of Class', in P. Anderson and R. Blackburn (eds) *Towards Socialism*, London: Fontana.

—— (1975) 'Radical Class Consciousness: A Comment', in M. Bulmer (ed.) *Working Class Images of Society*, London: Routledge and Kegan Paul.

Whipp, R. (1985) 'Labour Markets and Communities', *Sociological Review* 33: 768–91.

White, J. (1986) *The Worst Street in North London: Campbell Bunk, Islington, Between the Wars*, London: Routledge and Kegan Paul.

Whyte, W. F. (1943) *Street Corner Society: The Social Structure of an Italian Slum*, Chicago, IL: University of Chicago Press (2nd edn 1955).

Whyte, W. H. (1957) *The Organization Man*, London: Cape.

Wight, D. (1993) *Workers Not Wasters: Masculine Respectability, Consumption and Employment in Central Scotland*, Edinburgh: Edinburgh University Press.

Williams, O. P. (1971) *Metropolitan Political Analysis*, New York: Free Press.

Williams, R. (1958) *Culture and Society 1780–1950*, London: Chatto and Windus.

—— (1961) *The Long Revolution*, London: Chatto and Windus.

—— (1975) *The Country and the City*, St Albans: Paladin.

—— (1976) *Keywords*, London: Collins.

—— (1989) 'The Importance of Community', in *Resources of Hope*, London: Verso.

Williams, W. M. (1956) *The Sociology of an English Village: Gosforth*, London: Routledge and Kegan Paul.

—— (1963) *A West Country Village: Ashworthy*, London: Routledge.

Willis, P. (1990) *Common Culture*, Milton Keynes: Open University Press.

Willmott, P. (1963) *The Evolution of a Community: A Study of Dagenham After 40 Years*, London: Routledge and Kegan Paul.

—— (1966) *Adolescent Boys of East London*, London: Routledge and Kegan Paul.

—— (1986) *Social Networks, Informal Care and Public Policy*, London: Policy Studies Institute.

Willmott, P. and Young, M. (1960) *Family and Class in a London Suburb*, London: Routledge and Kegan Paul.

Wilson, E. (1991) *The Sphinx in the City*, London: Virago.

Willson, M. (1997) 'Community in the Abstract: A Political and Ethical Dilemma?', in D. Holmes (ed.) *Virtual Politics: Identity and Community in Cyberspace*, London: Sage.

Wirth, L. (1927) 'The Sociology of Ferdinand Tonnies', *American Journal of Sociology* xxxii, 3: 412–22.

—— (1928) *The Ghetto*, Chicago, IL: University of Chicago Press.

—— (1938) 'Urbanism as a Way of Life', *The American Journal of Sociology* 44, 1: 1–24.

—— (1995) 'Urbanism as a Way of Life', reprinted in P. Kasinitz (ed.) *Metropolis: Centre and Symbol of Our Times*, Basingstoke: Macmillan.

Wittel, A. (2001) 'Towards a Network Sociality', *Theory, Culture and Society* 18: 51–76.

Woodruff, W. (2002) *The Road to Nab End*, London: Abacus.

Wright, P. (1985) *On Living in an Old Country*, London: Verso.

Wright, S. (1992) 'Image and Analysis: New Directions in Community Studies', in B. Short (ed.) *The English Rural Community: Image and Analysis*, Cambridge: Cambridge University Press.

Wuthnow, R. (1994) *Sharing the Journey: Support Groups and America's New Quest for Community*, New York: Free Press.

Wylie, L. (1957) *Village in the Vaucluse*, Oxford: Oxford University Press.

Young, I. M. (1990) *Justice and the Politics of Difference*, Princeton, NJ: Princeton University Press.

Young, M. and Willmott, P. (1957) *Family and Kinship in East London*, London: Routledge and Kegan Paul (reissued 1986, Harmondsworth: Penguin).

Zorbaugh, H. W. (1929) *The Gold Coast and the Slum*, Chicago, IL: University of Chicago Press.

Zukin, S. (1995) *The Cultures of Cities*, Oxford: Blackwell.

INDEX

eBooks – at www.eBookstore.tandf.co.uk

A library at your fingertips!

eBooks are electronic versions of printed books. You can
store them on your PC/laptop or browse them online.

They have advantages for anyone needing rapid access
to a wide variety of published, copyright information.

eBooks can help your research by enabling you to
bookmark chapters, annotate text and use instant searches
to find specific words or phrases. Several eBook files would
fit on even a small laptop or PDA.

NEW: Save money by eSubscribing: cheap, online access
to any eBook for as long as you need it.

Annual subscription packages

We now offer special low-cost bulk subscriptions to
packages of eBooks in certain subject areas. These are
available to libraries or to individuals.

For more information please contact
webmaster.ebooks@tandf.co.uk

We're continually developing the eBook concept, so
keep up to date by visiting the website.

www.eBookstore.tandf.co.uk